ALSO BY CAROL LEE FLINDERS

At the Root of This Longing

Enduring Grace

The New Laurel's Kitchen
(with Laurel Robertson and Brian Ruppenthal)

The Making of a Teacher
(with Tim Flinders)

CAROL LEE FLINDERS

The Values of Belonging

Rediscovering Balance,

Mutuality, Intuition,

and Wholeness in a

Competitive World

 HarperSanFrancisco

A Division of HarperCollins*Publishers*

HarperCollins books may be purchased for educational, business, or sales promotional use. For information please write: Special Markets Department, HarperCollins Publishers, Inc., 10 East 53rd Street, New York, NY 10022.

HarperCollins Web site: http://www.harpercollins.com

HarperCollins®, ♛ ®, and HarperSanFrancisco™ are trademarks of HarperCollins Publishers, Inc.

FIRST EDITION

Library of Congress Cataloging-in-Publication Data

Flinders, Carol.
   The values of belonging : rediscovering balance, mutuality, intuition, and wholeness in a competitive world / Carol Lee Flinders. — 1st ed.
      p. cm.
   Includes bibliographical references and index.
   ISBN 0-06-251736-8 (cloth : alk. paper)
      1. Cooperativeness—Moral and ethical aspects. 2. Social ethics—History.
   3. Feminist ethics. I. Title.
   BJ1533.C74F58 2002 170'.44—dc21   2002068719

02 03 04 05 06 ❖/RRD 10 9 8 7 6 5 4 3 2 1

To Tim

Contents

Sedge Grass, Willow & Redbud

From sedge grass roots, willow shoots, and the bark of the redbud tree, stripped, peeled, painstakingly treated and cured, women of the Pomo tribe in Northern California wove baskets of extraordinary beauty and complexity.

The fact of those baskets and the women who made them, fasting and praying, as scrupulous of their mental state as they were of the coiled bundles of root and bark with which they worked, sustains me.

I am no weaver, and no basket maker. I deal in words and wild notions, and I can only barely imagine what it might be like to see a glowing length of fabric take shape in my hands, or the perfect ellipsis of a canoe basket, pale gold, traced over in a fine, reddish-brown design called "quail tip" or "grasshopper leg" or even "deer scat," or perhaps a design no one has ever seen that came to me the night before in a dream.

As a writer committed to making what sense I can of this world and of my place in it, I treasure what I know of the way those artists worked. That knowledge steadied my hand and nerve as I dealt with the several separate strands of this book and my desire to weave them into a meaningful whole—something sturdy, capacious, and serviceable. The weaving wasn't easy. There were moments, in fact, when I felt as if *I* were the one being stripped, peeled, treated, and cured. Throughout the process, Pomo baskets worked for me as both symbol of and touchstone for realities too deeply felt and too elusive to be seized straight-on. I am grateful to their makers.

Seeing Whole

When we want to understand something, most us begin by trying to isolate it. This approach can make perfect sense, but only as long as that isn't the end of the inquiry. Everything exists in the midst of something else, and before you can know *anything* for what it really is—animal or artifact, religious teaching or utopian vision—you have to be able to see it in context: figure and ground, all of a piece and interactive.

I'm acutely aware how difficult it can be to see the part without losing sight of the whole. I know that it can stretch one's cognitive powers to their limit, because I had to do something like it as a small child, and the memory of that struggle is locked into my neuromuscular system.

When I was just a few months old, it became apparent to my family that my left eye had no burning interest in entering a working relationship with the right one. Normally, the brain takes in information from both eyes, and as long as their readings differ only slightly, it can collate them, so that when we look at a tree or a face, we see just *one* tree, just *one* face, but we see it whole and in three dimensions. If the difference is extreme, though, and the brain can't reconcile the two images, it effectively ignores one of them.

In my own case, it turned out that the right eye was doing most of the actual seeing, and since the information coming in from the left eye was more or less random, my brain favored the right eye and the left one got weaker and weaker from disuse. If nobody had intervened, my visual world would have been one-dimensional and, because my ability to gauge distances was impaired, treacherous as well.

Fortunately, my parents and the best ophthalmologist they could find did intervene. Corrective treatment started when I was three or four years old, with a patch I had to wear over my right eye: this was the only way the left eye would find out what it could do and become strong enough to work in tandem with the right one.

I described the treatment once to a friend who teaches ballet, and he nodded in immediate understanding. When a dancer is learning a new position or routine, he said, he or she begins by performing exercises meant to strengthen each of the specific muscle groups that are involved.

"First you isolate, then you integrate."

And indeed, once the left eye began to get stronger, my mother and I started paying weekly visits to the doctor's office, where I would sit for an hour at a time in front of a series of machines that worked the muscles in my eyes much as a room full of exercise equipment works the muscles of today's eager body sculptor.

The machines were of several kinds, but the one I remember most vividly involved a lion and a cage. Through one eyepiece I could see a cage, through the other a lion, and my job was to turn the left eye in and hold it there for a few seconds so that the lion was inside the cage. There were several similar exercises. The uniting theme wasn't so much "cage the beast" as "place the free-floating entity in an appropriate context."

The integration phase of the treatment was desperately hard work, bordering on painful. Even now, when I think about it, my breathing becomes a little labored. But in time, everything fell into place. My wandering eye settled down so that I could see quite well with glasses, and I still do. But because of what I had to go through to become binocular—and because on a couple of unnerving occasions eyestrain has put me back at square one—I never take it for granted.

The language we use to describe how we learn and think is drawn by analogy from the language we use to describe what our bodies do: we may not "grasp" a particularly complex idea at first—may not be able to "absorb" or "assimilate" or "digest" it immediately—but once we do, we're able to "run with it" and even "build on it."

Maybe, though, "by analogy" is too weak a term. Perhaps the time we spent as a species learning to walk, climb, run, and throw was an actual apprenticeship for what our intellects would have to do further down the road. While the ability to coordinate the input from our two eyes develops in most of us without conscious effort, our having acquired that skill *as a species,* over vast reaches of biological time, may have constituted a long, drawn-out rehearsal for a task we would face over and over and over as we ceased to be foragers and moved out into ever more complex relationships with one another and the natural world, entering that phase of our collective existence that's commonly called "history."

The ability, and before that the willingness, to embrace complexity—to see things with both eyes, isolated *and* integrated, and address them in their wholeness—is perhaps the essential task of human understanding. It's invariably hard—at least as difficult as putting lions in cages. Ultimately, it requires that when we're constructing a hypothesis, that hypothesis must account for all the available data (even when the bits and pieces seem to contradict each other), and if it's a society we're constructing, that society must accommodate the whole range of human truths and human types—the fact that we are, for instance, relational *and* ambitious, reverent *and* innovative, idealistic *and* pragmatic, playful *and* industrious.

The easier thing always is simply to shut out information that doesn't fit. The easier thing always is, and always has been, to limit ourselves to what we can see out of just one eye.

The purpose of this book is to offer a fresh way of looking at the basic storyline of human history and what is usually called prehistory. That sounds a bit grandiose, even to me, but in a sense—the sense in which I hope to be taken—it's what we do all the time. A poem, an op-ed piece, or even a bedtime story plants a stake boldly, saying in effect, "*This* is the thing not to forget *ever,* the reference point that makes sense of everything else. . . ." Or even, "Here's what *really* happened at Camelot."

What we actually mean, of course, is, "Suppose we were to look at those events from this angle of vision, just look what comes into view," or "I *wonder* whether this might not be what really happened at Camelot."

Like the poem, the op-ed piece, and the bedtime story, the narrative I've constructed here is also an argument. It takes issue, for example, with most accounts of the historic origins of conventional gender arrangements, and it raises its own kind of questions about the relationship of religion and political reform. Because it is the product of a long drawn-out effort to "see with both eyes," it has its complexities.

But this attempt to explain a great many things is a story, too, with its own sweep, and lest the story be overwhelmed by argument, I have chosen to spin it out here at the outset, in its basic outlines, as a kind of aerial view of the terrain that will be covered in succeeding chapters.

There is a way of being in the world that recoils from aggressiveness, cunning, and greed, and there is a constellation of values that supports that way of being. Rooted in a sense of interdependence so profound that it extends to even the smallest life-forms, these values were the basis for human existence everywhere for our first several hundred thousand years. They arose directly out of the relationships our hunter-gatherer ancestors had with the natural world, one another, and Spirit—relationships that are most accurately understood in terms of mutual reciprocity and even symbiosis.

Pre-agricultural human beings didn't see themselves as sharply separate from the natural world, or superior to it, but as members of one family or tribe among many others, doing their best to stay alive. For a long, long time there was no uniquely human agenda. The deer, the rabbits, and the birds that human beings hunted were intent upon the same basic tasks they were: securing food and water, mating, and raising their offspring. And if with respect to these creatures human beings were predators, they were, with respect to others, prey. Many of our early ancestors knew as well as the deer and rabbits did how it felt to run for one's life.

Before agriculture produced food surpluses, most all human beings were nomadic, gleaning from one locale and moving on in a few days to another within a defined territory. They traveled in bands, but the bands were small, reflecting the limited food resources of most places. Interdependence was the basic law of life: what you found or killed, you shared, knowing that if someone else got lucky the next day, he or she would reciprocate. The individual's best hope for survival lay in connection with a group, and this meant that activities and behaviors that fostered cooperation between members of the group were, in the long run, as crucial to survival as foraging itself.

Pre-agricultural people didn't imagine for a minute that they were masters of the world they surveyed, and that may have been why they didn't imagine their gods to be their own masters. The keen sense of mutual reciprocity that defined one's relationship to the natural world defined one's relationship with the sacred as well. One knew oneself to belong in the particular watershed or canyon where one's people had always lived, and to the spirits who protected it and lived there right alongside oneself. God was multiple, fluid, and everywhere: God was the earth, and because the earth went on feeding us when we'd left our mothers' breasts, God was Mother.

I've chosen to characterize the values of pre-agricultural humanity with the word *belonging* for a couple of reasons. The word connotes the extraordinary dovetailing we see in any ecosystem—that special niche each life-form occupies in a perfectly functioning whole. But it prompts us, too, to consider how radically different two states of mind are: the one in which we look out across a forest or valley and say to ourselves, "This is where I belong," and the other, so intrinsic to Western civilization, in which we hear ourselves say, "This belongs to me." Out of that first state of mind, what I call the "values of Belonging" flow almost inevitably:

• *Intimate connection with the land to which one "belongs."* Not merely sentimental affection, but concrete knowledge of issues such as where the region's water comes from, what kinds of grasses and trees flourish there, and what threatens it.

• *Empathetic relationship to animals.* An appreciation for their diversity and splendor; an understanding of what they need, what they can teach me about myself, and what threatens them.

• *Self-restraint.* A holding back because greed kills. (Take one more quail than you need, and there may be none next year.)

• *Custodial conservatism.* Tremendous respect for the web of life as it exists, and reluctance to make changes whose impact we can't know.

• *Deliberateness.* The choice not to hurry but to be fully present always.

• *Balance.* The middle path through the contrarieties that we're always poised between.

• *Expressiveness.* Clarity and honesty with others; an understanding that secrets and grudges damage the trust that cooperation among individuals requires.

• *Generosity.* The unchecked flow of all things—information, resources, and ordinary kindness—so that everyone benefits.

• *Egalitarianism.* The belief that no one individual is substantially "more equal" than others, that the very best hunter is only one injury away from dependence.

• *Mutuality.* The ability to see oneself in others (and others in oneself) and to take differences lightly.

• *Affinity for alternative modes of knowing.* A way of viewing and processing the world that incorporates *all* the senses, but espe-

cially the sixth. (Intuition steps in where reason fears to tread.
Reason alone can't provide all the information one needs to
survive in nature.)

•*Playfulness*. A setting aside of seriousness that relieves tension
and facilitates intimacy.

•*Inclusiveness*. A primary corollary of interdependence (which
was the basic law of hunter-gatherer life) grounded in the
knowledge that excluding certain species, or believing them to
be expendable, may result in discarding something, or someone, crucial to survival itself.

•*Nonviolent conflict resolution*. The preferred method of problem-
solving, because violence has only *ever* begotten violence.

•*Openness to Spirit*. A belief that the fundamental reality is
Spirit, and that Spirit can be experienced firsthand.

These are the core values of Belonging, the values that guided our
hunter-gatherer predecessors. They aren't so much discrete elements
as components of a whole ethos. When scientists describe the structure of a molecule, they refer to the bonds that connect the various
particles to one another as "valences," and something like those mole-
cular bonds united the values by which our earliest ancestors lived.
Balance, generosity, self-restraint, mutuality, and intuition are so logically consistent with one another that they almost imply each other.
That may be why they turned up independently, in constellation, in
the human communities that came to occupy every continent.

The values of Belonging were "adaptive" to certain conditions—
specifically, to a nomadic, subsistence level life supported by foraging
and involving little contact with anybody outside one's own kinship
group. Yet while these values were "merely" adaptive, we lived by
them for so long that they've formed the equivalent of a thick geo-
logic stratum in human consciousness: they're deeply constitutive of
who we are and what we need, both as individuals and as a species.

So when the basic conditions under which human beings lived changed radically with the rise of agriculture ten thousand years ago, and those values were displaced, the psychic cost was inconceivably high.

CHANGE IN THE AIR ALWAYS

While it's correct to emphasize the stability of the pre-agricultural world, and the full integration of human beings into it, it's also true that throughout those long stretches of time, the seeds of change were germinating: slowly, but irreversibly, human beings were inching out of the realm of pure instinct. They captured fire, and they invented tools and weapons that gave them a widening edge over other creatures; they became artists (noticing, presumably, that while they were painting antelopes on the walls of caves, the antelopes themselves were doing nothing of the kind); and they understood the basic concepts involved in farming long before they took it up in earnest.

The forces behind the shift from foraging and clubbing to farming and herding were several, and even now they're only partially understood, but the Agricultural Revolution appears to have had an exuberant, almost explosive quality. One of those "tipping points" in human evolution must have been reached, because agriculture got underway within a few thousand years, and not in just one part of the world but five. Its adoption marked a radical shift in the relationship of human beings to their environment. Paleontologist Niles Eldredge helps us grasp the full magnitude of what happened: "Taking control of our own food supply, we became the first species in the 3.5 billion year history of life to live outside the confines of the local ecosystem."[1]

Human beings took charge now. They would decide what to grow and where. They would domesticate animals to work their fields, and they would divert water from rivers and lakes to irrigate them. In a sense, the idea of mastery was born along with agriculture—mastery, as opposed to connection—and from that idea flowed an altogether new set of values. These new values, which were adaptive to survival in agricultural economies, I've chosen to call the "values of Enterprise."

The empathic openness, for example, that hunter-gatherers had cultivated—toward land, animals, and other human beings—had to be suppressed now. For the farmer, land, animals, and even human beings were resources that he must bring under control, and the man most adept at exploiting those resources was rewarded.

He was rewarded, too, as he hadn't been in the past, for his own industry. Beyond survival itself, the hunting-gathering life had had only modest rewards for those who worked hard. In the absence of technologies for storing food, enough was enough. There was no point in piling up food that couldn't be eaten right away. But once food surpluses could be produced and stored, they could be bartered as well—for goods, animals, more land, or the services of others. The concept of ownership took on new meaning, and for that matter, so did the concept of poverty. More complex economies evolved, within which it was worth a farmer's time to take risks and experiment. There was more to gain now, and more to lose as well. Social and economic inequities divided humanity, as they really hadn't in the past, into "haves" and "have-nots."

The trait of competitiveness suited a person to prevail in this new environment. So did acquisitiveness, ambition, recklessness, irreverence, and the ability to keep secrets—values that were anathema, all of them, in the world of hunter-gatherers.

It was no coincidence that as all of these societal changes were taking place, God underwent a transformation as well. The growing prestige of "big men" required that He be correspondingly masculine, on the one hand, and supreme, on the other: the One God. *Capo da capo,* boss of the bosses. And as the earth was tamed, and wildness itself was banished—from forest, stream, and meadow—belief in an immanent God eroded steadily. It made more sense, finally, to relocate Him altogether, into the heavens. From there He could oversee human affairs, which were becoming more complicated by the minute. Human beings would see to making the earth bountiful; they would *wrest* crops from the soil if need be. What they needed from God now was a firm hand: a king and a judge who would inspire fear and compliance in people who had never really learned, as hunter-gatherers, to be subject to anyone.

If the values that shaped the hunter-gatherer's life reflect the need for connection, the values that fueled the Agricultural Revolution (and the subsequent rise of civilization as we know it) reveal disconnection—from nature, from other people, and from Spirit. The two constellations of values couldn't have been more deeply at odds.

One eye looked at the world and saw relationship. The other looked and saw opportunity. So powerful was the emerging culture, and so magnificent the promises it held out, that it simply took over. In breathtakingly short order, one way of being in the world gave way to another. One way of seeing the world was closed down.

A culture of Belonging ceded to a culture of Enterprise.

THE MISSING HALF OF WHO WE ARE

With the advantage of historical hindsight, it's tempting to imagine another, better arrangement—one that, in effect, might have kept both eyes open. Couldn't the inventiveness, curiosity, and industry that drove the Agricultural Revolution have coexisted in some kind of creative tension with the deep commitment to balance and sustainability that marked the pre-agricultural world?

Conceivably, they could have. As we'll see, though, there was tremendous momentum to the changes that were taking place, and that momentum would only intensify over time, right into the present. Each new technology gave rise to another and another, and with each technological breakthrough there came new economic and social arrangements—new roles for people to play and new choices to make. Social complexity intensified, and so, surely, did anxiety. A growing number of people lived in cities now, and archaeologists' reconstructions of some of those cities suggests that population density was extremely high. Epidemics broke out regularly under these crowded conditions, and so did food shortages. Social unrest was often acute. Wars, for which there was no real precedent in the pre-agricultural world, could flare up at any time.

Nothing was certain in this new environment except continued change and chronic, perpetual imbalance. Any hold the values of Belonging still had on people's hearts and imaginations was challenged severely by the harsh realities of their daily lives. So it was that, finally, those values were set aside.

It isn't difficult to understand why with the advent of agriculture, human beings found it impossible to integrate the values of Belonging with the values of Enterprise—why, in effect, they allowed one eye to languish and the other to become dominant.

But here, now, in the most technologically advanced nation in the world, where inventiveness, competitiveness, ambition, and acquisitiveness are cardinal virtues, the consequences of that choice are chillingly clear. Because the values of Enterprise have prevailed, and because the pace of change has only kept on accelerating, the entire world stands in acute and perilous imbalance.

When I first began to think about that imbalance (and indeed, for a couple of decades), I would understand it, and inveigh against it, in terms of gender. It seemed to me that as a society—as a species, for that matter (because the situation wasn't appreciably better anyplace else)—we weren't just trying to see with one eye, we were trying to breathe with one lung and walk on one leg: the silencing of women, and the systematic devaluing of their talents and contributions to society, had effectively removed them from the stage of history. Women, I was quite certain, were the missing half of contemporary civilization—the missing eye, lung, and leg. Their absence was the reason everything felt so precarious.

Though my assessment wasn't altogether wrong, I now believe that it didn't go far enough. The reality is much more interesting, and more hopeful as well. The missing half of who we are isn't just women, but the constellation of values that defined pre-agricultural life—a coherent, radiant whole that's much more than the sum of its parts. The retrieval of those values would be the best thing that could happen to humanity generally, and also the best thing that could happen to women.

CREATING A CLASS OF LOSERS

The values of Belonging didn't vanish altogether. Even as technologies multiplied, even as the "great civilizations" came into being, rose, fell, and were reconfigured, the ethos or culture of Belonging never really disappeared. At intervals it resurfaced, in an individual or a movement or even a work of art, and humanity glimpsed the extent of its losses. But the culture of Belonging has remained at the margins, barely audible; and of all the reasons why this is so, one stands out above the rest: rigid and highly contrastive notions of gender. Though such notions aren't the *source* of all our problems, they play a crucial role in perpetuating them.

It has long been conventional to associate values such as empathy and intuition with women, and aggressive mastery of circumstances with men. But the values of Belonging aren't inherently feminine, and the values of Enterprise aren't innately or exclusively masculine. As we'll see, male hunter-gatherers displayed the same reverence for the earth that women did, and nobody who's spent time on a mixed-gender playground can pretend that little girls are any less managerial than little boys.

The values of the pre-agricultural world couldn't be discarded altogether because they were too integral to being human. But they did need to be subordinated, lest they impede the emerging culture of Enterprise. And there was a relatively simple way in which that could be done. Because Enterprise values involved domination—over the land, resources, and human beings—people fell now into two groups: winners and losers, the powerful and the powerless. If the values of Belonging could be linked with the growing class of losers, that would in itself ensure that the values wouldn't be taken seriously.

So it was that the values of Belonging came to be seen as "women's values." They were placed in the custody of women, assigned to women, and identified with women—but not for the reasons one might think. Not because women were seen as inherently more empathetic, closer to nature, or more reverent than men, but because women were the undisputed losers in the adoption of agriculture. Their most important role in the new economy was to produce offspring to work the fields and fill the ranks of the military. Once women were sedentary and relatively well fed, and once cereal gruels were available as weaning foods, their fertility doubled, meaning that they were pregnant and caring for infants almost all of the time. Domesticated now much as sheep and cattle were, women incurred sharp losses in mobility, agency, and authority. Nothing could have been more natural, therefore, than to associate a banished culture with them, a defeated sex.

Identifying the old constellation of values as feminine put a human face on what might otherwise have been something of an abstraction. The face was a woman's, but not a woman as women *had* been, moving about on an equal footing with other members of their band or tribe. A woman, rather, as women had come to be—enclosed, subdued, and surrounded by hungry offspring.

Men would live out the values of competition, expansion, and exploitation, and women would go on being (or being expected to be) as relational, restrained, and reverent as before. But they would do so alone now, as women, and with the understanding that living in this way marked them out as the underclass.

For the foundations of modern civilization to be laid, then, something had to be suppressed, silenced, subdued, and (perhaps most important) broken apart. That something was a constellation of values that was fundamentally incompatible with the buildup of city-states and empires. The profound consequence of the domination of the Enterprise value system over that of Belonging was that women lost power and voice, and for decades we've interpreted women's role in history from the perspective of that dual loss. But what we've failed to realize is that it wasn't just women who incurred massive losses. The lost "half" of who we are, collectively, is that constellation of values; and that loss has impacted men as injuriously as women, though in different ways.

I don't believe that I would have arrived at this understanding, or begun drawing the many implications I have from it, if I'd known that set of values only as an abstraction. Before I could begin to see the culture of Belonging as a living reality and stop confusing it with "the feminine," I would have to come to the end of a certain kind of rope. I would have to come up against the limitations of the feminist perspective that so many of us had spent decades constructing. I would have to revisit cherished theories and explanations.

OUR WHOLE LIVES

Like most women my age, I grew up believing that life is essentially about men—that history is the history men make, poetry and painting are the creation of men, and so on. Not really seeing women, not always hearing them, and worse still, not questioning their absence—from film festivals or literary reviews, history faculties or police departments, lists of Fortune 500 CEOs or the United States Senate—was as habitual for me, until my early twenties, as it was for anybody else.

But then, so was white bread. And for many of us who came of age during the 1960s, "refined" was a dirty word. Wholeness was the standard by which we measured food and a great deal else besides, and the women's movement grew out of the recognition that the lives of women in our society were far from "whole." As we came to understand how long and how thoroughly half the human race had been silenced, what struck many of us most forcibly was the sheer wastefulness of such a system. As the uncharted half of human experience came into view, in a flood of women's biography, memoir, art, history, and literature, we grieved at the depth and beauty of what had been excluded. As a species, human beings had made certain choices that seemed more and more curious—arbitrary and ultimately impoverishing.

So it was that I spent the better part of two decades plumbing the half of human experience that I'd grown up ignoring. I "isolated," in effect, occluding the eye that knew only the male-centered vision of things and concentrating exclusively on the particulars of women's experience and achievements.

I knew all the while that eventually I would want to relax my study of everything female and integrate what I'd learned into a bigger picture and a better paradigm. Once I had a reasonable grasp of women's history, for example, could I fit it into a broader, more comprehensive historical narrative? Would existing handed-down narratives work for this purpose ("Add women and stir"), or would the very inclusion of women so destabilize the old stories that they would have to be recast altogether? Could I learn to read women poets both as poets who were women and poets of particular times and places (for "poets" read filmmakers, novelists, painters, photographers, musicians)? And if I did, what effect would such a reading have on my understanding of poetry itself and its place in human experience—its transformative power?

That was the plan. But time passed, and that second, integrative phase never quite happened. It appeared that one couldn't just "add women and stir," even imaginatively. Reinserting women into the historical narrative helped, but the whole story that I'd so eagerly anticipated—three-dimensional and vivid—didn't emerge.

Gradually I began to suspect that the missing half wasn't just women after all, or even the body of "what women know." Rather, what was in exile was a way of being in the world, an *ethos* or a *gestalt*. I realized that a culture that allowed women to live in comfortable parity with men would differ from the one we live in now in a great many other, nongender ways as well: gender equality would only arise as the symptom or byproduct of more far-reaching changes.

But before I could arrive at that conclusion, I had to get the sort of perspective on my own culture that you can get only by stepping outside it, and I had to experience that other way of being in the world much more directly.

THE PREVIOUS TENANTS

I live near what's called the Sonoma Marin Coast, and until very recently I've been more oriented to the San Francisco Bay Area than to the far less populated country to the north and east. The first time I drove north to Ukiah felt like a guilty pleasure. It was one of those late September days when the sky was as sharply, uncompromisingly blue as the roadside cottonwoods were yellow-gold—so spectacularly autumnal that some part of me kept thinking I was supposed to be in school.

I was on my way to see a museum exhibition of Pomo baskets. Woven from materials native to Sonoma County's creeks and rivers by women who'd inherited their skills from mothers and grandmothers in a lineage that went back thousands of years, Pomo baskets are renowned all over the world for their extraordinary workmanship and for the beauty and intricacy of their designs. This particular collection was on display for a limited time: it was on its way to the Smithsonian Institution, where it would be housed permanently.

Set out among the baskets were enlarged photographs of the weavers themselves that dated, in some cases, back to the nineteenth century. I couldn't get enough of looking at them. One especially pretty elderly woman, her face creased with laughter, sat behind what looked like an enormous spider made of reeds. This was a "thousand-stick basket," still in the making, and the woman holding it (the caption said) was Elsie Allen. I recognized her name, because a local high school is named in her honor, and now I learned why.

It was Elsie Allen (1899–1990) who had led the revival of Pomo basketry. Her dedication was the reason that this collection existed. To create it, she'd had to challenge at least two longstanding Pomo traditions. One was that, because a Pomo woman's baskets were believed to be so much a part of her, they were customarily buried with her; the other was that no one who was not a Native American should be initiated into the art.

Walking around the museum that day, learning the difference between "coiling" and "twining," and what it means when you see a break in one of the colored bands that circle a basket or a bit of reddish brown worked into a band of a lighter color, was the beginning of an ongoing revelation for me.[2]

In an entirely unsystematic fashion, but steadily and hungrily, I began to research Native American women such as Elsie Allen. It was shocking to realize how little I knew about the people who had lived in my neighborhood just a hundred and fifty years before I got there: the Coastal Miwok and the Pomos in particular, and the Ohlone nearer the Bay Area.

I began walking the hills behind my house, as well as Dillon Beach, Point Reyes, and the shore of Tomales Bay, mentally lifting off the fences and barns, the houses and highways, trying to imagine what the area must have looked like a hundred or two hundred years ago. Because certain local heroes and heroines have kept development in reasonable check, that imaginative leap wasn't as hard as it might have been.

Before long, I'd found places where I could sit quietly and begin to feel, after half an hour or so had passed, that I was not altogether alone. It wasn't a great stretch to sense the presence of others who must have sat by this same creek—generations of women and men, listening as appreciatively as I was now to a red-winged blackbird, watching the shadows of clouds move across the same green hillside I was looking at.

I began bringing home piles of books from the local libraries that taught me more about the men and women who had lived for upward of several thousand years along the Sonoma Marin Coast. Although they left hardly a trace, the archaeological record shows clearly that warfare played almost no part in their existence. What makes this all the more impressive is that nowhere on the continent of North America had so many Indians lived so closely with as much linguistic diversity. It appears that then, as now, all kinds of people had wanted to live in the Bay Area, and that if doing so meant putting up with other people's idiosyncrasies, so be it—small price to pay for a perfect climate, ocean views, and abundant food.

The Pomos, I learned, hadn't been a *single* people at all. They'd spoken seven related but mutually incomprehensible languages, and they'd lived in a variety of social structures governed not only by "chiefs" but by an elite of ceremonial leaders, shamans, professional craftspeople, traders, and heads of families. While each community could be seen as an independent village-state, they were all joined to other villages by reciprocal religious obligations, intermarriage, trade, and military links. They'd worked out a balanced complexity that allowed them to prosper and live in harmony.

It came through very clearly that first day at the museum that these were a people who honored women, particularly their female elders. I saw little evidence that anything like a "goddess culture" had existed here, but something far more mundane (though, as far as I was concerned, just as valuable) had clearly been present: a simple, ordinary sense of respectful mutuality. Men and women performed different tasks and played different kinds of games, but the things that concerned women most urgently concerned men also.

When an Ohlone woman was pregnant, for example, she was hedged round with restrictions: to protect the health of her baby, she would eat no meat, fish, or salt, she would make no use of the basketmaker's awl, and she would be especially careful in her behavior toward people and animals. But the husband of a pregnant woman was just as mindful: no meat or salt, no tobacco, very little hunting, and careful governance of his emotions.

Among the Pomos, nobody who became a parent hadn't heard the legend of Slug Woman, a truly terrifying figure said to lurk still around the darker byways of the northern Sonoma Coast. Pomo custom dictated that the father of a newborn baby was to stay close to the mother and infant for four full days after birth. When once upon a time a young father had scoffed at the stricture and left his home to go out hunting, Slug Woman is said to have come after him, carrying a cradle decorated with abalone shells that tinkled as she ran. Tirelessly she pursued him; then, having found him, she dragged him to the inside of a hollow tree, apprised him of his error, and, over the next few days, burned him to death. (The rest of this grisly little tale has to do with his son, who grew up making smarter choices.)[3]

These were a people who took parental leave seriously!

As my impressions of the former tenants of Northern California accumulated, I began to understand why I was gathering them in so hungrily. The elusive wholeness that I'd been looking for and failing to find in my painstakingly reconstructed "add women and stir" version of history was palpable here, in a culture with which I was still just barely familiar.

Erosion of the Social Matrix

On the morning when breaking news bulletins informed the country that twelve Littleton, Colorado teenagers had died at the hands of two of their classmates, many of us knew that, collectively, we had reached a defining moment.

One Littleton resident interviewed by a television news caster drew a connection in the days that followed between the Columbine High School shootings and what she saw as "the stunning erosion of our social matrix." Her choice of words struck me forcibly.

My own feminist awakening, chronicled in *At the Root of This Longing,* had had much to do with the violent deaths of three young women. Struggling to reconcile the anger and helplessness I felt at those deaths with my commitment to a meditative spirituality, I'd found myself envisioning something I really knew only by its absence.

What I'd envisioned was that around every human being (not just girls, but every one of us, vulnerable as all of us are at different stages of life), there should be—there *could* be—a kind of force-field. Radiant, almost palpable, that force-field would deflect injury as surely as if it were made of steel. Rooted in a simple baseline horror of doing harm, it would be the counterpart at the level of the whole society of the fierce love each of us has for our own children.

In the past, I'd had no evidence that such a thing had ever really existed outside my own imagination and desire. I couldn't have said what values a society would have to hold in order for that kind of protective zone to be in place. But the more I learned about the life-ways of Northern California's native peoples, the more certain I was that something like that force-field or matrix had practically *defined* their culture, and that it had a great deal to do with the baskets and those who wove them. Over and over it came up in anthropologists' interviews—memories of a mother or grandmother working silently in the early-morning hours, weaving prayers for a young bride into the gift basket she was making, weaving prayers for her children into baskets she would store their food or clothing in. A family's wealth was gauged by the number and quality of baskets in its possession, and this wealth wasn't the equivalent of money or real estate, but of solid-ity and strength—"capital" of a very different kind.

The very structures that made Pomo life comfortable appeared to be extensions of "what women knew" as weavers. Linguistic differences may have broken the region up into innumerable tiny patches, but over time, bonds of trust and affiliation had been thrown out across lines of difference, weaving tribe and tribelet together in ways that didn't re-quire homogeny. Tribes that didn't speak the same language could meet nonetheless for all-night "sings," because they knew a shared body of songs that were made up of "vocables"—words whose meanings weren't known, borrowed from a third language or from spirit or ani-mal language.

No two foraging societies were exactly alike—that's the beauty of their being so closely adapted to their particular settings. But they did resemble one another in certain basic ways. Gradually, as I became familiar with a fair number of these societies, a composite picture began to emerge. From that picture, and from the understanding that variations are myriad, I could begin to extrapolate meaningfully with respect to the foraging societies that existed more than ten thousand years ago, before the rise of agriculture.

As I came to see how these cultures operated, I realized, for example, that the same thickly woven cloth of custom and connection that evolved over long periods of time among people such as the Pomos and the Ohlones must have evolved among our pre-agricultural ancestors as well. That cloth was the protective force-field I'd envisioned, and the values of Belonging that formed the base of those earlier cultures were the "social matrix" that had deteriorated too badly to protect the kids at Columbine High School. The cultures of Belonging may be gone, but collectively we still feel their loss. We know that we need the protective medium they wove to keep our own children safe.

A Crisis in Values

Human beings embraced the values of Belonging for our first two and a half million years of existence. Our nervous system evolved along with those values: they are who we are.

Only they've never been *all* of who we are.

Sunspots didn't cause the Agricultural Revolution, and the Devil didn't make us do it. Our own human desires and our own irrepressible ingenuity moved us along, and when the culture of Enterprise first announced itself, *it* must have felt like the missing half of who we were.

We honored that powerful eruption in consciousness, but it compelled us to set aside long-cherished values of Belonging, and that in turn meant losing the secure niche that those values had created in a Spirit-filled universe. It meant the loss of matrix, and the end of simply *belonging*.

So of course relationships between men and women were thrown out of kilter. Mutual reciprocity had defined those relationships in earlier days as surely as it had defined people's relationship to the earth. The Enterprise paradigm wasn't about mutuality at all, but about competition. The defining change wasn't that men would henceforth be privileged over women, but that *privilege itself would be privileged:* class, race, religious persuasion, sexual orientation, and gender would all be employed to justify the elevation of some of us over others. The existing social fabric would be rent, and free-floating insecurity would replace it.

To recognize this pattern is to recognize that the situation of women won't improve measurably until everybody else's does too: the wholeness of a society within which women are fully and meaningfully included won't return until the very idea of privilege begins to lose its validity.

Odd as it might seem to say so, this new understanding of men and women, in the context of the values of Belonging and Enterprise, struck me as good news.

Because now it no longer looked as if half the human race just woke up one morning unable to stand the other half. Our male ancestors didn't arbitrarily or cold-bloodedly decide to put their daughters and wives under a permanent, systematic oppression on a whim. Everyone was caught up in a crisis of conflicting values—a crisis whose full consequences no one could have predicted. Women probably had a voice, very early on, in some of the decisions that would ultimately damage them the most.

It seems appropriate to pause over that point. During the period when our ancestors made the crucial shift from foraging to farming, much about that change would have cheered women: a dependable diet for their families, permanent shelters that could do more than just keep out the rain, and the stimulation of being around more people, at the very least.

It wouldn't have taken long for women to start recognizing the disadvantages, however, including new kinds of illness, loss of dietary diversity, rising militarism, and the particular losses they experienced as women in this rapidly changing environment. But I don't think that they could have recognized easily (if at all) the ideological shift that was taking place—a shift that would in the long run affect the status of women far more catastrophically than any of the specific forms of oppression that were increasingly a part of their lives.

It wasn't just that women were being dominated, in their homes and communities, to a greater extent than before. Worse yet, the very idea of domination was rapidly taking on a sanction that it had never had (and that it wouldn't lose). It is that idea, and its almost complete acceptance in Western society, that women must ultimately combat if they're to gain the genuine and lasting equality they want.

Today, a considerable number of women do understand this. They see how damaging the paradigm of dominance is to men and boys as well, and it seems only reasonable to them, therefore, that men should see it too, and begin to challenge it. And in fact, some men are doing exactly that. But their number is small, and their voices are all but drowned out by a chorus of mostly male voices, indignant that women should find fault with the gender scripts intrinsic to the culture of Enterprise and outraged that men might too, for those scripts make nothing clearer than that "whining" is something only women do. Real men do their suffering in silence.

(Tellingly, two of the most important current books on male depression are called *The Pain Behind the Mask* and *I Don't Want to Talk About It*. Urgent as it is for men and women to confront the "gender knot" together, they won't be able to until men begin to break their silence and acknowledge their pain.)

To recognize that the glories of Western civilization don't altogether outweigh the costs isn't to argue that our ancestors should have gone on eating roots and berries and the odd wild critter. Still, if (knowing what we know now) we revisit that extraordinary historic watershed wherein one value system trumped another, it's impossible not to wish the transition had been better handled.

Fortunately, it isn't too late to act on that wish. The hard task that our ancestors either couldn't see or understandably dodged—the task of integrating the two halves of who we are (the culture of Belonging and the culture of Enterprise)—is still right where they left it. Thanks to about ten thousand years of uninhibited Enterprise, we know a few things that they didn't; and some of those things can help.

PART   I

The Values of Belonging

On the Willamette Valley farm in Oregon where I spent my child-hood, it wasn't uncommon to find arrowheads chipped out of obsidian flakes or flint, and one spring when my father was plowing the bottomland near the creek he turned up a bowl made of stone. Nearby was another stone that fit a hand nicely and looked as if it had been used for grinding. We kept these on the hearth, never using them to crack walnuts or filberts because they seemed precious to us—antiquities from the remote past.

Not long ago I realized that the grinding bowl and stone could well have been in use as little as a hundred (maybe a hundred and twenty) years before we found them. If you'd told me that as a child, I'd have thought a hundred and twenty years was an eternity, but now, well aware how quickly three, four, and even five decades can pass, I see how brief the interval actually was between our tenure and that of the Native Americans who'd lived near that creek for hundreds, maybe thousands of years before the first white settlers arrived.

That small epiphany became part of a larger one. I began to think about the culture that preceded the arrival of white settlers, when the Native Americans who lived by "our" creek were still hunter-gatherers. Their way of life had effectively vanished from most of the world thousands of years earlier. Realizing this, I began to see the displacement and near annihilation of American Indians by white settlers and their government in a light that I hadn't before.

When Europeans spread out across this continent, what actually took place was a head-on collision—in fact, innumerable head-on collisions—between representatives of a culture fast outstripping all others in the world in its technological prowess, and small bands of people who hadn't taken even the first steps in that direction.

When my grandmother's grandmother crossed the Great Plains on her way to Oregon, therefore, and met up with Indians along the way, those brief encounters (and innumerable encounters like them) had extraordinary historical significance. Across an immense cultural divide, humanity as it had been for its first few million years gazed at humanity as it had become over the past ten thousand years. For a time, at least, the culture of Belonging was right here, plainly visible to the culture of Enterprise. Here at the far end of the extraordinary trajectory that has been Western civilization in the making, Americans in particular (the greatest beneficiaries of that civilization) have had the chance, and the obligation, to reflect upon all that had been set aside, silenced, and discredited in order to get us here. To the extent that that obligation has been taken seriously at all—to the extent that this continent's indigenous people have been honored, studied, and recompensed even a little—to that extent, the impetus of Enterprise culture has been slowed here and there, and its more destructive impact grasped.

That same terribly important scrutiny has been taking place in other parts of the world where the last hunter-gatherer cultures have all but succumbed to the same pressures the American Indians did— among them Australia's Aborigines, the Kalahari San of southern Africa, the Bambuti Pygmies of the Ituri Forest in the very heart of Africa, and the Inuit of North America's Arctic region. By awakening the rest of us to the strengths of these cultures, several generations of anthropologists have helped us substantiate the intuitive feeling that all is not what it could be in this wealthiest, most powerful society ever. But their work also compels us, by way of pursuing that intuition, to revisit and even reconstruct our sense of what constitutes human history.

Until very recently, everything that happened before the rise of agriculture was labeled "prehistory." By extension, our earliest ancestors were "pre-humans." Today, though, we know way too much about hunter-gatherers to go on pretending that the two or three million years of human existence that preceded recorded history was a vast emptiness.

Long before people lived in cities, wrote letters, and cultivated and stored food, they lived in community. They told stories and sang songs that preserved the memory of their collective experience. Beauty dazzled them, and they found ingenious ways to reproduce it. They loved each other and lost each other, and grieved at the losing, struggling to make sense of it; and, they did all of that just as we do, inside a framework of values—a complex of values that is fully within our capacity to grasp.

Among the important insights into those early life-ways that anthropologists have given us is the understanding that those values are, in fact, adaptations. They arose directly and even organically out of the relationship of human beings to their environment and one another as surely as the capacity to walk upright did, or the visual astuteness to tell ripe berries from green ones.

CHAPTER I

A Sturdy Web, Closely Woven

Before the advent of agriculture, all human beings were foragers. They didn't till the earth, and they didn't domesticate animals. They relied on the plant and animal resources of their own locality. The foraging strategy has been called mankind's most successful and persistent adaptation. What that word "adaptation" implies in this context is that human beings spent their first couple of million years becoming the ideal inhabitants of specific niches in a wide range of local ecosystems. Through the mechanism of biological evolution, they gradually became fine-tuned so as to fit perfectly into the more-or-less steady-state equilibrium of the shoreline or foothills or ice-scape they called home.

Human beings had to be able to eat whatever was available in their bioregion from one season to the next. Carnivores in some places, omnivores in most, they developed strong jaws, teeth that could tear as well as grind, a long digestive tract, and all kinds of enzymes for breaking foods down. Because in areas where food resources were few or sporadic in their appearance, the ability to walk long distances without tiring was an asset, as was the capacity to store calories as fat until needed, human beings acquired those traits in due time too.

The fact that our earliest ancestors were foragers shaped us in innumerable other ways, among them the physiology of infants and mothers. Helpless for a much longer time than other mammal babies, and unable to obtain their own food, the children of foraging mamas stayed on their hips and at their breasts well into toddlerhood. That extended propinquity allowed human offspring to learn by osmosis and observation much of what they would need to know as adult foragers.

Biological adaptations take place slowly, and they're not swiftly undone just because surrounding conditions change. When most of us stopped being hunter-gatherers about ten thousand years ago—which in evolutionary terms is no time at all—our diet changed sharply, reducing the variety of foods we ate even as food itself became more easily available. Life scientists across the spectrum have noted over the past hundred years the many areas in which health is compromised because our bodies have still not adjusted to that shift. Cardiovascular disease and diabetes are just two of the illnesses that are caused and/or exacerbated by diets composed largely of separated refined foods such as butter-fat, corn oil, sugar, and white flour.

But biological adaptation involves much more than biochemical interactions. Exercise, for instance, plays a crucial role in health. Our bodies were clearly designed, by the long process of genetic "sculpting," to flourish at high levels of activity. Muscular exertion stimulates the growth of bone mass, for example, sweating removes toxins from the bloodstream, and deep breathing strengthens the muscles in the heart. All these relationships can be traced back to our having been very active while we were evolving, and we ignore them now at real cost.

There's still another dimension to the adaptations that made us who we are. Take a troubled mind for a long walk in the woods, and watch the tensions dissipate as you fall into a rhythmic pace. As anxiety levels drop, the likelihood of developing stress-related digestive and circulatory problems drops as well. In addition, the natural "high" of released endorphins is palpable—that is, if we move in the ways our bodies need to move, we receive the immediate bonus of feeling great.

As for the infant on her mother's hip, the hormonal secretions released in the long-ago mother while she nursed her baby made it unlikely that the woman would conceive again soon, which was typically a good thing for hunter-gatherers, because it was important that the size of the group not exceed the carrying capacity of their environment. But delaying the next pregnancy also meant that the child would have her mother's exclusive companionship all the longer. In addition, hormonal secretions induced in both mother and child feelings of deep delight in one another.

All around, it was a nice package.

Our unconscious emotional needs, then, were shaped as powerfully by the experience of foraging as our physiological characteristics were; they didn't develop separately. We don't have to meet those needs in exactly the way they once were met (even nonhuman primates avail themselves of babysitters: anthropologists call them "allo-mothers," or "other-mothers"), but we do have to reckon with them, because they're so deeply a part of who we are. They were "adaptive" to the conditions we lived in for our first few million years, but they haven't gone away just because external conditions have changed.

VALUES AND DESIRES

The massive sum of adaptations that allowed hunter-gatherers to live successfully and sustainably on every continent extended beyond the physiological and the emotional. What enabled human beings to live in such finely tuned harmony with their environment was that particular constellation of values listed earlier, universal among hunter-gatherers, hammered out over time in the context of a foraging life as inexorably as peripheral vision, the opposable thumb, and "fight-or-flight" reactions to immediate danger.

We'll describe the relationship between a foraging life and the values it generated much more extensively in the next chapters. But for now, consider the following:

In a nomadic, subsistence economy it was folly to be anything but generous and forbearing toward one's companions, because everyone depended entirely on one another: parents and children, gatherer and hunter, woman and man, old and young. Intimate knowledge of the natural world was synonymous with survival, and so was restrained use of that world's resources.

The simple fact that over long reaches of time a band or tribe had been able to eke out its subsistence in a particular region gave rise to a strong sense of connection and mutual reciprocity with that place—a sense that you and I would be tempted to call "reverence" or even "worship." Though most of these cultures didn't have a word for "religion," a strong sense of the sacred, and of sacred presences, pervaded the whole of life.

Cultivation of a rich interior life, a certain serenity and balance, the capacity to take great pleasure in small things: all of these were survival skills in societies where external stimulation and intellectual engagement were minimal.

These values support and imply one another, forming together the living constellation that I've chosen to call the culture of Belonging: a system of meanings within which the interdependence of all life-forms is the central truth—a way of being in the world that presumes connection, balance, mutuality, and self-restraint.

The values of hunter-gatherer cultures aren't the cardinal values of contemporary postindustrial life. But because we lived by them for so very long, I would argue, our current slighting of them comes at great cost. Because we act against their promptings so regularly, social, political, and spiritual problems have arisen that are as real and palpable as diabetes, hypertension, appendicitis, and asthma.

Admittedly, the mind does stumble over the word "values." Family values. American values. Christian values. End-of-season, empty-the-warehouse, blow-out-the-competition shopping values. Popular usage has rendered the term all but meaningless. But we need it, so I want to take just a moment to administer etymological CPR.

The word "value" is rooted in the Latin verb *valere:* to be strong or well. The value of a coin is the measure of its strength in the market-place—the weight it can pull compared to other currencies: the euro up against the dollar, the peso facing down the ruble. If I'm wavering between two courses of action and one calls me more powerfully than the other, that's a value declaring itself.

A value, then, isn't an idea or an abstraction; it's a force in conscious-ness closely connected with desire. In the Upanishads, it's said that a man is his deep, driving desire. As his desire is, so is his deed; and as his deed is, so is his destiny. To find out what someone's values are, you don't *ask* her; you look at the choices she makes. From deep down, well out of sight, values direct the course of our lives like the rudder of a ship. Just so, the values shared by an entire people are forces in their collective consciousness.

The values of pre-agricultural people weren't thrashed out in parliament or fine-tuned on radio talk shows: conscious choice played almost no part in the process. Their values arose directly out of the contingencies of their lives. So to know what those values were, we need to know how people lived before the so-called Neolithic Transition. If we had to depend only on the archaeological record, our knowledge of pre-agricultural life would be very limited indeed.

But in fact, thanks to the work that anthropologists (both amateur and professional) have carried out this past century and a half, we know a great deal about more recent hunter-gatherers. Combining their information with the rich archaeological record yields a picture of life that is rich and suggestive. I draw gratefully on the work of these many dedicated scientists to elucidate the relationship between the hunter-gatherer lifestyle and the values of Belonging.

Vocabulary, of course, is problematic. The more we learn about the "prehistoric" people in question, the more unsatisfactory all of the conventional labels become:

Prehistoric is accurate in that what happened in the world wasn't recorded as "history" until there were alphabets, but the term feels injurious nonetheless.

Hunter-gatherer is bulky, and since it implies that more calories came from hunting than gathering, it doesn't describe all hunter-gatherer cultures accurately. Gatherer-hunter is an even bigger mouthful, though. Since we know now that a bit of cultivation did slip in here and there, neither term is strictly applicable to everyone we'll want to discuss.

Tribal is dicey also, given that anthropologists distinguish meaningfully between "bands" and "tribes" (the former being smaller than the latter), and yet there's no parallel label "bandal," even though anthropologists say that most hunter-gatherers in fact lived in bands.

Aboriginal—from the Latin *ab,* meaning "from," and *origine,* meaning "beginning"—is arguably appropriate, except that most people assume it to apply only to the natives of Australia or New Zealand, and they often hear in it the connotation "primitive."

Somewhat arbitrarily, then, and for the sake of clarity, I'll use only the term "pre-agricultural" with reference to people who lived before agriculture arose, and "hunter-gatherer" to describe later groups who didn't adopt agriculture. I'll call this latter group "foragers" too, especially because that label underscores the fact that gathering, not hunting, was in most situations the primary source of calories.

Achieving clarity with respect to timelines is even more difficult. When we speak or write about the traditional culture of the Apaches or the Australian Aborigines or the Congo Pygmies, should we use the present or the past tense? With indigenous peoples in every part of the world fighting to retain and revitalize connections with their past, describing their traditional life-ways in the past tense feels like a cruel discounting of their struggles.

And yet, in its pure form, the hunter-gatherer way of life is over. The extensive land-base it requires is gone, and contact with contemporary culture has altered traditional life-ways irretrievably. It may be true that a handful of Pomos or Apaches are still making baskets (or bows or canoes) in the way their ancestors did. But they certainly aren't making them in the context of a subsistence, preliterate, tribal or "bandal" life, and it's the *whole* life that concerns us here.

Past or present—dead or alive? The only right answer may be that the question isn't ours to decide. As a writer, though, I've *had* to decide, and it has felt most honest to me to adopt the past tense, for the most part.

CHAPTER 2

At Home in the World:
The Life-Ways of Hunter-Gatherers

A value is a tug in consciousness that shapes the choices we make. A value is also a strategy for survival, however, as we saw in the last chapter.

The values of Belonging evolved as adaptations to the conditions of pre-agricultural life. So when people like the Kalahari San and the Congo Pygmies are described as kind, generous, affectionate, and hospitable—which they are, and regularly—we must ask ourselves what it was about their life-experience that "selected" for kindness and generosity (or at least the appearance of kindness and generosity). We need to understand what the parameters of that way of life actually were.

By ten thousand years ago, human beings had colonized virtually every corner of the globe, and nearly all of them were foragers. Most were nomadic too, though the range they traveled for food varied dramatically depending on the resources available. They all lived at the subsistence level: the essential business of their life was simply staying alive. They had no written language, but through oral transmission they preserved large bodies of story, song, and precept. They lived in small bands, smaller in some places than others—from two dozen to perhaps four or five dozen.

Most of the more recent foragers whose lives have been available for study the past hundred and fifty years were people who had been edged out of their traditional territory onto lands deemed uninhabitable by everybody else. It makes sense to assume, then, that prehistoric foragers probably had an easier time of it overall than did the desert-dwelling Kalahari San or Australian Aborigines. In fact, we know that some had more in common with the Indians of the San Francisco Bay Area, who lived near the sea in a temperate zone and were effectively sedentary, shuttling summer and winter between the coast and warmer interior valleys, a distance of only a few miles—foragers, yes, but affluent, adept at trade, admired for their artistic accomplishments (notably basketry), and skilled at keeping the peace.

Living near the sea was one way out of the nomadic life: easy access to shellfish, fish, seabirds, and seaweed allowed foragers to be sedentary year round in some places. Figuring out that meat could be preserved by freezing it was another. In the Central Russian plains, the remains of several small villages have been discovered that date back as early as thirty thousand years ago. The houses had been built out of mammoth bones and been covered, probably, with skins. Deep holes in the ground appear to have served as storage lockers through the coldest winter months, when food supplies were scarcest.

Early evidence of sedentism is important, because being settled is a precondition for social complexity, which in turn leads to technological breakthroughs, specialization, and accumulated wealth. Sedentism also signals some facility at resolving conflicts, which hunter-gatherers often handled by simply dispersing.

On the other hand, it's also true that even in the absence of agriculture, sedentism and affluence can precipitate some of the less benign developments we associate with the rise of agriculture: sharp class differentiation, for example, and the oppression of one group by another, both of which characterized Indian tribes who lived near what is now the border between California and Oregon (and must have characterized some prehistoric hunter-gatherers as well).

All of which is to say that we have to be careful when we generalize about our pre-agricultural ancestors. Their lives weren't necessarily as stripped-down as those of the most stressed of the modern hunter-gatherers. Even so, when we take into account the differences among later foragers—what the "spread" is, and what seems to be most typical—a composite picture of pre-agricultural life-ways does emerge, and that picture is consistent with the idea of a culture of Belonging. Even as foraging cultures began to edge toward the agricultural model—planting seeds to grow water gourds, for example, or attaching themselves to herds of migratory animals—most of them tended to retain, in large part, the cardinal values of Belonging. In fact, some of the most instructive situations are exactly those transitional moments when a traditional culture is teetering toward a very different model but still holding on.

Why Generosity Worked

Among hunter-gatherers everywhere, subsistence itself was the basic objective—necessary and sufficient.

In the absence of techniques for storing food, whatever was gathered or hunted had to be consumed within a day or two. There was no advantage, then, in getting more than you needed, except that sharing out whatever you'd killed set up the conditions for future reciprocity.

So generosity worked. So did trust and the willingness to overlook slights and forget quarrels quickly.

So, obviously, did a capacity to be contented with what was available. Anthropologist Marshall Sahlins has described foraging as "the original affluent society . . . in which all the people's wants are easily satisfied."[1] But the claim hides an implicit proviso: for all the people's wants to be easily satisfied, those wants have to be relatively modest.

And wants were modest indeed among most foraging peoples. Not only was there no point collecting food that couldn't be eaten in a day or two, there was also no reason to pile up possessions beyond what was essential: whatever you acquired was also yours to carry, and any seasoned backpacker can tell you how that equation plays out.

Of course, one happy side effect of living such a materially minimal life was that it obviated one of the perennial motives for warfare. One might feel wary about the band of people camping one valley over, and concerned that there might not be enough game for everyone, but one had no illusions about their possessing treasures you wished you could get hold of. And on the more intimate level, couples could break up if they needed to without the burden of property settlements.

PLAYING AROUND

The word "subsistence" needn't connote a grim struggle from one desperate repast to the next, though. Playfulness was intrinsic to foragers' lives. In some of the most daunting circumstances, observers have noted among the Kalahari San, for example, an astonishing readiness to laugh—not because they're "childlike" or giddy or frivolous, but because life is so unrelentingly difficult, and being bitter doesn't help.

Hunter-gatherers everywhere enjoyed decorating themselves elaborately: adorning oneself—and one another—was (and still is) one of very few artistic outlets available to nomads. Fantastic markings of face and torso, intricately designed headdresses, and bracelets, anklets, and aprons made of braided fiber and handmade beads—all of these crafts took hours and hours; but once subsistence needs had been met, there was no more actual work to be done, so there was often time for whimsy and the sort of handwork that has always relieved mind and spirit.

Sahlins's description of foragers as "affluent" might be an exaggeration, but so are terms such as "stark" and "grim."

Anthropologist Richard A. Gould, who spent several months hanging out with a family of Australian Aborigines makes the rigors of their life unequivocally clear in his account of the visit but he also describes walking several miles with one of the men and his pregnant wife to reach a small stand of pale blue flowers from whose roots the women extract a key ingredient for a fragrant ointment they like to smooth onto their limbs.[2]

SOCIAL FLUIDITY

Pre-agricultural people were for the most part nomadic, because no ecosystem ever evolved with the express purpose of supporting human beings. A forest or a meadow is an incredibly complex mosaic of interdependent life-forms. Providing three square meals a day for mobs of bipeds wasn't the first priority of *any* habitat.

In fact, for every bioregion there's a rough rule of thumb: the sustenance of a single human being will require so many acres (assuming the most rudimentary of tools). If the area is resource-rich, the ratio will be low: two or three acres per person. If it's basically a wasteland, the ratio will be much, much higher: thirty or forty acres and counting. Human beings could, of course, have distributed themselves across their vast territories in groups of two or three and thereby kept their traveling needs to a minimum. But there was safety in greater numbers; and besides, we're preeminently social beings. I suspect that the nomadic life gradually selected for relatively gregarious individuals who didn't mind picking up and moving on every few days.

The evolutionary process had equipped human beings rather well in other ways for the peripatetic, foraging life they led for their first couple of million years. Being bipedal and upright, for instance, means that human beings suffer less from the heat of the day than four-footed animals do, whose whole bodies are exposed to the hot vertical rays of midday sunlight. Human beings catch more of the cooling breezes too, and they absorb less heat from the ground.

Membership in nomadic foraging bands was fluid, not static, and it needed to be. Anthropologists report hunter-gatherers to have been surprisingly individualistic, given the high degree of cooperation they displayed. Each time the band moved, the camp could (and usually did) reform in a slightly different way. Friends who had fallen out would build their shelters farther away from each other, and new friendships and alliances would be created. In fact, if group dynamics or environmental factors dictated—if tempers flared, for example, or food resources in a particular area were too thin to support everyone—a small group would sometimes break up into two or more still smaller groups. These subgroups would often coalesce again later when everyone had forgotten what the fuss was about—or when the rains came, and with them times of dance and celebration.

Mobility allowed for a constant realignment of friendships and work units, then, and it helped dissipate latent disputes. In addition, it allowed for a constantly shifting locus of authority, which was important because foragers were rather fiercely egalitarian. If more recent foragers complained about one another to a visiting scholar, it was often to the effect that someone else was "bossy."

For a people to enjoy social fluidity, it helps if no one has made a substantial investment in private, personal accommodations. (Think about the difference between switching roommates in a college dorm and getting your aged mother to move from her home into a retirement center.) That lack of investment certainly characterized hunter-gatherers. Whatever shelter the climate called for was something that could be thrown up in hours: a framework of sticks covered over with grasses and leaves, or sometimes just a windbreak to protect the campfire. Such impromptu shelters could last for a stay of months, but they were so easy to construct that abandoning them after only a few days was no problem either. If it was time to move on, or if your near neighbor had annoyed you, it was a moment's work (and probably rather satisfying) to kick such a structure down and walk away.

Living in the Matrix of Nature

The foraging life was arduous—more so, from our point of view, than foragers themselves would often admit. Anthropologists have marveled at the endurance, strength, and resourcefulness of the hunter-gatherers they've lived with. But they've seen, too, that those qualities were deliberately cultivated in each generation of children: the more rigorous the life, the more exacting the initiation rites. The pain of circumcision, for example, and of subsequent "subincisions" performed on older men, was explicitly linked, in songs accompanying the ritual, with a male's capacity to be a tireless hunter. And yet even those initiation rites were imbued with joking, teasing, and laughter.

A key to understanding hunter-gatherers' lives is that such people didn't make the same kind of distinctions you and I do between work and play. Heading into the Ituri Forest to collect honey or track an animal, the Bambuti Pygmies would sing, laugh, and jump up at intervals to swing from tree branches. They brought to their play the same intensity they brought to their work.

Furthermore, hunter-gatherers didn't calculate the time or effort that a particular task would take in the way we do today. They just *did* the task. The Pomo Indians, for example, used to speak of the autumn as "food fall," referring to the native oak trees, which in most years shed far more acorns than the people could eat. "Food fall" sounds effortless—divine bounty, lavishly dispensed. But in truth, no fewer than seven separate processes had to be carried out before the acorn was edible (and that doesn't count the prior construction of large baskets so tightly woven that they would hold water). In the final stage, acorn meal and water were placed in the baskets and rocks that had been preheated in the fire were dropped in. Diligent stirring with wooden paddles kept the rocks from burning the basket while the mush cooked. The end product was highly nourishing and had a somewhat buttery flavor, like the Peruvian grain *quinoa*. Delicious, but hardly a convenience food.

In other words, the rigors of that life were absolutely real, but they were offset in large part by the wonderfully improvisational quality of what went on. There were no scripts, but there were other actors—an ensemble, if you will, who'd been working together forever. This dimension of hunter-gatherer life helps explain why many contemporary hunter-gatherers "held out" as long as they did.

The Kraho of Central Brazil, for example, had always lived by hunting. When there were no more wild animals—white hunters having killed them off—the Brazilian government offered the Kraho startup herds: they could be cattle ranchers like the white men were who had moved into the area.

The Kraho accepted, but with great reluctance. "We are hungry," one of them reflected. "Our children cry out for meat. We must have cattle to survive. But we do not want to give up our village community and live in scattered families like white people. It is no fun."[3]

In the Matrix of Kin

When a band of Kalahari San set up camp for the night, the fires weren't lit randomly.[4] The oldest male member took out his fire sticks and produced the first sparks. He fed the fledgling fire with tinder, then kindling; and only once it was well established did the heads of each of the families in the band approach and take burning faggots from it to light the fires for their own families. Each nuclear family had its own fire, and the nuclear families that were related to one another built their fires close to one another's. But all the fires had the same source.

That ritual seems to me to capture something intrinsic to the way in which hunter-gatherers lived wherever they lived: a very real measure of personal independence experienced within a framework of communal unity and interdependence.

What, we might wonder, held a society of hunter-gatherers together? What gave its members the sense of common identity that, from what we can gather, was the only version of identity they knew?

Kinship bonds were vital, though among hunter-gatherers they were often defined more loosely than in modern societies. Among the African hunters British anthropologist Colin Turnbull studied, for example, children were brought up to regard as a parent any adult who lived in the same camp, and as a brother or sister anybody who was about the same age. These were real and effective relationships, he maintained. They shifted and changed as the composition of the bands changed, but they had solid survival value[5] as a way of organizing food production and distribution and as a way of ensuring that children would be taken care of no matter what.

Childrearing customs among hunter-gatherers were very permissive, by the measure of modern societies. There was no need for them to be otherwise. Children learned what they needed to know by working and playing alongside their parents. Nobody had to tell them what the consequences of selfishness or laziness were because they could see that firsthand. The qualities that were adaptive for their life developed quite naturally. They grew up to be hardworking, generous, and affable.

They also grew up to be resistant to authority, and that too was adaptive. Every member of the band had to have roughly the same encyclopedic knowledge of her environment, and each had to be able to make her own decisions on the spot. Top-down hierarchical authority structures had no utility for hunter-gatherers, nor did elaborate specialization. In a subsistence life, moreover, the flow of resources needed to be unobstructed through the whole group. In very small societies, the individual's security lies in one's relationships with other people and with the group as a whole. Formal authority structures rarely do much to enhance those relationships.

The integrity of the band or tribe was crucial to the existence of its members—so much so that one's sense of individual identity came to be subsumed under that larger unit. The fact that one's sense of self was so deeply bound up in the group shaped attitudes toward death in fundamental ways. Among the Kalahari San, for example, the elderly or infirm person knew very well that if the band needed to move on for its own survival and he couldn't keep up, he would be left behind, with a fire to keep him warm and a barrier of thornbush to keep off the hyenas. If his kin found food and could get back to him in time, they would. If they couldn't, they would avoid that place for several generations.

On the other hand, there's good evidence that pre-agricultural hunter-gatherers took care of elderly people long past the time when they'd have died on their own. In September 2001, a skeleton was discovered in the southeast of France that suggests human beings have cared for their elders more than fifty thousand years longer than had been believed.[6] In a rock shelter known as Bau de l'Aubesier were found the remains of a pre-Neanderthal individual who had lived somewhere between 175 and 200 thousand years ago. The person was toothless and had clearly been very old at the time he or she died. In fact, it appeared that this person had been missing teeth for quite some time.

When nonhuman primates lose their teeth in the wild, they die. But someone had clearly cared enough about this old soul to have softened whatever food was available. The archaeologists who found the skeleton believe that the meat had been both cooked and pounded up. In fact, it's possible, even likely, that the cooked meat had been pre-chewed by a loving child or grandchild.

RESOLVING CONFLICTS

Observers of a band of Kalahari San describe a hunting expedition that climaxed in the death of giraffe.[7] Ebulliently, but following a long-established protocol, the four hunters carved the animal up and parceled out the meat. They returned to camp and subdivided their spoils yet again, everyone still in good spirits.

But no sooner had everyone finished eating than someone found fault with the man whose shot had downed the giraffe and who had therefore been in charge of its distribution. A fight ensued, and the bystanders thought it best to let them work off their aggressions *mano a mano*. They confiscated the arrows the men had been hunting with, though, because the arrows were tipped with deadly but slow-acting poison. A man could be fatally hit and yet be capable of killing off his opponent before he died. The very word "fight" was thus synonymous among the San with "unspeakable catastrophe."

In her important 1997 book *Blood Rites,* independent scholar Barbara Ehrenreich opens a window onto what lies behind scenes such as this, and onto the immense threat fighting posed for the band itself. *Blood Rites* was written with the intention of determining why human beings are fascinated with war—so fascinated that not only do we go on waging war, we make it a veritable sacrament.

The traditional argument is that we wage war because in prehistoric time we were hunters. Ehrenreich disagrees. For our first two and a half million years, she argues, human beings weren't hunters at all; we were hunted. We weren't predators; we were prey, scrambling up trees, hiding in caves, and hoping like hell not to be eaten alive. It wasn't until about fifteen thousand years ago that bows and arrows were invented, and even after that development the relationship between men and predatory animals would reverse itself only sporadically and slowly.[8]

The compulsive attraction war exerts, Ehrenreich concludes, is that it allows us to reenact and celebrate, over and over, first the initial terror and then the fierce satisfaction of the prey-to-predator transition. The image of a man perpetually reenacting a transition from prey to predator because he can never fully convince himself he's succeeded in making it contrasts sharply with the image of a high-spirited hunter/warrior who's just doing what comes naturally. The glamour is gone, and the real poignancy of the situation is evident.

What Ehrenreich lets us see in the earlier cited story of the Kalahari hunters and the conflict that erupted among them is that a successful hunt (even of a nonpredatory animal such as a giraffe) always has the potential of reawakening the commingled anxiety and ferocity that the first hunters experienced. Her perspective also lets us see that the explosive force of those troubling feelings can ignite something very like war.

Seeing the San's small but very real skirmish in this light makes the actual outcome extremely interesting. By evening the conflict had still not been resolved, and tensions were running high. As night gathered in around the camp, the women sat in a circle around the central fire; sat in a circle around it and began to sing and clap with slowly mounting urgency. The men began to move in a circle around the women, chanting, while strings of rattles attached to their legs made a rhythmic, swishing sound. For hours they danced, the rhythms building in intensity until at last one man led the others into an opening between two women and they began dancing around the fire itself. Eventually one of them fell into a trance—then another, and another. The medicine man actually fell into the fire itself, keeping his head in the hot embers for ten seconds or so, then helped other men to enter a trance state. As a man lost consciousness, someone would come pull his tongue out so that he wouldn't swallow it.

The next morning, the observers recorded, the camp was once again harmonious, and the medicine man showed no trace of injury. The destructive energies of the previous day had been dissipated: nobody had had to die in order that someone else could savor victory.

Nonviolent conflict resolution was crucial to the life of small communities. The San weren't alone in resorting to dance. The Bambuti danced at any excuse (or none at all), and when they did, it was often

as if they were affirming their collective unity over and against whatever might be threatening to divide them.

"One dances as one drinks, as one eats," an elderly Bambuti woman
told her interviewer. "It is a necessity."[9]

MEETING AT THE MIDDLE: GENDER MUTUALITY

A gendered division of labor was undoubtedly the norm among pre-
agricultural peoples, as it would be of later hunter-gatherers. But
those divisions were probably not as rigid as was once believed, or as
meaningful in terms of status. Men would have done most of the
hunting, and women, children, and elders most of the gathering. But
if the behavior of contemporary hunter-gatherers is indicative of pre-
agricultural hunter-gatherers, there was considerable overlap.

While they were digging roots, for example, and picking nuts or
berries, women would also have been gathering valuable intelligence:
What kind of animal tracks had they seen, and how fresh were they?
Furthermore, women and children often joined in the hunt—particularly when the game animals were small and when much of the work
consisted of driving animals into prepared enclosures and clubbing
them to death. Inuit women fished, and still do, and a number of them
have made a name for themselves as hunters of larger game. Modern
male hunters, for that matter, have been observed digging up a particularly succulent root and bagging it to take home without appearing
to think they've compromised their male identity by doing so.

What keeps emerging in reports of hunter-gatherer life is that the
work of men and women was profoundly complementary: the hunter
and the gatherer required one another, and because everyone understood this very well, a baseline of mutual respect was more than evident. A fisherman of the Pacific Northwest could bring home a huge
catch of salmon, but if his wife wasn't there to bone, fillet, and dry the
fish, it would simply rot. An Inuit man might have been a tremendous
hunter, but his skills would have been meaningless if his wife weren't
his match at the craft of turning seal and walrus hides into the warm,
waterproof clothing that made the region habitable. And the fact that
she didn't stop at simply making the clothing—that besides the most

utilitarian boots and parkas she turned out magnificently beaded and embroidered garments for special occasions—attests to a certain joie de vivre that speaks volumes about Inuit women and how they felt about their lives.

SELF-RELIANT WOMEN

Foraging women are now thought to have been considerably less dependent on hunting males than early researchers believed. As much as seventy to eighty percent of the caloric intake of hunter-gatherers came from food gathered by women and children. Earlier researchers may have attached excessive importance to the high protein content of the meat that successful hunters brought in. While there's no question that everyone would have been thrilled to have meat, we know now that if a plant-based diet is varied enough—if it includes seeds, berries, and small grubs, for example, in addition to taro or mandioca root—it provides adequate protein, vitamins, and minerals.

Women could support themselves as foragers, then, and the very nature of their work gave them a lot of autonomy. Foraging men couldn't control women's resource base in the same way agriculturists would be able to, nor could they restrict their movements. In fact, foraging women could be mobile in the extreme. Among the Kung of the Kalahari Desert, women carrying their infants traveled as far as fifteen hundred miles in a year!

As foragers, women led very public and active lives. Scarcity of water and unavailability of weaning foods compelled them to nurse their infants around the clock. That fact may have been the origin of the so-called String Revolution, a tremendously important technological advance that took place around twenty to thirty thousand years ago, when some genius hit upon the principle of twisting handfuls of little weak fibers together into one long, strong thread. Perhaps the genius in question was a woman who needed to construct some kind of a sling to carry her baby around in while she foraged. We haven't a clue as to what the first use was, because evidence of sewing, spinning, and weaving suddenly turned up all over the archaeological record.

Because a foraging woman nursed day and night until her child was old enough to walk about and digest adult food, her pregnancies were spaced—spaced *themselves,* in fact—at four- and five-year intervals.

Foraging women were effective at building supportive networks for themselves and their children. The evolutionary importance of the granny and the auntie have come to be fully appreciated in recent years. Scientists used to wonder why female reproductivity doesn't extend through women's entire lifespan as it does in most other female animals. What use does nature have for postmenopausal women?

It was one of those questions whose answer seemed ridiculously obvious once it had been demonstrated scientifically: mothers lucky enough to have a surviving postmenopausal female relative—some-one who was active but didn't have babies of her own to feed—had help feeding their babies. So in families whose women were particu-larly long-lived, infant and child mortality rates would have been significantly lower. Thus sturdy postmenopausal women offered a genetic advantage to their whole lineage.

Indeed, the whole band would have benefited from the presence of elderly women (and elderly men as well). The longer a person had lived, the more likely it was that he or she had lived through lean times—drought, for example—and could remember which plants were edible when the preferred ones weren't around. Could remem-ber, probably, all *kinds* of things.

It appears now that in prehistoric times those who were adept at forming alliances also had better reproductive prospects. You and I may be here today because our great-granddaddies were more sexually aggressive than others, but it's just as likely that we're here because our great-grandmothers were better at networking than their peers.

One of the more disconcerting observations that fieldworkers study-ing indigenous peoples have made is the degree to which the foraging mother's commitment to a newborn infant can vary. "Maternal ambiva-lence" has been documented throughout European history, and it appears to be a persistent and distinctly human trait. (It isn't observed in nonhuman primates, at any rate.) Unlike her primate antecedents, and precisely because of her bigger and more complex brain, a woman is able to think ahead and ask herself pointed questions:

Is there enough food available now to allow me to nurse this child successfully?

Is this child strong enough to survive?

Am I strong enough to care for it?

Can I provide for it without jeopardizing my older children?

Knowing that I can get pregnant again next year, is this the child—as opposed to another who might be of a different sex, or more attractive—that I want to raise?

If the answer to these or similar questions was no, and the various biological mechanisms that would otherwise ensure maternal commitment hadn't had time to kick in yet, the baby could well be abandoned or killed. The welfare of the whole community outweighed individual desires—a concept that each mother (indeed, each member of the band) would have internalized powerfully.

It's important to recognize that the qualities associated with nurturance—unhesitating tenderness or self-abandonment, for example—aren't the sole domain of women. However, it may be just as important to realize that these qualities aren't even *in* the domain of all women all the time. In fact, the work of primatologists and anthropologists suggests that competitiveness is as nascent in women (surely we haven't doubted this) as in men.

Primatologist Sarah Blaffer Hrdy feels strongly on this point. If it's shown, she argues, that there are no important differences between males and females in intelligence, initiative, or administrative and political capabilities—a view that most social scientists generally now concede—then one has to accept also that these potentials didn't appear gratuitously as a gift from nature. "Competition," she points out, "was the trial by fire from which these capacities emerged."

She goes still further: "The feminist ideal of a sex less egotistical, less competitive by nature, less interested in dominance, a sex that will lead us back to the 'golden age of queendoms, when peace and justice prevailed on earth,' is a dream that may not be well founded."[10]

In fact, feminists don't all believe that women are less egotistical or interested in dominance than men. By conditioning, maybe, but certainly not "by nature." I appreciate mightily, though, the distinction Hrdy draws here, because it underscores my own contention that the gender straitjackets into which we've all been laced have very little to do with who any of us really is. She's right: fantasies about ancient "queendoms" won't get women anywhere.

EASYGOING MEN

It appears now that pre-agricultural men didn't enjoy the unequivocally superior status that the modern world used to attribute to them. Aggressive male dominance developed later, for the most part; it wasn't the natural consequence of men's skill as hunters.

On the other hand, prehistoric man wasn't under the same unrelenting pressure to provide that he would be much later, as a farmer; and that had to have had its merits. If he brought home a tapir, great. But if he didn't, fine. He could still pull up a leaf mat, light into the huckleberries, and talk about the ungulate that got away: a good story is a long way from nothing.

Unburdened by the exaggerated expectations around heroic manliness that would develop later, men probably had the option of a more easygoing affect. A certain kind of comfort and camaraderie could exist between the sexes that would evaporate once women came to be more lopsidedly dependent on men, as they would when agriculture had replaced foraging. Observers have noted, too, the affection and demonstrativeness that hunter-gatherer men displayed routinely toward their children.

At the same time, to the extent that there were threats to life, men had a special role to play. The male hunter-gatherer, like his primate antecedents, understood himself to be expendable. Because the integrity and survival of the community was crucial, the male hunter-gatherer knew that in contrast with the females of his band—who could bear and nourish offspring—he himself was nothing. When the band or tribe was under attack, there was no question as to who would have to stand and face the enemy.

That he should have understood and accepted this role is all the more impressive when you realize that his instinctive willingness to sacrifice himself in defense of the band had to be strong enough to override the comparably strong instinct that evolutionary biologists attribute to all living creatures: to see that his own genes were replicated. This particular adaptation would shape "manliness" in ways that we're still sorting out.

It would be a mistake to idealize the hunter-gatherer way of life or the individuals themselves. The values these people honored were directly and pragmatically linked to the survival of the band and therefore the individual. The empathy that's so marked within a band or tribe didn't necessarily (or even typically) extend to members of other bands or tribes.

In fact, one might argue that many hunter-gatherers felt more meaningfully connected to the land they inhabited than to fellow human beings who were strangers. One's sense of belonging had as much to do with one's relationship to the environment as it did with kinship bonds. The small or large piece of the natural world that was home to a particular tribe or band constituted its identity. Intimate knowledge of that homeground was handed down through time and marked an individual indelibly as its child, sibling to all its other children. Indeed, among certain Australian Aborigines, pregnancy is linked to the movement of the "dust" or "essence" of something on the land—a bit of rock, for example, or the soul of an animal—into a woman's womb.[11]

But we can't begin to grasp the importance of either kinship bonds or connection to the land if we try to imagine them apart from their religious significance. We'll see in the next chapter that for pre-agricultural human beings, a sense of the sacred, present and alive, lay at the heart of identity. The culture of Belonging is in its very essence religious.

CHAPTER 3

The Sense We Made of Things:
Religion and the Hunter-Gatherers

"This is right-brain paradise," said Mary Norbert Korte, laughing. "Sheer heaven for a poet."

Mary is a poet whose work I'd enjoyed in the 1950s and 1960s. As a Dominican nun (until the late 1960s), she'd been something of an anomaly in the Beat Poetry crowd that included the likes of Gary Snyder, Lawrence Ferlinghetti, and Allen Ginsberg. When I heard a couple of years ago that she'd been working for the past twenty years as a teacher and environmental adviser at a Pomo reservation outside of Ukiah and lived nearby in a cabin surrounded by redwoods, I couldn't wait to talk to her and get her impressions of a people with whom she'd clearly formed deep, strong bonds.

I was particularly curious about the Pomos' religious practices. In the twenty-some years she'd spent working with them, what had she been able to learn about what they believed and how they worshiped? She sat very still for a moment, collecting her thoughts, and when she finally did speak she leaned forward and looked straight into my eyes as if to be sure I was really hearing her.

"First of all," she said, "what they know is almost never put into words, so it's very hard to learn anything about it that would feel tangible to us. You catch it only in a look, a gesture, a silence. Second, everything in their life revolves around it. Third, it survives everything you'd think could destroy it—poverty, illness, alcoholism, violence, *everything.*"

As I was driving home, I realized that with those three assertions, and the fact that she'd referred not to "what they believe" but to "what they know," Mary had said of Pomos and their relationship to the divine exactly what the ancient sages of India had said of their relationship with the Ground of Being they called Brahman (which they too said was fully and directly knowable): that relationship is ineffable, all-pervasive, and indestructible.

And when I realized this, I smiled, thinking how much Huston Smith would appreciate that parallel. In 1998, Smith, distinguished longtime scholar of world religions, published a new edition of his classic work *The Religions of Man.* He retitled the book *The World's Religions* and made several other changes, the most important of which may have been the addition of a final chapter, which he called "Primal Religions."

Arguably, Smith should have placed this chapter first, since the faiths it examines—those of the Australian Aborigines, Native Americans, and Congo Pygmies, among others—offer as good a window as we're likely to get into the religious practices and beliefs of our earliest ancestors. Primal religions are the *Ur*-religions out of which Hinduism, Judaism, Islam, and the other "historic religions" all sprang.

But the beauty of those primal religions being encountered last in Smith's book lies precisely in the questions that they raise about the religions of temple, tabernacle, cathedral, and mosque that the reader has just visited in his preceding chapters. Even the most cursory comparison reveals in how many ways, and how powerfully, early religious impulses were reshaped and redirected into organized religions that suited the needs of the exuberantly expanding civilizations in which they arose. We see, too, in how many ways the reform movements that sweep regularly through all historic religions look like attempts to recapture exactly what Mary Korte described: direct, unmediated experience of an all-pervasive, indestructible Ground of Being that words cannot capture.

The religious life of hunter-gatherers has long fascinated professional and amateur scholars. But the general public's interest in that life has leaped in recent years for the same reasons that its curiosity about eastern religions has grown. Belief in the possibility of direct encounter with divinity is as fundamental to both preliterate and Eastern spiritual traditions as it is foreign to most Western religions, and a great many Westerners are turning to them now to assuage hungers that their own traditions haven't met.

Among the scholars who've helped open Western eyes to the beauties of paths not their own, few have been as effective as Professor Huston Smith. Because his particular focus is comparative religion, Smith offers us a somewhat different view of indigenous peoples than a more general anthropological account would yield—a view that almost *defines* them in terms of their religiosity.

He distinguishes primal from historic religions in several key regards, all of which are helpful as we try to understand how the values of Belonging evolved within foraging cultures.

EMBEDDEDNESS: A CIRCUITRY OF THE SACRED

Among peoples such as the Australian Aborigines, Native Americans, and Congo Pygmies, Smith notes, the concept of a separate and personal identity wasn't merely unfamiliar, it was practically incomprehensible. Like a tiny glass chip in an elaborate mosaic, one understood oneself to be held safely in not one, but three respects.

The individual was effectively embedded, first, in a kinship network: being born into a particular lineage determined which tracts of land you had access to, who your ancestral heroes or heroines were, whom you could appropriately marry, and what sort of ceremonial or political responsibilities you had (if any).

If you were a Brazilian Kraho Indian, for example, you were born into one of two political groups that took turns governing the settlement: one took charge during the six summer months; the other ran things through the winter. You were also born into one of two groups with respect to feasts and rituals. The relatively complicated affiliations that this sort of twofold division produced must have made for a sense of connection across lines of difference. Similar arrangements exist among the Indians of the American Southwest. As a Hopi, you might be born into the Badger Clan, which would determine (among other things) whom you could properly marry, and you could at the same time hold membership in the Snake Society, which would define your religious ceremonial obligations.

Families, clans, and tribes, moreover, were embedded just as firmly in the particular part of the natural world that sustained them. The names of different American Indian tribes often mean nothing more specific, in their own tongue, than "the people of the land." For the Aborigines of the Australian desert, sacred landmarks are the bodies of totemic beings that were transformed during the era of creation "Dream-Time," into individual waterholes, trees, ridges, and rock alignments. The Aborigines' sense of kinship extends to all of these landmarks: when they're passing through the desert and see one of them, they respond as warmly as if they'd seen a beloved human being. This almost familial intimacy with the landscape translates into an elaborately detailed knowledge of the land, which guides them through it. It translates, too, into the strong sense, expressed by foragers everywhere, that one is truly alive, truly *whole,* only out on the land.

Smith also observes that indigenous people typically see themselves as embedded in the sacred—"in a single cosmos, which sustains them like a living womb"—and that imagery seems to me crucial to what Smith is getting at: because while the word "embedded" suggests a certain rigidity, the reality he describes is clearly, in fact, fluid and organic.

The Indians of the Pacific Northwest Coast, for example, believed that salmon were people with eternal life who lived in a large house far under the sea. In spring the salmon people swam up out of the sea disguised as salmon and offered themselves as food to the Indians. When the first Coho salmon of the year were caught, the fisherman greeted them joyously: "Welcome, swimmer! I thank you because I am still alive and you have come back to our good place." The fisherman's wife added her own prayers to his, and that night his whole lineage gathered to eat the salmon and pray yet again: "O supernatural friends: we know that only your bodies are dead, in order to provide us with sustenance, but your souls watch over us."[1]

Moreover, to ensure that each salmon person was able to return to his home beneath the sea, the skeleton of each fish caught was returned to the water whole. One reason that the Indians were reluctant to sell salmon to white people was that in our ignorance we would fail to act correctly (and thus would jeopardize for everyone the yearly and timeless cycle).

Living in intimate, reverent connection with the earth places one within a circuitry of the sacred, in which something is understood to flow from nature, through oneself and back into nature, and then back around again to oneself in exactly the way that blood circulates in the body of a pregnant woman from her heart to the placenta, to the infant it sustains, and back again. To live in attentive harmony with that flow is to open oneself to mystery and power.

Salome Alcantara, a skilled Pomo basket-maker who was a healer as well, recounted in her own broken English the experience that told her she was called to become a medicine woman:

> When it was starting on me . . . I just did what it told me.
> . . . Then one day it took me, it told me to walk up the hill
> where we live. . . . I just listen. . . . It was water running; . . . it
> was going over the rocks and it made funny rippling sounds, . . .
> pretty sounds, . . . real sounds . . . that was Indian songs, and the
> Indian medicine song. . . . I know that it was giving me a job . . .
> when they call me, then, to go and help them, . . . so people
> come and get me. [2]

When Alcantara and other Pomo basket-weavers spoke of their work, it was as if the natural world had met them halfway. In providing them with the sedge root, for example, nature had been extraordinarily beneficent, for the root's fine, woody fibers dress down into sewing elements as fine as thread, only much sturdier. The most admired and costly Pomo baskets—durable, strong, woven with extraordinarily fine and even stitches—are "root baskets." Their makers have seemed eager to deflect praise for the baskets away from themselves and back to what they see as the real source:

"If you just listen to the roots," one weaver used to tell beginning students, "they'll tell you what to do."

"You walk into the woods," said another, "and you come out with a basket."[3]

MUTED DISTINCTIONS

The second respect in which Huston Smith believes primal religions differ from the historic religions has to do with "the muted character of distinctions . . . distinctions that in the historical religions explode into opposites."[4]

A missionary who spent time among the Kalahari San in the nineteenth century is said to have asked a San youth what was the most wonderful creature he had ever seen. The clergyman was immensely disappointed when the young man replied that no one thing was more wonderful than any other and that all the animals were the same. How typical of the savage mind, the missionary wrote later, that it was incapable of discriminating between His creations.[5]

Foragers and other tribal peoples aren't blind to nature's differences, Smith reminds us; on the contrary, their powers of observation are the stuff of legend. But they see distinctions as bridges, not barriers. What's significant for them about the difference between two phenomena is where they meet, and that they do meet (and typically overlap), however much they might differ.

Many Native American tribes, for instance, regard a "manly woman" or a "womanly man" as spiritually gifted (and in fact as a gift to their tribe). Like Tiresias, a figure in Greek mythology who was both man and woman, such people know the things that women know, and they know the things that men know as well. Called "two spirits" by California Indians, they're believed to be able to see the world whole and in depth, because they see out of both eyes.

By the same token, spiritual seekers in India regard twilight and dawn as the ideal times for meditation: these are the moments when darkness and light touch one another and give way to one another, a juncture called *sandhya*. Even children are expected to stop their play when *sandhya* occurs, and to repeat their mantras for a moment. Between sleep and wakefulness, too, the Indian tradition hold that for just an instant a door into deeper consciousness swings open: if you're alert enough to be repeating a mantra at that juncture, the charged syllables can slip inside and work in mysterious ways.

The idea of absolute good and absolute evil that pervades so much of historic religion, associated with dichotomies such as spirit and matter, light and darkness, doesn't appear to have had a foothold among foraging peoples; thus it couldn't predispose them to categorize people, objects, animals, ideas, and so on in terms of their distance from God (or the angels, or light, or the Prime Mover).

The border between the animal world and the world of human beings is typically fluid in the primal worldview, and so is the border between the living and the dead. For the Bambuti, for example, the Ituri Forest is filled with spirits who can take human *or* animal shapes. If the totem animal of your clan is a leopard, you know that when you die your breath might be embodied in a leopard; and you know that your ancestors were able to call out the spirits from the forest and turn themselves into leopards at will.

The possibility of metamorphosis—of shape-changing in either direction—is just as prevalent in the Americas. Among the Northwest Coast Indians, for instance, a whale hunt was known to be terribly dangerous, and one man recalls his father preparing months in advance, not only reciting special prayer songs that would enhance his power, but also all but becoming a whale himself. "Sometimes he swam to the cliff beyond the surf, diving and spouting water like a whale; he made us believe he was a whale to show that in his heart he was good."[6]

The people of this stormy region must often have felt themselves barely equal to its demands. They certainly harbored few illusions about any innate superiority they might have had over the creatures they shared it with. A creation myth from the Haida Indians of the Pacific Northwest conveys charmingly how small and vulnerable they must sometimes have felt, and how much *consciousness* they attributed to creatures such as Whale, Raven, Bear, and Otter. It conveys, too, the high value that they attached to playfulness. It goes like this:

Raven Yel was walking all by himself down the beach one day, bored as could be, when he came upon a giant clamshell that was open just a crack. He bent down, peeked inside, and saw that it was full of the tiniest creatures, who were peering back at him fearfully.

Yel applied all his well-known seductive powers, coaxing and enticing: "Come out, come out—we can play!" Shyly then, and fearfully, one by one they ventured out. And they were strange-looking indeed: two-legged, like Yel, but with no feathers! Covered with pale skin, they were naked, and they had no beaks. Just long black hair on their round heads, and sticklike appendages instead of wings.

But Yel was pleased. He knew that he would enjoy his new playmates.[7]

SYMBOLIST MENTALITY

The third important feature of primal religions, Huston Smith believes, and possibly its most important, is its "symbolist mentality." For indigenous peoples, the material world is the window onto the world of Spirit: one's task as a human being is to learn to see through its richness to the even greater magnificence it conceals.

At the simplest level, this meant that when an Alaskan Indian killed a polar bear it wasn't just *one* bear, it was *Bear,* and had to be treated with the respect it deserved. But at the more complex level, a symbolic reading of the natural world meant that everything had both an ordinary and a profound meaning.

French anthropologist Joel Bonnemaison has written movingly of his stay with the people of Tanna, in Micronesia, who conflate the geography and mythic history of their island almost completely, and speak reverently not so much of its Dream-Time (as do Australian Aborigines) as of its Dream-Space.

For human seekers of the divine, Bonnemaison explains, water, land, sky, fire, a volcano, a mountain, or even a rock aren't simply natural elements; they're hierophanes. That is, they reveal the sacred dimension of the world. In Tanna, space itself is a live hierophane, and therefore the best way to learn a myth on the island is to walk with "one who knows."

"Within a lattice of places," Bonnemaison notes, "each myth generates a magical, symbolic territory that in turn gives the myth a tangible reality that makes it familiar and always present."[8]

For the Australian Aborigines, for Native Americans, and for the Bambuti Pygmies, the visible world was an allegory and even a sacrament (much as it was for the mystics of medieval Europe). In other words, the natural world was the "outward and visible sign" of sacred realities that are invisible to ordinary eyes.

The word "symbol" is a bit bloodless for what's really at stake here, however. When people, who are as vitally connected with the natural world as these people were, spoke in this manner, they weren't disparaging the natural world at all. A bear, otter, or deer didn't just "point to" Bear, Otter, or Deer; it also really *was* Bear, Otter, or Deer, vibrant with the deeper reality to which it was directly connected.

BEING WITH GOD

The Tewa Indians, descendants of the mysterious Anasazi, live in what's now northern New Mexico. But they also live in a timeless world animated by spirits. Repeatedly throughout the year, the Tewa gather near their ceremonial kivas and dance the world back into balance. Their pueblo's dusty plaza couldn't look more ordinary, but from that plaza the *sipapu,* or "spirit hole," leads down into another universe: to the world where the Cloud Beings, or *kachina*s, are said to live, and where the souls of the departed go. In the course of the ceremonial dances, energy from shrines on top of the four magic mountains that surround the ancestral land is focused as if by a lens, and at the *sipapu* the four directions converge, each associated with a color, an animal, a god, and a sacred lake.

For the Tewa, as for indigenous people all over the world, everything is connected in a single fabric. A disturbance anywhere in that fabric is believed to ripple out across the whole. To avoid disturbances, the opposing spirits that life is full of—heat and cold, ripe and unripe, magic and witchcraft—must be kept in balance.

And that's why the Tewa dance. Attentive to the smallest ceremonial directive, costumed as they have been for centuries, they perform the Turtle Dance, the Rainbow Dance, the Corn Dance, and many others. Their task is to emulate (and thereby reinforce) the essential orderliness of the universe, counteracting the anomalies that could otherwise bring a drought, a famine, or a miscarriage.[9]

The one distinction that isn't "muted" for indigenous peoples, says Professor Smith, is the one that separates ordinary time-bound experience from those moments when an individual transcends time and enters a realm that the Aborigines call the Dream-Time or "the Dreaming." Smith notes that the Aborigines draw that distinction with unique sharpness: while there are analogs to Dreaming in other, similar cultures, nowhere is the notion of two parallel realities so fully and elaborately embraced. (The terms "Dream-Time" and "The Dreaming" tend to be used interchangeably, though the latter term refers not only to the "timeless realm" in question but to the human activity that gives one access to it.)

The Dreaming is a backdrop to the ordinary world, and in it, time is suspended. Its events take place, Smith notes, "everywhen." The Dreaming is peopled by legendary heroes who are much like us, only on a grander scale. Their special genius is to have modeled everything that is (maleness and femaleness, bird, fish, antelope) and everything that human beings do (hunting, gathering, fighting, lovemaking, etc). The myths that arise out of the Dreaming provide virtual scripts for the Aborigines. They can literally lose themselves—lose all sense of separate self—in following these scripts. The term "Dreaming" is in fact paradoxical, because it's when Aborigines conform most closely to the models left by their heroes and heroines that they feel most truly alive.

Parallels to the Dreaming motif exist in foraging cultures worldwide, Smith acknowledges, and I want to underscore that fact. What we see writ large in Aboriginal religious practices and sketched in more subdued forms in other "primal religions"—and what sets them all apart from nearly all the historic religions—is their emphasis on *being with God* ("God" being understood here as a placeholder for far less anthropomorphized or even specified entities), as opposed to *worshiping God* or *fearing God*.

What allows human beings to feel genuinely effective performing the ceremonies of world renewal, or balance, or re-creation that they do all over the world is the certainty that, with the right kind of effort and attention, they can align themselves with the forces of renewal, balance, and re-creation that exist in the natural world—forces that they can see plainly, and that are way too mysterious and powerful not to be, in some sense, God; and they can even be conduits for those forces. If in order to pull off such a tremendous feat they must suffer, sometimes even experiencing something very close to death, that effort doesn't feel out of proportion to them.

For hunter-gatherers, religion has never been a question of belief or doctrine. As noted earlier, in most of their languages there's no word for "religion." The closest approximations mean something like "the way we live," which sounds very mundane. But hunter-gatherers understand that through a variety of means one can enter exalted states of consciousness, and that so doing is to the advantage of the individual and community alike. Indeed, it's in these elevated states, however they're attained, that the fluid borders between the dead and the living, animals and human beings, plants and people, become most porous.

No ethnographer I know of has pretended that all the members of a particular community are equally religious in temperament or orientation. In fact, the recorders of the Trance Dance I mentioned in the previous chapter noted that only half the men were able to achieve the trance state. However, the benefit of the trance state was nonetheless understood to accrue to the whole community; and the direct experience of the sacred by some, far from alienating them from others, appears to have integrated them even more deeply into their communities.

The Aborigines aren't unique in believing that the most ordinary of everyday activities hides a springboard to the extraordinary. While trance states brought on through fasting, thirsting, vigils, chanting, dancing, ceremony, and the use of hallucinogens are common among foragers everywhere, there are even less dramatic routes to what we might call transcendent states. Many American Indians maintain, for instance, that an individual can be lifted up out of herself—can become one with "First People," for example (the progenitors of her tribe)—in the course of everyday life. States of heightened awareness can take place when one is weaving a basket, provided concentration is complete and every step is carried out in the ritually prescribed manner; and the prayers a weaver makes in that state on behalf of family or community are thought to be powerful.

RELIGION IN THE CULTURE OF BELONGING

Religious practice and belief among foraging peoples, and among a great many other groups that haven't moved far from the primal model, is deeply consistent with the notion of a culture of Belonging.

For we've seen that, in these societies, the individual typically derives a sense of identity from intimate and reciprocal connection with kin, nature, and Spirit—so much so that the very idea of autonomy strikes people not just as peculiar, but as life-threatening. The practice of making distinctions that don't polarize is logically compatible with such a view of oneself and others: drawing lines or building categories that emphasize one's separateness or superiority would be counterintuitive.

In fact, a symbolist mentality that lets one see through the created world and glimpse a timeless, uncreated reality behind it is in itself an example of a muted distinction, for it says, in effect, *Yes, there is a difference, and it isn't unbridgeable.* The assumption that the human being's task in life is to be with God, and make oneself available to the work of world renewal and balancing, simply extends—into the sphere of action—the belief that Spirit surrounds us and supports us "like a living womb."

CHAPTER 4

The Constellation We Steered By:
The Values of Belonging

The values of Belonging arose out of the convergence of what foraging people experienced and the meanings they attached to their experience. They reflect the individual's sense of herself as a meaningful part of a vast, orderly, and integrated whole. They're consistent with a reluctance to make the sort of distinctions that polarize. They're informed by a deeply symbolic reading of reality. They allow for, and in fact facilitate, direct encounters with the sacred.

By acceding to certain interior pulls—by honoring them over and over, even at the cost of immediate personal comfort—foragers developed a constellation of values that was impressively consistent from one part of the world to the next and that would endure to a surprising degree even as those cultures began to diverge from the foraging model.

It may be useful to think of the values of Belonging as habits of the heart. However adaptive they might have been to the conditions of life before agriculture, and however pragmatically they might have been embraced in the first place, they became so deeply engrained in human behavior (in our responses to other people, for instance, and in our unconscious expectations and needs) and we carried them with us for so long (thousands of years) that it would prove impossible for us to slough them off gracefully when external conditions changed, however radically they changed.

The values of Belonging are, in effect, the *symptoms* of a particular way of being in the world. Together, they form a dynamic whole—a syndrome, if you will, or an orientation or ethos. Within that whole, each value reinforces and all but implies the others, and the source of their power as a constellation is the synergy between them. As we look more closely at the values, we'll approach them not so much as a catalog, then, or a list, but as points on a circle, windows onto a single reality.

CONNECTION WITH THE LAND

Fundamental to the culture of Belonging is a strong sense of reciprocal connection to the land where one lives. Poet Mary Korte told me a couple of stories that allowed me to understand this in ways that I don't believe I could have otherwise.

The Pomos of Coyote Creek Rancheria, where Mary works, had actually been removed from their tribal lands in 1957, when Warm Springs Dam was built. They were able to regroup later and buy the land they occupy today, but their original lands are under water, at the bottom of what's called Lake Sonoma.

It's been forty-five years, then, since they lived on that homeland. But still, on festival days, the oldest women go to a hill above the dam early in the morning. They set up their folding chairs in a line, and they sit down.

"They sit there all day," Mary said, "just looking at where their homes used to be, not saying anything—and when the sun goes down, they fold up their chairs and come back here."

Haunting as that image is, I think I might have missed the point of the story—might just have filed it under "nostalgia"—if Mary hadn't already given me an account of a dramatic dispute that had taken place at the Rancheria a few years earlier. Federal authorities had discovered that a couple living on the reservation had been harboring a man who was later convicted of a terrible crime. After his arrest and removal, the tribal council met at length to decide whether the couple themselves—who weren't Pomo and had been troublesome in other ways—would be allowed to stay. When after careful deliberation it was determined that they would have to leave, the ruling didn't say that the couple had been an offense to the community itself; it said that they had dishonored the land.

Empathic Relationship to Animals

People who hunt to live cultivate in themselves and their children the ability to think like their prey: "If I were a rabbit, what would I do now?" That habit alone could help account for the empathic connection to animals that hunter-gatherers have universally displayed, to the bewilderment, sometimes, of people who get their meat from butcher shops. Propinquity itself could also help explain it: the antelopes of the Kalahari Desert and the giraffes of the Ituri Forest weren't just "dinner" to the people who shared their habitats; they were companions—creatures who got hungry and thirsty just as human beings do, who were lovely to watch, and who were as poignant in their death throes as human beings. Inuit hunters would often place fresh water in the mouth of a freshly killed seal so that "Seal" would know that the hunter respected its willingness to be hunted and killed.[1]

Toward the end of his life Colin Turnbull became a Tibetan Buddhist monk, and when he made his prostrations to his foremost teachers, he always included the Bambuti in the lineage. For during the years that he lived with the Bambuti, he had seen that compassion was central to their lives. They were hunters, yes; they lived by killing. But they had devised systems to keep themselves from killing more than they needed, and they believed, sadly, that there was a connection others might call karmic between their own deaths and the deaths they inflicted on other creatures in order to live. If they didn't have to hunt to live, they told their British friend, they would probably live forever.[2]

To know animals intimately is to know—and accept—the parts of oneself that are animal as well.

SELF-RESTRAINT

Implicit in the sense of responsibility toward the land that runs through all the cultures I've been describing is the willingness to exert restraint in the use of its resources—if for no more selfless motive than the desire that one's own grandchildren will be able to live there. Over time, indigenous people developed a finely tuned sense of just how much traffic their stretch of land would bear. They knew when it was time to move to a new location, and they knew how large their group could get before it started eroding the resource base; and for the most part, they behaved in keeping with those limitations. When we see any divergence from that model, as we will in Chapter Eight, we can usually also see quite interesting reasons for it.

CUSTODIAL CONSERVATISM

Foragers tended to remain, for thousands of years, inside the territory they defined as home—"the land." To have left would have been to go into a region that they didn't know as well, and that would have been an invitation to danger.

The driving desire of foragers was to keep the natural world exactly as it was—which is to say, perfect. The very idea of change was thus suspect. Yet even as I write this, I have to acknowledge that in the mythologies of hunter-gatherers, transformation—of fish into woman, man into leopard, cloud into mountain—is an immensely popular motif. It would probably be more correct, then, to say that changing the natural world wasn't thought to be the human being's job; that his job was, rather, to change *himself*—into a better inhabitant.

If the universe was found to be in good working order, it wasn't only because it had been ideal to begin with, but because our great-grandparents had left it that way; so the highest human duty was to emulate them. If there were problems, the highest human duty was still to emulate the ancestors—in ceremony, dance, or the way one carried out simple tasks—because by doing so one could revitalize the original models. Oral tradition made that possible: there was a correct way to carry out every activity and honor every plant-spirit so that natural processes would go on unfolding as they always had, and that information was preserved in the song and ceremony of a people.

Hence the need to be absolutely conscious about everything one does . . .

DELIBERATENESS

Among the Australian Aborigines, a young man's rite of initiation into manhood included learning the names and locations of watering places through songs and dances that conveyed myths about them. The initiate might well have visited the actual places and imprinted the look of them with as great care as if his life were going to depend on it. And in fact it would, as would the life of everyone traveling with him.

Because the hunter-gatherer's understanding of the natural world was holistic—because he understood very well, having observed it throughout his life, that everything in nature is connected to everything else—he knew that one small bit of carelessness on his part could reverberate through his whole local ecosystem and come back to haunt him.

Haste was anathema in this worldview, and so was imbalance. In fact, it could be said that balance was the linchpin in this system of values.

BALANCE

Among the people of Bali, the ordinary term for the period before the coming of the white man was "when the world was steady." Implicit in that idiom is the understanding that traditional cultures value "steady-state equilibrium" to a degree modern societies do not.

Gregory Bateson, one of the founders of the cybernetic revolution, spent several years in Bali in the early 1930s, and his understanding of the systemic nature of social structures was clearly influenced by what he experienced there.[3]

The Balinese, he remarked, particularly those in the plains, enjoyed an economy of plenty. While some of them were poor, nobody was in danger of starving, and it shocked them to learn that in the urban West poor people did indeed sometimes starve. They disliked the idea of maximizing wealth or property, and in fact they were wasteful of food by most standards, spending a great deal of their time in what appeared to be unproductive activities: artistic events or religious ceremonies in which food and wealth were lavishly expended.

None of these ceremonies seemed to have as its object the propitiation of gods or the outdoing of one group by another: nothing like a Mardi Gras or a Potlatch. What *was* going on?

In direct contrast with societies built on the idea of competition, Bateson notes, the Balinese strove for stability—*but not the stability of motionlessness*. Any ballerina can tell you how many continuous, minute adjustments it takes to stay *en pointe* in apparent stillness. Similarly, Balinese society functioned "rapidly and busily," carrying out ceremonial and artistic tasks that weren't economically or competitively determined, in their effort to remain stable.

In other words, the people of Bali were constantly correcting for the absolutely natural tendency of things to *tip:* life is in a thousand different ways precarious, because it's fundamentally and implacably dual. Conflicts will invariably arise, therefore, between human beings. But conflict needn't result in combat; in fact, combat only exaggerates the imbalance that precipitated it.

EXPRESSIVENESS

Almost universally, ethnographers studying foragers marvel at how talkative the people are that they are observing, and how much they laugh, comparing them sometimes to a flock of birds or a playground full of children. Do they wish, some of these professional academics, that faculty meetings back at their universities could be so happily raucous? Because it's clear how many tensions get released among indigenous peoples, and conflicts resolved, through the simple medium of talk laced with laughter.

When people live in small, interdependent groups, the keeping of secrets tends to be destructive. What you have, you share. And that brings us to one of the more complex issues . . .

GENEROSITY

The Bororos of sub-Saharan Africa are a nomadic pastoral people whose herds of zebus must be strong enough to survive long months of heat and drought that abate only during a mildly wet season that runs from June to September. During those cooler months the separate families converge in the northern part of their territory to celebrate marriages and births and conduct the business of the herds. If a family has lost cattle to disease, famine, or taxes, their kinsmen make up the losses readily, knowing that they could be in the same position next year.

Just so, when hunters share their kill with one another, they're merely strengthening the welfare net that supports them all. If one of them has acquired even something small—a knife, say—that his companions admire, he's likely to give it away rather than stir up envy.

But there's another side to the generosity of hunters, and that's the prestige that a man can amass who is a consistently successful hunter—prestige that helps him win a wife (or a second wife, or a lover). Among the Indians of the Northwest Coast, the tradition of potlatch appears to have begun as a simple redistribution of food resources: villages that needed food for the winter received it from villages that had more than they needed—nobody was permitted to starve. Later, though, the same institution would become a competitive exercise. "In the old days," one Nimkish chief recalled in 1921, "the potlatch was my weapon, and I could call down anyone with it."[4]

There are tensions within most hunter-gatherer societies, as we'll see in the next chapter—tensions that, if they erupt, tend to move a society toward a more complex economic model. One symptom of that sort of change is the emergence of leaders—"big men" and chiefs—which traditional foraging societies tend to resist.

EGALITARIANISM

Father Alphonse Sowase, O.S.C., a missionary to the people of Asmat, headhunters of Papua New Guinea, recalls trying to teach the children to play soccer and realizing after a while that the game invariably ended in a tie.[5] His experience has been duplicated in mission schools all over the world, where Eskimo or Navajo children have preferred to sit in silence rather than best one another by so much as dividing twenty-five by five successfully.

Hunter-gatherers are notoriously noncompetitive. Authoritarian structures are simply not adaptive for their way of being in the world.

Captain James Cook reached the Micronesian island of Tanna in 1777 and noted in his diary the graciousness of the people themselves and the beauty of the gardens in which they grew their yams. He was struck, though, by the absence of anything he could recognize as authority. He asked if there were a chief or a king and was taken to the home of an old man wreathed in smiles who lived in a hut that appeared to be no different from anyone else's. He did wear a belt made of *tapa* pounded bark with black and red stripes, but nothing else distinguished him. Meanwhile, one of Cook's associates tracked down another supposed chief on the same island, but this fellow couldn't even persuade any of his people to climb a coconut tree and bring down a few nuts for their guests. The old "chief" ended up having to do it himself. Understandably piqued, he gathered all the nuts on the tree, giving some to the guests and keeping the rest for himself.

The Tannese were apparently the kind of people who needed *sort* of a chief for *some* of the time and knew it, but weren't about to expand his role beyond what was strictly necessary. Nothing could have separated them more definitively from the British, who had come after all, halfway around the world on the strength of a tightly organized hierarchy.

Along the same lines, Bateson discovered that among the Balinese, oratory was almost totally lacking. The very idea of demanding someone's continued attention was just . . . well, *distasteful;* and if someone were foolish enough to try to exert emotional influence on a group, that person would find the task impossible: as if on cue, everyone's attention would begin to wander.[6]

Which may have been more or less what happened when Captain Cook's "chief" got carried away with the moment and actually tried to give an order.

MUTUALITY

A recurring question raised by Native Americans when the first white explorers came to this continent was, "Where are your women?" It seemed odd to them that these men should have been willing to separate themselves so radically from women.

Implicit in the imagery of balance and inclusion of opposites that I've touched on above is the notion that, as individuals, we do better to emphasize our commonalities with one another than our differences. A gendered division of labor, even if it's relatively slight, can exacerbate the perceived distance between men and women, so devices to overcome that distance were a common feature in traditional foraging cultures. The Sun Dance, for example, performed by the Plains Indians in particular and involving real ordeals—fasting, thirsting, piercing of the body—was undertaken by men in order that they might experience something of the pain that women undergo in childbirth. And among the !Kung of Africa's Kalahari Desert, a girl who has had her first period is said to have shot an eland. The Hadza of Tanzania say in the same situation, "She has shot her first zebra!" The dangers of hunting and war are understood to be no more or less dire than those of a woman's reproductive life.

When men and women live with one another as intimately as they do in foraging cultures, the sexes don't inhabit different worlds. Women have nothing to prove to men by way of courage or capacity to endure, and men have nothing to prove to women. The habit of drawing muted distinctions encourages that understanding, and so does a general commitment to modes of knowing that aren't strictly rational.

AFFINITY FOR ALTERNATIVE MODES OF KNOWING

It's often been noted that hunter-gatherers aren't specialists—that their ability to survive depends on their retaining a tremendous volume of information about their environment. Some of that information they inherit, by way of the oral tradition and, more directly, by working alongside their elders. And much of it, probably most of it, is wordless: fine distinctions made by the nose, the ear, the eye—the precise way the breeze feels on one's face, for example, when a cold front is moving in.

But as any decent educator knows, possession of a great many facts doesn't in itself constitute intelligence—not the sort of intelligence, anyway, that makes one effective in life. Hunter-gatherers have to make decisions from one moment to the next—which animals to follow, for example, and how far, and where to spend the night and when. To make such decisions they must be able to marshal everything they know—about the animals themselves, the proximity to watering holes, the weather—but they must also make judgments about the relative importance of the facts they possess. Some such decisions are routine, but others involve so many factors and are so crucial to a band's well-being that ordinary reasoning processes aren't equal to the task. Just as students and writers sometimes turn a daunting project over to the unconscious—by going for a long run, say, or playing a musical instrument—the hunter-gatherer regularly seeks to bypass ordinary deductive reasoning through dreaming.[7]

In fact, it would appear that much of what indigenous people do, from Trance Dance and vision quest to sweat lodge and artistic projects, is undertaken as a means of shutting down ordinary thought processes, for a time, to allow intuitive wisdom to come to the surface.

PLAYFULNESS

Where had I seen figures like this before? In paintings by Paul Klee perhaps, or Marc Chagall—maybe even Picasso. A seal with a human face, a human body with a bird's head, a raven growing arms: hybrid creatures, these, vibrant with color and life, dancing across the wall hangings of Irene Avaalaaqiaq.

Irene, a member of the Caribou Inuit, lives near the shore of Baker Lake, in Canada's Northwest Territories. Like all Inuit women, she's an accomplished seamstress, and today she uses the sewing skills developed making clothing from caribou skins to create arresting wall hangings with titles such as "Possessed by Demons" and "Birds Transforming into Inuit."

When Irene was a little girl, she lived with her grandmother, who told her traditional Inuit stories about olden times, when animals and human beings spoke the same language and could change into one another at will. Those stories of transformation, fundamental to shamanic practices the world over, are the wellspring of her artistic work today. "Wall hangings and whatever else I make do not come from my mind," she maintains. "They come from my grandmother."[8]

The knowledge that nothing is what it seems to be, and that nobody is altogether who he seems to be, is a constant in hunter-gatherer life. So are humor and impatience with pretense, and the three are of course intimately linked. Among the *kachina* honored by the Hopi Indians of the American Southwest are comical figures known as "mudhens," who give the sacred gift of laughter. When the Indians of the Pacific Northwest hear stories about Coyote told by Shoshone Indians, or Crow, or Nez Percé, they smile and say, "We know that story, only we tell it about Raven." These are stories of immense cleverness and overweening pride—scatological, irreverent, and profane. Raven/Crow is at once the Promethean bringer of fire and the amoral trickster, greedy and lecherous; and the other characters in the stories—Whirlwind Woman, the Mouse Girls, Horned Toad—aren't noticeably more honorable than he is. And the fact that he's so many different things at once is intended to remind us that we, too, are a mass of contradictions.

Nothing for it but to laugh and move on.

INCLUSIVENESS

The hunter-gatherer's reluctance to elevate one species over another— her unwillingness to see hierarchies in nature—extends to her fellow human beings and the anomalies she finds there. I've mentioned the high esteem in which the "womanly man" and the "manly woman" are typically held. Among the Yoruba of West Africa (who, though not hunter-gatherers, nonetheless retain certain of the values of that culture), it's believed that the god Orishanla is responsible for creating human beings—and that he does so "as he chooses." Orishanla is responsible for the existence of albinos, hunchbacks, dwarfs, and those who lack the power to walk or speak; thus the Yoruba consider no such individual to be imperfect or expendable. They are, like all human beings, sacred.

Nonviolent Conflict Resolution

Built into the "steady-state equilibrium" of Balinese society, Gregory Bateson observed, were any number of customs and habits that headed off extreme behaviors before they got started. One of these was a patterned avoidance of what he called "cumulative interaction" and you and I might call "escalation." When two men had quarreled, for instance, they would go formally to a local authority and there register their quarrel, agreeing that whichever spoke to the other should pay a fine or make an offering to the gods. Later, if the quarrel terminated, the contract could be formally nullified.[9] In other words, a kind of plateau took the place of a climax.

Customs of this sort distinguish the Balinese rather sharply from other agricultural societies but ally them with foragers everywhere. Hunter-gatherers are no more innately nonviolent than farmers and city-dwellers would be, but typically they have much less to gain from violence and much more to lose.

Simple avoidance is, as we've seen, one solution: a Bambuti Pygmy might simply leave the camp for a while and set up his shelter elsewhere, returning when he feels like it. Immersion in trance states is another powerful alternative to violence among many groups, as are laughter and casual talk. Elaborate protocols typically govern occasions when members of one band show up at the camp of another: weapons are set aside, direct eye contact is avoided, polite exchange of talk is initiated, tobacco is shared—and then, if all goes well, a party might take place in the evening.

Hunter-gatherers aren't pacifists; they'll resort to violence if pushed. But they have a healthy respect for the consequences of striking out at one another: violence isn't an abstraction for them. So they strive to circumvent violent confrontation when they can, and they bring their children up to do the same. Anthropologist Hugh Brody has spent decades working with the Inuit, and he notes that while anger is tolerated in children, it's unacceptable in adults. When his linguistic informants taught him the question "Are you angry?" it was clearly "somewhere between a tease and a reproach."[10]

OPENNESS TO SPIRIT

I balked initially at characterizing spirituality as a particular value of Belonging, because spirituality suffuses the entire constellation of Belonging values and breathes life into it. Everything about hunter-gatherer life—economics, art, social relations, parenting practices, healing systems, and so on—presumes a spiritual orientation. As I noted earlier, all of the values I've discussed allow for and facilitate direct encounters with the sacred. But since the shift to agriculture would entail exactly the separation that hunter-gatherer life does not—that is, the creation of spirituality or "religiousness" as a category of experience distinct from all others—it seems useful to underscore the place of spirituality in the constellation of Belonging values.

At the same time, I have to acknowledge that the word "spirituality" is problematic. To say of oneself that one is "spiritual" as opposed to "religious" can be a way of letting oneself off the hook that a substantive religious commitment involves, and pre-agricultural people don't appear to have let themselves off that hook at all.

POINTS ON A CIRCLE

The values of Belonging imply and reinforce one another in a powerful dynamic—which makes entire sense, given that they arise out of a way of being in the world that is coherent and venerable.

Certain of these values could perhaps be identified as cardinal, in the sense that the others flow from them logically: reverent connection with the land, inclusiveness, empathic relationship to animals, balance, and openness to Spirit. But note how all of them shade into one another:

Intimate connection with the land strengthens one's identification with its nonhuman residents as well, building empathic relationship to animals; and both these connections prompt self-restraint in use of resources and an overall reluctance to change or manipulate the environment for one's private ends.

A conservator's care for the natural world is compatible with a deep respect for the sort of equilibrium that cultures can achieve through gradual fine-tuning, and nonviolent conflict resolution is an ideal way to sustain that sort of equilibrium.

Expressiveness allows for the open flow of important information between people and makes for emotional health.

Generosity lets food and other resources flow where they need to, and egalitarianism is consistent with the sort of respect for one another that makes that kind of generosity feel intuitively right.

Mutuality between men and women is on that same continuum, and it's enhanced enormously by the use of alternative modes of knowing (such as imagination, intuition, and whole-body knowing) and by ordinary playfulness.

No human population ever embraced any of these values in an absolute sense, or abandoned them absolutely either. When anthropologists describe a society as being gentle, generous, and good-humored, they must be understood to be making relative statements. (Some could even be understood to mean no more than that these people are gentler, more generous, and better-humored than most academics!) Still, the values I've listed are ascribed with remarkable consistency to the Kalahari San, the Inuit, the Ituri Pygmies, the Pomos and other American Indians by the people who have studied them most closely. However harsh the conditions of their life might be, hunter-gatherers have left generation after generation of ethnographers with the indelible impression that they possess something immensely precious that "civilized" people lost a long while back.

I have come to see in the clustered values of Belonging, and in the various cultures of Belonging that they foster, the essence of what it was we lost.

Matrix: A Metaphor for the Values of Belonging

Something like the closely woven protective zone that I referred to in Chapter One does exist in our collective memory or imagination, and when it pops up in myth or fairytale, it's almost invariably associated with women. In the *Odyssey* and the *Iliad* women are always spinning, weaving, and washing linens, and at critical moments in the plot, protective garments—ordinary or magical—are abruptly thrown around a hero by one female figure or another. In the classic fairytale *The Wild Swans,* a princess weaves cloaks out of nettles to free her twelve brothers, who've been turned into swans.

The word "matrix" has several dictionary meanings, and they all seem to me to be pertinent to the idea of a culture of Belonging. One meaning, of course, is "uterus" or "womb"; and that meaning has been extended to include anything that's "a place or medium in which something is bred, produced, or developed." By extension, too, the word "matrix" can refer to any point of origin and growth or an "embedding or enclosing mass." In mathematics, the word "matrix" has a specialized use, describing "a rectangular arrangement of quantities or symbols"—a *weave,* in short.

For all our national wealth, our technological genius, our military dominance of just about everybody out there, I believe that many Americans feel themselves, as a people, to be in the position of infants "ripped untimely" from something that should be close around us—"an embedding or enclosing mass"—the "place or medium on which something is bred, produced, or developed." That perception is probably the reason that nostalgia is such a staple in film, music, and literature. Nostalgia for the stability and security we like to imagine our parents and grandparents enjoyed, but nostalgia, in particular, for a time when women were readier than most of them are today to weave the linens, stitch the quilts, and knit the sweaters that have been the traditional symbols of maternal love.

To use the word "matrix" as a metaphor for the clustered values of Belonging would seem to reinforce the notion that what I'm really talking about is "the feminine." But I would hope that everything I've said about the values of Belonging would discourage that reading. To classify as feminine values such as mutuality, imagination, and intimate connection with the natural world is to declare those values off-limits to men and boys, and nothing could be farther from the spirit of the pre-agricultural world.

Linguist Malcolm Margolin has had a longstanding love affair with the entire Native Californian tradition. In his classic work *The Ohlone Way,* he conveys what he knows of the Ohlone tribe, who lived around the San Francisco Bay, in a series of intimate sketches. My favorite of these narrates the birth of a baby.[11]

When an Ohlone women was about to give birth, her husband would absent himself while the older women of the community helped her through her labor. But as soon as he learned that the baby was born and everyone was safe, the husband would swing into action. Digging a long pit and lining it with smooth stones, he would fill it with wood and build a fire. When the stones were hot, he would rake out the ashes and pile fresh herbs and grasses on top to make a soft, thick mattress. Some hours after giving birth, the mother would be taken to the stream to bathe herself and the baby; and when she returned the two of them would settle into their warm, fragrant bed, be covered with deer hides, and begin to sweat profusely.

Over the next few days the fire would be rekindled several times and the bed refreshed. Baby and mother would enjoy a long, delicious rest, held close in a nest—a womb, really—of the father's contrivance.

And when in time, the infant was placed in a cradle, that too was of her father's contrivance. Among the Pomos, as among most of the Indians in Northern California area, basketry is a woman's art. But the cradles—made with boughs that are thicker and require more muscle to work—are made by men.

In these examples, and in the many illustrations throughout this book of values at work, we see that the values of Belonging aren't the values of women in particular. Rather, they're adaptive, for men and women alike, to a particular way of being in the world. When that way of being in the world is disrupted, the old values can quickly come to be maladaptive, as we'll see now.

PART II

The Values of Enterprise

With the adoption of agriculture, human beings stepped out of the matrix of kin, earth, and the palpably holy, and into a new dimension altogether. More than ten thousand years ago in the "Fertile Crescent" of the Near East, they began to alter radically their relationship to one another, to the natural world, and to the sacred, abandoning cultures of Belonging and replacing them with cultures of Enterprise. "Civilization" entered the world at that point, and if we wince at that word—at the implicit assumption that hunter-gatherers were "uncivilized"—it's good to remember that its etymological meaning is just "citification."

Animals and plants were first domesticated in the region that's now northern Iran, Iraq, Syria, and southern Turkey. The first farmers were really horticulturists, growing wheat and barley in small plots in the rainy hill country north and east of Mesopotamia. Raising a few sheep and goats, they met no more than their families' immediate needs. Initially, the vast, arid plain formed by the Tigris and Euphrates Rivers must have seemed thoroughly unpromising. Still, they came, and they built mud huts near the marshes, and within a few thousand years, they had mastered the science and technology of irrigation.

A network of dikes and canals allowed Mesopotamian farmers to put vast stretches of rich alluvial soil under cultivation, and the surplus of grain that resulted was the basis for Sumerian civilization. By the year 3100 B.C., a string of magnificent cities had sprung up along the valley formed by the Tigris and the Euphrates. These cities in turn were welded into city-states, and then a nation. To carry out the business of these cities, and to record the great deeds of the nation, and to set down permanently the poems and stories the people loved, the Sumerians invented the first form of writing.

History had officially begun.

About two thousand years later, it began in Egypt too, where the Nile, with its violent seasonal flooding, presented even more complex challenges than the Tigris and Euphrates had. By 3000 B.C., those challenges had been met, and immense fields of barley, emmer, and flax were in cultivation. That accomplishment, along with the consolidation of Egypt's cities under one ruler, opened the way for the dynasties of the pharaohs.

Meanwhile, beginning around 2500 B.C. (independent of what was happening in the Middle East), a series of cities came into being in the floodplain of the Indus River, in what's now Pakistan—most notably, the twin cities of Harappa and Mohenjo-Daro, with their ingenious sewer systems, indoor plumbing, and huge, well-designed municipal granaries. Intriguingly, no palaces or temples were built in either city, and nothing in the archaeological record indicates what the system of government was (or whether one of the two cities held sway over the other). In that region, too, a system of writing developed.

In China, the Agricultural Revolution couldn't take off in earnest until about 2300 B.C., when construction of an immense network of dikes and drainage canals confined the treacherous Yellow River within its banks.

Mesoamerica was next, with cities emerging around 2100 B.C. based on an agriculture of maize, squash, beans, and bottle gourds, along with llamas, pigs, and guinea pigs.

From these centers of origin, agriculture spread steadily and swiftly. The first archaeological record of European farming, for example, found in Greece, dates to around 6000 B.C.; and within three thousand years, the remotest areas of northern Britain were being farmed. And in nearly all the places where agriculture took hold, cities and city-states emerged as well.

The extent of the changes involved is almost impossible to take in: for a couple of million years, the vast majority of human beings had been nomadic, tribal, egalitarian, subsistence-level folk with a very modest inventory of tools; after a remarkably brief period of transition—just a few thousand years—they developed settled, politically centralized, socially stratified, economically complex, and technologically innovative societies.

They had become *us,* in other words.

Until the very recent past, the Agricultural Revolution was seen as an unmitigated blessing and triumph. Today, among environmentalists in particular, another perspective is emerging. Its focal point is the threat to the global ecosystem posed by the runaway population growth that agriculture eventually permitted. But the environmental critique of agriculturally based civilizations tends to substantiate certain misgivings one might feel on other grounds about humanity's "great leap forward."

When human beings became farmers, they became the first species in the entire history of life to live outside the local ecosystem, as was noted earlier. And they didn't stop there: in taking it upon themselves to identify certain plants as *crop* and others as *weed,* and then displace everything that was weed so that crop could take its place, human beings effectively reimagined the natural world as if it existed solely for human use. They reimagined it, and then they remade it in the image of their own desires.

In short, they played at being God. Except that in the pre-agricultural world, the kind of God they were playing at being—anthropomorphic and all-powerful—hadn't been around to emulate. To take the tremendous step human beings were taking, therefore—by elevating themselves above the Spirit-filled local ecosystem—they really needed a new concept of divinity as well. That's exactly what the first two chapters of Genesis provided. The creation story narrated there, which is in fact two stories, can be read as a thinly veiled account of the radical relocation of human beings outside, over, and above the natural world. The argument embedded in the biblical narrative—that human beings are intended, *by God,* to have dominion over every other living thing—may well be, of all existing threats to the global ecosystem, the greatest. It is, in any case, as opposed as it could possibly be to the values of Belonging.

When human beings left foraging for farming, they entered an altogether new territory—one in which qualities that had been maladaptive in the past, such as innovativeness, competitiveness, and acquisitiveness, were newly and unequivocally adaptive. There's no reason to pretend that our earliest ancestors weren't innovative, competitive, or acquisitive. After all, they too were *us.* It's just that hunter-gatherer societies held those riskier impulses in check by a number of means. The engaging, ambivalent figures of Raven and Coyote, for instance—so smart, so dumb, so tricky, so vulnerable—provided cautionary tales for the man or woman who might presume to challenge traditional, conservative ways and pursue his or her own private ends.

We have to wonder, therefore, as we look at the rise of agriculture, why those traditional checks fell away when they did. In the following chapters, we we'll look at that whole process of change, addressing the following questions:

First, in Chapter Five, what brought agriculture into being, and why did it continue?

Second, in Chapter Six, how did the adoption of agriculture transform human life-ways?

Third, in Chapter Seven, how were religious views affected by the rise of agriculture, and what happened to women (and why do those two questions have so much to do with each other)?

Fourth, in Chapter Eight, what are the values that support this new way of being in the world? Why call them the values of Enterprise, as opposed to the values of Dominion or even Domination?

CHAPTER 5

Tearing the Web:
The Genesis of Agriculture

There was a time when scholars speculated about *the* trigger for the Agricultural Revolution. One theory had to do with technological breakthroughs such as polished stone tools, which would have been as important for the grinding of grain as for its cultivation. Tools of this sort don't appear in the archaeological record until the beginnings of agriculture. So maybe, some speculated, the real trigger for agriculture was the invention of those tools.

But there was no obvious reason why those tools should have been invented when they were and no sooner, and in so many different places that had no direct contact with one another. Not unless, in fact, the cause-and-effect relationship was exactly the opposite of what the above theory suggests. In other words, the ability to make such tools may not have been a deep, dark secret at all, but rather one of a great many things that human beings had already figured out but hadn't taken up in earnest until they decided to live on cereal grains.

The question was therefore refined. Instead of asking what started agriculture, archaeologists began asking why it started in so many places at once.

One popular answer was population pressure. Slowly, over hundreds of thousands of years, the argument went, hunter-gatherers had spread out and occupied all the land that supported their lifestyle. There were just too many of them at that point; and so, in response to increased population density, and in many parts of the world at once, they took up farming. That theory seemed plausible enough too, and overpopulation undoubtedly *was* an important factor in some areas. But in some of the centers where agriculture began, population density was relatively low.

Climate change was a third candidate, for a couple of reasons. At the end of the last Ice Age, the great ice sheets that had covered most of the earth began to melt, and as the ice receded, many of the large game animals that people had hunted went north too, or became extinct. So it would have been increasingly difficult to live by hunting.

In addition, in the warm, wet soil that was left as the glaciers receded, huge fields of cereal grasses sprang up—notably, in the area that's now Iraq. Long before cereal grains were actually cultivated, these fields attracted great numbers of human beings to their periphery. In the presence of such abundance, "gathering" took on a whole new character. People could stay in one place, and they did: "sedentism" became a real option. And it would have been advantageous, in that setting, to make polished stone tools for grinding grain, especially since those tools wouldn't have had to be carried around much.

So the change in climate was clearly pivotal.

But in fact there had been significant warming periods before the time in question that *hadn't* prompted the adoption of agriculture. What was different this time?

The consensus today is that it was social complexity, and our attraction to it, that tipped the scales toward agriculture: the human hankering for human company—for culture itself.

As people congregated around those fields and settled down, building permanent and semi-permanent dwellings, they found themselves living in much closer proximity to one another (and in larger groups) than they had as nomadic hunter-gatherers. When the ancient Syrian village of Abu Hureyra was first occupied between 11,500 and ten thousand years ago, for instance, just a few hundred hunter-gatherers lived there as "sedentary foragers." But when it was reoccupied about five hundred years later, as a farming community, several thousand people lived there, crammed into a space of not much more than twenty-five acres.[1]

Changes of that order have to have challenged ordinary conflict-resolution strategies mightily, and a great many other problems must have arisen as well. But none of them came close to diverting the course that human history had decided to take.

Some scholars see cultural complexity as the outward expression of an increasingly complex and bigger brain. They view the shift to agriculture in evolutionary terms, because all at once and everywhere, human beings appear to have *realized* that adopting a settled and stratified social and economic order would allow them to do things that isolated wandering bands or tribes could not.

What sorts of things might we do?

Oh, but all kinds of things! We could build dams and harbors and roads, aqueducts and storage facilities, great temples that would function like lightning rods and attract supernatural juice. We could build fortifications and fisheries and great libraries (because look, we just figured out how to write!).

None of which could happen, of course, without a dependable supply of food.

Initially, the simple fact of all those cereal grasses didn't herald the beginning of agriculture. It simply meant that people could begin to harvest what they needed without having to travel so far. But once they did settle down near fields of cereal grasses, more babies were born; and with a steady supply of food, more of them survived; and as populations grew, so did inventiveness. In short enough order, the various technologies required for storage and transport of grains came along. Anthropologists have determined that the rate of innovation jumps in direct proportion to growth in population size and density. More people means more inventions—and more *culture*.

So there you have it:

Two bands settle in by a huge meadow, watching one another warily at first, and the next thing you know, the Neolithic counterpart of a David Packard and a William Hewlett have met and discovered their mutual fascination with . . . widgets. One has figured out how to make especially sturdy widgets with a bright glaze—just collectibles, really. The other has developed half a dozen uses for the admittedly more fragile ones he's been working on. In no time flat they've put their heads together and emerged with absolutely terrific widgets, and everybody wants one.

And the worldwide web is only minutes away!

The "trigger" for agriculture, then, appears now to have been a global awakening to ourselves as a species (to our *genius,* if you will)—an awakening prompted by proximity and sedentism.

Foraging gave way, then, to farming, and it makes *sense* that it did. But why did our ancestors *stay* with agriculture?

It's a serious question, because in fact farming involves considerable hardship. Farmers back then would have had to work harder and longer than foragers, and for much higher stakes: a flood, drought, or windstorm could wipe out a year's crops in a matter of days. Indeed, a general impression is growing among anthropologists that farming in its early days was unremittingly harsh. Archaeologists have shown that the first farmers in many areas were smaller and less well nourished, suffered from more serious diseases, and died on the average at a younger age than the hunter-gatherers they replaced.

The wives of the first farmers fared no better. One northern Mesopotamian archaeological site of the era, rich in skeletal evidence, revealed that the toe, knee, and shoulder bones of women were deformed by the pressure from kneeling and pushing heavy objects— grinding stones, presumably—with the arm and shoulder. Male remains often reveal similar deformities.

From a nutritional standpoint, moreover, the far more limited diet of farmers would have predisposed them to diseases unknown to their more omnivorous ancestors. For that matter, diseases of all kinds were a serious threat now that people were living more closely together (and typically were surrounded by their own refuse).

Nostalgia for the "golden days" of foraging would persist for six thousand years after the adoption of agriculture. Preserved in oral traditions, that nostalgia is visible in all the earliest written poetry and epics.

So why did the new farmers persist?

One reason stands out above all others, and that's the emergence of a positive feedback loop. In other words, as people began cultivating crops and domesticating animals, surplus food made it possible for their numbers to rise. But with more and more land given over to growing crops, to grazing, and to human habitation, the wilderness retreated, decreasing the opportunity for foraging and making farming even more imperative.

Other factors undoubtedly helped accelerate the shift from foraging to farming. Some of these become evident when we consider (even in broad terms) what basic changes agriculture effected in ordinary lifeways.

CHAPTER 6

Taking Control:
The Life-Ways of Farmers

It's fruitless to generalize extensively about farmers, because the diversity of their patterns of living is even more considerable than that of hunter-gatherers. The trajectory from simple horticulture, involving a single family working a small plot of land and meeting just its own subsistence needs, to the large-scale agriculture along the Tigris and Euphrates, the Nile, and the Yellow River of China, varied widely in the different centers where agriculture took hold. So did the forms of social organization that arose afterwards. The cities of Uruk (in Mesopotamia) and Harappa (in what's now India), for example, differed from one another dramatically.

Initially, most farmers would have followed a mixed strategy—some hunting and gathering along with a bit of farming and herding. Some environments would have lent themselves much more readily to cultivation than others. The changeover was inexorable, but it would have taken place at different paces and followed any number of different patterns.

It's possible, though, to outline the most obvious ways in which farmers parted company from foragers. (I'm speaking here in broad terms of changes that took place over several thousand years.) We see that parting of company most clearly if we think not just of farming but of agri*culture* in its fullest sense—a culture which, as it expands and its technologies multiply, becomes diversified and powerful, giving rise to cities and then city-states. In fact, there's no small irony in the contrasts I keep drawing between farmers and foragers with respect to Enterprise, because of course with the growth of city-states, most *actual* farmers were reduced to the lowest class level, thoroughly exploited, and marginalized.

It's also possible to recognize what kind of changes the Agricultural Revolution brought about in the values by which most people lived. I'd like to pause here and anticipate in certain regards the discussion of those values that will take up later chapters.

In Chapter Eight, we'll look more closely at each of the values of Enterprise as they manifest themselves in the first agricultural economies. But it seems useful to list them right here as well, in a barebones fashion, by way of suggesting what radically new territory our ancestors were entering as they took up farming.

THE VALUES OF BELONGING	THE VALUES OF ENTERPRISE
Connection with land	Control and ownership of land
Empathic relationship to animals	Control and ownership of animals
Self-restraint	Extravagance and exploitation
Conservatism	Change
Deliberateness	Recklessness and Speed
Balance	Momentum and High Risk
Expressiveness	Secretiveness
Generosity	Acquisitiveness
Egalitarianism	Hierarchy
Mutuality	Competitiveness
Affinity for alternative modes of knowing	Rationality
Playfulness	Businesslike sobriety
Inclusiveness	Exclusiveness
Nonviolent conflict resolution	Aggressiveness and violence
Spirituality	Materialism

When, with the rise of agriculture, qualities such as competitiveness, acquisitiveness, and aggression became not just socially acceptable but openly admired, it wasn't as if they'd suddenly appeared out of nowhere. These and similar impulses had always been part of the human repertory; but they'd had to be discouraged in pre-agricultural society, because to act them out would have been to risk destroying the all-important fabric of communal life. But now, in this fundamentally different landscape, these traits must have looked as crucial to survival itself as connection with land, kin, and Spirit had been in the past.

In other words, embracing the values of Enterprise didn't signal a fall from grace. The values of Belonging define the relationship that human beings had enjoyed with the natural world before agriculture. They describe the kind of people we'd had to be in order to live in synchrony with the other inhabitants of our particular bioregions. They're the outward and visible signs of "embeddedness." The qualities that would surge to the forefront now had always been with us— human beings are just as competitive, curious, and innovative as they are cooperative, reverent, and custodial—but at last those more disruptive qualities could be lived out without shame.

If we thought we could walk away from the values of Belonging, we were in error, because they're part of us. By trying to live as if they weren't, or as if they applied to only some of us and in only certain contexts, we've created enormous problems for ourselves and for the global ecosystem as well. But on the other hand, that alluring old way of being in the world had real limitations.

The habit of making *muted distinctions,* for example, does create an atmosphere of tolerance and empathy that's all but unavailable in cultures governed, as our own is, by oppositional thinking. But in fact there's nothing inherently wrong with the capacity to make smart, quick, definitive choices when and where they're called for.

And as haunting as the imagery of *embeddedness* is, one senses its constraints. A womb is, after all, something we *leave* as we come into our own.

The *symbolic vision* of things, for that matter, can wear on one after a while so that we cry out like the poet Wallace Stevens for "not ideas about the thing, but the thing itself." The natural world is no less miraculous for our having come to understand how it works. Quite the opposite.

Most of us wouldn't for a minute—well, perhaps a minute—wind the clock back to the world our early ancestors left. What's worth wishing, though, is that the values that supported that world—the values of Belonging—hadn't been swept away so summarily. Couldn't some kind of balance have been struck? Couldn't the two sets of values have been integrated? In the individual? In the societies we built?

On the face of things, that *could* have happened. But foraging swiftly gave way to farming, and farming to commerce, and in the process a fateful imbalance developed—an imbalance that would set in motion a whole train of negative consequences.

To understand why imbalance seems to haunt cultures of Enterprise, it's imperative to see that the Enterprise paradigm has, in fact, two phases: one in which the primary impulse is ingenuity or inventiveness, and another in which the will to control drives all other concerns.

If we're ever to achieve the sort of balanced life that our great-grand-ancestors did *not*—a way of being in the world that acknowledges and employs the most exuberant and innovative parts of ourselves (rather than simply holding them down)—we need to understand how those phases are related. Once we do, we can also understand how it is that the one slides so easily and perennially into the other. Only then can we begin to think constructively about what kind of integration and balance might actually be possible.

THE TWO PHASES

Initially, wherever in the historic record we see an explosion of human innovativeness, we see ingenuity, curiosity, industry, and tremendous exhilaration at what people can do together. This first phase of Enterprise draws into it just about everyone with a good idea. No sooner does the new technology announce itself, though—within minutes, often—than we're in Phase Two, characterized by anxiety, acquisitiveness, secretiveness, and a thirst for control, which bring in their wake hierarchy and separateness.

The reasons for this shift are understandable. When the conquistador ethic asserts itself at the sudden opening of a new frontier (whether it's geographic, economic, or scientific), it isn't only because so much of life is now about exploring, conquering, and fortifying, and it isn't only because we are, among other things, greedy and violent. It's also because when we're out there throwing open all those doors, relational ways of living are typically disrupted. And whenever that happens, a vacuum opens up. When traditional sources of identity and connection fall away, so do the constraints that were keeping in check our greedier, more aggressive impulses. The sheer joy of conquest is supposed to fill the void: better a sense of self built on acquisition and accomplishment than none at all—or so it must have seemed reasonable to believe.

The first phase of Enterprise tends to "morph" so unresistingly into the second that it is easy to forget there even *is* a first phase and speak, rather, of the values of control, or dominance, or mastery. But if we do that, we ignore the deeply human and admirable side of this ethos and oversimplify the task that awaits anyone who wants to integrate meaningfully the cultures of Enterprise and Belonging.

Let's look now at the specific changes that took place in the lives of the people who first took up farming.

Readapting

It's an interesting paradox that while hunter-gatherers have a relationship to the earth that's more reverent and intimate than that of most farmers, they're nomadic, while farmers are relatively sedentary. Farmers lay claim to the land that they cultivate, and they stay close to it lest someone else make off with the crops. This means that nothing that hunter-gatherers had done *specifically because they were nomadic* would have any necessary relevance to their lives once they became farmers. They might as well build permanent homes now, for example, and get comfortable. And they could have the enjoyment of more extensive possessions, because they wouldn't have to carry them around anymore.

With this change, a less obvious one took place—a change whose effects would be, in a certain sense, even more far-reaching: people's time and attention were taken up considerably less now with relationships (with other people, animals, land, and Spirit) and considerably more with things. For men and women alike, the generosity, mutuality, and inclusiveness of the hunter-gatherer world would be tested now as materialism began to eclipse the sort of spirituality that had quite literally "come with the territory." Leisure time, which is relatively ample among most hunter-gatherers and which makes the cultivation of relationships one of the great pleasures of the foraging life, was reduced now, because one had the option of working, instead, for profit and increased buying power.

The option of ownership made trade more attractive too, and prompted the development of currency and counting. The subsistence model of living fell away: if one could store food, and if there were others around to sell (or barter) it to, there was plenty of motivation to work much harder than one had in the past. Industriousness paid off: the easygoing playfulness of the forager didn't.

On the other hand, as they built homes and accumulated material possessions, farmers also risked arousing the interest of thieves, working singly or in gangs. So it made sense to build walls around their homes, and/or congregate in increasingly large villages or networks for mutual self-defense. (The logic didn't stop there, of course; it would give rise to kingdoms, in time, and empires.)

With these changes, a new seriousness entered life—or rather, a sharp falling off of the improvisational tenor that life had often had before agriculture. Because competitiveness was no longer inhibited by the need to retain harmony in the small hunter-gatherer group, social inequalities became more acceptable. Indeed, they were inevitable, given that some families and individuals were better positioned than others to prosper, and that with a growing sense of control over nature, they all felt themselves to be less dependent on the goodwill of others. Resistance to hierarchy, so visible in foraging peoples, was steadily dropping.

A farmer's primary affiliation was not to his band or his tribe, but typically to his father and sons. Nor would he experience the land as a living relative: land was *owned* now, and it was passed on, in most parts of the world, to sons. Even if a man picked up and left the region he'd been born in, he would retain a sense of connection to his forefathers—preserved orally at first, and then, in time, in written form.

Acceptance of centralized authority was inevitable as villages joined together, forming cities and city-states that in turn began interacting with other cities and city-states. The consensual decision-making processes that small foraging communities favor would have been unworkable in the new political landscape. Military actions needed generals, and large public works (such as irrigation projects and the construction of storage facilities, temples, and monuments) required foremen and bosses. To feel defended on the one hand, and effectively aggressive on the other, one had to be willing to give over some agency.

Entering alliances, declaring fealty, and accepting the existence of a ruling class also entailed the payment of tribute and taxes. With the emergence of chiefdoms, what biologist Jared Diamond calls "kleptocracy" had also arrived: the steady, unembarrassed transfer of wealth from the lower to the upper classes that has characterized virtually all forms of government ever since.[1] (The literal meaning of "kleptocracy" is, of course, "government by theft.")

The military model of command-and-control gradually edged out the egalitarian individualism of hunter-gatherer cultures. Childrearing practices changed to reflect the new commitment to hierarchy. Being able to think on one's feet was less "adaptive" for children now than docility and industry.

Some of the strategies by which foragers had prevented violent conflict were abandoned now, because whatever losses might be incurred in combat, there were possible gains as well: war was no longer seen as an unmitigated evil.

And in fact, as history teaches us, agriculture and war are symbiotic. They work together in another of those positive feedback loops:

In the first place, as agricultural technology improves, a single family can cultivate more and more land. For that matter, a large family can cultivate more land than a small one. Agriculturalists tend, therefore, to be prolific: in contrast with the one or two children typical of hunter-gatherers, the average number of European children in rural families varies between four and eight, with some even larger.[2]

Second, as more labor makes for increased productivity and the ability to feed still more offspring, those offspring are born; and within a couple of generations, their paterfamilias, whose brood is now quite sizable, has begun to eye the fields next door—or across the river, or on the other side of that low mountain range. If no one else is cultivating that land, fine. If someone is, but his sons aren't as many or as able-bodied as one's own, annexing the land is easy enough. And if the only people on the land are foragers, it will not only be easy enough to force them out (given that foragers are rarely well set up to wage war), it will also be easy to justify doing so, because the foragers clearly aren't making adequate use of the land. They aren't carrying out the task God assigned to human beings!

Still, it's helpful to be able to rally an entire army to fight such battles—so helpful that people are increasingly willing to pay taxes and swear fealty to a regional chieftain.

Farming almost invariably gives rise to war—war fought over land, water, seaports, enslaveable populations, and access to minerals. Militarism is a direct function of agriculture's inherent expansiveness. The doctrine of Manifest Destiny has been around since the first Mesopotamian peasant dragged a bent tree branch through the soil and saw a long, straight furrow opening up behind him.

Agriculture also saw specialization replace the encyclopedic knowledge that hunter-gatherers possess of the land where they live and the ways one can extract a subsistence from it. While all hunter-gatherers hunt and gather, everybody who lives in an agricultural economy doesn't necessarily grow food. Only people who own land can grow food. But as humanity moved away from the subsistence model, its desires multiplied and diversified, meaning that people with special gifts—jewelers, carpenters, potters, metallurgists—could make their way in the world without owning property.

Even as they were coming together in more densely populated villages and cities, then, human beings began to experience one another as distinctly "other" in ways that hunter-gatherers rarely had.

The sensation of existing side by side, but in sharply separate spheres, has to have been particularly acute between men and women. By no stretch of the imagination could one argue that the lists of Belonging and Enterprise values that appear on page 71 represent "the feminine," and "the masculine." But from the time of the Agricultural Revolution onward, they would be understood as exactly that. Even now, in our own culture and most others, a young man is far more likely to be rewarded for embracing the values on the right side, and a young woman for honoring those on the left.

THE FADING OF GENDER MUTUALITY

During the horticultural phase that typically preceded the adoption of agriculture, women are believed to have fared rather well, and largely for reasons of scale: everyone lived in autonomous villages, the plots were small, grain was hand-tended, and large draft animals weren't in use yet, so women and children could handle most of the work.

Small-scale, face-to-face economies are universally woman-friendly. Indeed, it was probably women's expertise as gatherers that brought the first garden plots into existence; and just as a successful male hunter gets to decide how he'll share out the antelope, women who cultivate typically get to decide what they'll grow, how much, and how their vegetables and fruits will be distributed.

On the other hand, once women are no longer nomadic or far-ranging, men can more easily control them, if they're so moved, as well as control the fruits of their labor.

And men may well have *been* so moved in that rapidly changing world. Because once the wild animals were reduced in number and pushed back, and once horticulture had replaced gathering, a great many men would have been at a real loss. Anthropologists studying warfare among American Indians of the Southwest believe that war broke out there when women learned to grow crops single-handedly and (with the children) could care for domesticated animals, so that there was no longer anything for men to do that was both indispensable and unique to men. It may be that the best way to explain men's willingness to forego their independence, relinquish the autonomy of their villages, and become footsoldiers to the state is in terms of that sense of displacement.

In any case, the emergence of war always hardens cultural norms for gender, narrowing the options for men and women alike, and placing them in increasingly separate spheres. As the forms of social organization evolved among our ancestors to facilitate the waging of war—and as large-scale farming replaced horticulture, for that matter—women drifted steadily on outward to the periphery of public life. Their primary role now was to give birth—to farmers, ideally, and footsoldiers.

Attempts to pin down what actually happened to women with the rise of agriculture are hindered immensely by the difficulty of determining what their status had been in the pre-agricultural world. In the ethnographic work carried out on recent hunter-gatherer societies, no area is more vexed and beclouded than that of gender relationships. In the first place, one sees a great many different patterns. (That's in part why ethnography is such a fascinating exercise.) But in addition, the meaning of gender is so controversial in Western culture that the observers themselves aren't sure how to describe what they think they're seeing! It doesn't help that the lion's share of fieldwork has been carried out by men, who, however objective they might have been, couldn't have had the kind of access to indigenous women that female investigators would have.

In recent years fieldworkers have developed more sensitive protocols. For instance, they've learned to distinguish more subtly between "status," "authority," and "power," and that's helped account for situations in which women appeared to have low status (having little or no role in ceremony, for example) but clearly wielded considerable influence in the community.

THE ROOTS OF MALE DOMINANCE

If we want to make educated guesses about what happened to women with the advent of farming by extrapolating from recent hunter-gatherer models, it's helpful to know something of the range of possibilities. What situations have been more advantageous for for-

aging women than others? What are the "risk factors" for male dominance?

It turns out that if we leave aside the subtler questions and focus
only on egregious male dominance, some fairly clear and interesting
answers are available.

Anthropologist Peggy Sanday examined more than 150 cultures
that she describes as "preliterate"—not foraging cultures exclusively,
but also many that are making the transition toward agriculture—to
determine the relationship between "female power" and "male dominance." Her working definition of male-dominant cultures is unequivocal: it requires not only that women be excluded from political and
economic decision-making, but that males be actively aggressive
against women (as indicated by evidence that males are expected to
be tough, brave, and aggressive; that men have specific gathering
places where women may not be; that wife-beating is permissible and
frequent; that rape occurs regularly and/or is sanctioned, and that
other groups are raided for wives).

In preliterate cultures where gender imbalance is that severe, three
conditions are typically present, according to Sanday's findings:[3]

1. *A culture of separation by gender.* Sanday observed that no matter
   how separation of men and women is produced (for example,
   by a strict delineation of male and female roles), it creates two
   worlds—one male and the other female—each with its own
   set of meanings and its own prescribed code of behavior.

2. *Limited food resources.* The status of females seems to be lowest
   across the board, with respect to ceremony, marriage customs,
   food allotments, and physical assault, when food shortages are
   a serious and recurring threat. When men feel that they're
   struggling for subsistence in an environment that's not behav-
   ing like a "living womb," they tend to take it out on the
   women around them. It's in societies plagued by shortages that
   women's reproductivity is most likely to be described as *threatening* or *polluting*—descriptions that may be just a roundabout

way of expressing the fear that more babies will be born than the environment (and the men themselves) can feed.

3. *Creation stories based on male symbolism.* Third, and decisively, in order for aggressive male dominance to come into play, the society in question must embrace a creation mythology that excludes female power. Even if women and men are separated, and even if the environment is inhospitable, women will be safe if the creation mythology of their people includes positive depictions of female power.

Peggy Sanday's analysis helps us realize that even in the pre-agricultural world there would have been a range of possibilities where the standing of women was concerned, because of course the economies and the environments of foraging societies would have varied. Some, for example, would have emphasized hunting more than others—and in fact there's a correlation between latitude, hunting, and male status: the further north a people is situated, the more dependent they are on hunting, and that tends to increase the male's prestige.

Overall, though, Sanday's work seems to strengthen the likelihood that the pre-agricultural foraging world was relatively comfortable for women. Her findings associate aggressive male dominance with increasing technological complexity, as well as with an animal economy (not just hunting, but pastoralism) and separation of women's work from men's. The examples she offers of markedly male-dominant cultures are typically farmers, pastoralists, and/or people who've been pushed onto marginal lands by other populations.

In other words, the changes that took place as agriculture replaced the hunter-gatherer life constituted a virtual prescription for aggressive male dominance.

From Immanent Spirit to Transcendent God

The whole premise of hunter-gatherers' spirituality was the conviction that all living things (defined much more inclusively than we see life today) are connected to one another. By living in the right way, one moved into an ever deepening experience of that interconnection.

With agriculture, that orientation changed radically. The natural world couldn't be one's mother. It was there to be exploited—and to as great an advantage as possible. So even as farmers learned how to drain the marshlands and redirect the waters of great rivers, they learned to drain the earth of the sacred meanings they had always found there. Soil, water, plants, and animals were only material elements now. Spirit, no longer immanent, took the form and shape of a transcendent God.

The creation story in Genesis (with its account of Adam and Eve's eviction from the Garden of Eden) conveys the overwhelming sense of exile that must have accompanied this great change. The possibility of experiencing the sacred directly vanished along with the intimate connection to earth and its life-forms that had nourished spiritual impulses in the past. From here on out, human beings could reach God only indirectly, through intermediaries.

A Dark and Toxic Stream

The changes I've outlined took place over several thousand years—the actual timeframe varied, of course, from one place to another—and that sounds like forever. But measured against the millions of years that human beings have been evolving, it isn't long at all. By the time the Agricultural Revolution took place, human beings were essentially who we are now. They looked like us, and they had the same brains, the same hormonal and nervous systems we do. And they had *become* us in the context of the foraging life. When foraging gave way to agriculture, the social equilibrium that had sustained human beings in a more or less steady state for eons was severely disrupted. But so was a great deal else besides.

So many things were happening at once—molecules dancing, synapses crackling, brilliant ideas flaring up—all because for the first time people could concern themselves with something besides keeping themselves fed.

How do we begin to imagine what a mixed blessing that was? Gone was the whole-body knowing that would allow you to walk through a forest sure that you were its beloved child—but look! Here come potter's wheels, and water wheels, and plows made of bronze, and calendars. And not far behind, steam engines, the Bolshoi Ballet, satellite weather systems, and John Coltrane.

And from the very beginning, all those technological advances, innocent as they may have been in themselves, were taking place in the context of the steadily consolidating state—Egypt and Mesopotamia in particular, prototypes for the Roman and other empires.

Among those early innovators, there were plenty who loved what they were doing for its own sake. There were men—maybe some women—who supported each other's work, sharing information and materials as freely as their foraging ancestors would have, and who did it all for the joy of figuring things out.

But right alongside, peering over their shoulders and looking, looking, looking for how each new discovery might be turned to military advantage, were the warlords. Like a dark and toxic stream, they were a presence from the beginning, gripped by the need not just to understand the natural world, and not just to tease out of it relief from human suffering, but to *master* it.

It's so easy to demonize them. Yet if Barbara Ehrenreich is correct, those individuals have only ever been acting on an impulse that's part of our shared evolutionary past: the need to keep on proving to oneself—in hunting, in warfare, in relationships—that one is not prey, but predator. In that simplistic, binary view of the human condition, there's no middle ground; and that very model, enshrined in the "law of the excluded middle," would become the basis for Western philosophy and science as well as for agriculture.

To clear a piece of land and grow what one chooses in place of what's there is to shatter the delicate balance of plant and animal communities that have co-evolved in that place over long reaches of time. However noble the motives might be, and happy the outcome in other regards, the decision to cultivate the earth is, with respect to those interdependent communities, a declaration of war. "This I declare a weed," said First Farmer, "and this a valuable plant. This one will die, and that one I will allow to live."

Thus it is that with agriculture, a working metaphor emerged, anathema to the worldview of hunter-gatherers, which would tacitly legitimize war. Just as there are useful (to us) plants in the world, that view maintains, and people we recognize as like us, so are there are plants we have no use for, and people who feel distressingly foreign.

That perception is nothing that a band of hunter-gatherers might not have entertained, mind you—only typically they wouldn't have found in it a motive for violent assault. Gravitate toward the plants you can use; steer clear of people who make you nervous. Fine. But if you kill them, you could be unleashing destructive energies that will come back to hurt you and yours.

If it's true that a binary vision of the world was born along with agriculture—a vision that would offer sanction to the emerging and companionate idea of war—then it isn't surprising that the fortunes of women went into freefall (as women's historians have concluded they did) at the very same juncture. "Difference" had come to be synonymous with "division" and "domination." As the hierarchical model for life impressed itself more and more deeply on human societies, it came, inevitably, into the home and family. As God was to the heavens, and humanity to the earth—magisterial and distant—man was to wife and child.

On New Terrain

Our altered relationship with the environment, and thus with one another, raised other questions that had rarely, if ever, come up before. Given that we could do more now than merely meet subsistence needs, how would we decide what "enough" was? What would "enough" look like?

Because there's a sharp difference between the knowledge that it makes no sense to expend more effort than is needed to assuage hunger, and the realization that you could not only produce large quantities of food but could also store that food and later barter and sell it. Vexing questions arise in the latter case:

How hard can I work? How able a man am I?

Do I need enough for comfort, for long-range security, to impress and even intimidate my neighbors, to support my great-grandchildren?

Or to support my as-yet-unborn children, for that matter, in the style that they believe befits them? A letter preserved from the time of Hammurabi, the great lawgiver of Babylon, startles us with its contemporary ring. The son of a government official wrote to his mother almost four thousand years ago (his mother, note, not his father!), chagrined because his wardrobe had fallen behind current fashions and she'd shown no interest in paying for new clothing. The letter closes on a petulant note: "You, you do not love me!"[4]

We were on decidedly new terrain.

However zestfully we strode into this brave new world, everything about it was at odds with the values—the ethos—that had kept us going for our first couple of million years. Connection to the land was attenuated or broken, and as people moved into villages and cities, kinship bonds were strained or broken as well. Most important of all, the human being's relationship to the sacred was completely redefined. To understand why, though, and how, we must look more closely still at the standing of women as this crisis in values unfolded—and before *that* we need to grasp the real nature of that crisis, and its flawed resolution.

CHAPTER 7

Wherein Women Are Enclosed, and We All Get Religion

My friend Charlotte had had a revelation about her marriage, and she knew I'd want to hear about it. She'd been telling Malcolm about something one of their three children had done: a situation. She needed his input and just wasn't getting it. They were fast approaching impasse, and she couldn't figure out why he was being so noncommittal and remote. Suddenly, in a great white wave, the truth broke over her.

"I had never realized it before, but now I did. In his mind—I saw this now as clear as day, and I said it—we had signed a contract. He would make the money—the serious money to cover house payments and college tuition—and *I* would have the feelings."

"It was your job," I said.

"It was my job," she agreed, grinning broadly, knowing that the full, delicious irony wasn't lost on me: not so much that she has a full-time job, thank you (a job that, while it pays less than his, is good for groceries and car payments), but that Malcolm himself (a psychiatrist who works primarily with veterans) spends the better part of his working hours helping other men figure out what they feel—and *that* they feel, and that it's all right to feel.

"Oh," said Malcolm, hearing his wife's assessment—or maybe even *"Ouch";* and as couples do who've weathered worse, they found their way toward even terrain.

It's probably been ten years since I heard the story, but I've thought about it often, because on a very intimate scale it reflects something a great many of us have wondered about.

Where does it come from, this sense that somewhere back there our ancestors did indeed sign a contract on behalf of all of us: the male would lay waste for our daily bread, and the female would hang back and preside over a small, intimate, enclosed universe where no one would jostle or shove or speak harshly—a world pointedly and blessedly unlike the one "out there" where he was compelled to spend his days.

The more we know about the transition from foraging to farming, and about the resultant crisis in human values, the better we understand where this arrangement originated.

THE COMPROMISE THAT COULDN'T BE STRUCK

Theoretically, the cultures of Belonging and Enterprise could have found a common ground. If humanity in general had possessed a clear sense that by embracing Enterprise values so unrestrainedly they were losing something precious, they could conceivably have identified what that something was and resisted the floodtide of change.

Why *was* our response to the new model of things so unrestrained? Inclusiveness is, after all, a byword of the paradigm by which our earliest ancestors lived. Couldn't this new set of impulses have been absorbed and accomodated?

Theoretically, *it could have.* In reality, though, the defining modality of the new paradigm was Exclusiveness: The model of individual heroism is basic to Enterprise. Precedence matters more than anything else. The emergence of the exceptional individual is of paramount interest, and so is the emergence of a single ruling idea.

So perhaps it was, in fact, inevitable that the two cultures would clash and that the paradigm of hierarchy and winner-takes-all would take precedence over that of inclusion and connection.

I asked readers earlier to notice the synergy of the values of Belonging—the manner in which mutuality, inclusiveness, and empathic connection to land and animals, for example, all imply and strengthen one another. They *cohere,* and they work toward the same ends.

Just so do the values of Enterprise cohere and work toward the same ends. Acquisitiveness prompts industry, curiosity sparks exploration, envy goads us to competitiveness, and soon everything is moving along so quickly that nobody's observing the consequences of what they're doing.

Marxists think of this new paradigm in economic terms, calling it "capitalism," but that may define things too narrowly. The term "Enterprise" captures the exhilaration and open-endedness of this new ethos, and it reminds us as well that its initial phases were as blameless as a baby's first steps.

Hunter-gatherer peoples everywhere have shown themselves able to make significant innovations in the basic template of foraging life without shattering the ethos itself. But the changeover ten thousand years ago to agriculture, and then to towns and city-states, was truly dramatic. Collectively, it was as if humanity were stirring, stretching, and recognizing needs that we/she/it hadn't really known about until then; and it's hard to imagine how those needs could have been met within traditional structures.

For the most curious, risk-taking, independent, and materialistic individuals, and for that side of *every* individual, the new constellation of values worked well enough. And yet the needs for connection, continuity, and "Dream-Time" didn't go away.

This was the quandary facing humanity as a whole as we moved into the tremendous new adventure that beckoned with agriculture and all that it made possible. We were looking at two radically different ways of being in the world. Any psychologist will tell you that an important criterion for psychic health is the ability to deal with paradox, but there are paradoxes and paradoxes, and this one was huge. The collision of deep, human truths we were up against six or eight thousand years ago, collectively, was inconceivably far-reaching.

So what did we do in the face of the unprecedentedly complex challenge of balancing the radically opposed claims of Belonging and Enterprise?

We sidestepped.

We punted.

We finessed.

Instead of integrating the values of Belonging with the values of Enterprise, making the appropriate adjustments as we went along, we decided (if that isn't too strong a term, for the process was surely wordless and unconscious) that the values of Belonging were the values of women and that the values of Enterprise were the values of men. We "decided," moreover, dazzled by the possibilities we saw in Enterprise, that these new values—and therefore men—would take absolute precedence. It was an odd stratagem, but it did mean that the ascendant culture of Enterprise wouldn't have to figure out what to do about the culture of Belonging. And that was probably a relief.

When the ethos of Belonging came up against the ethos of Enterprise, contradictions occurred at almost every salient point. Rather like a tectonic plate, too massive and too real to simply crumble or vanish, the old one slid beneath the new.

And women slid with it.

That was the solution—jerrybuilt, slapped together—and it held. Women would carry the values central to the constellation of Belonging, and men would build a civilization on the basis of the values of Enterprise.

Why did this solution hold?

One wonders, because it really *shouldn't* have held. It flies in the teeth of what we know about ourselves. Women aren't innately more playful than men, and men aren't congenitally more industrious, more competitive, or more essentially serious than women; and even if they were, it's hard to imagine what advantage there might be in deciding that women must be *unremittingly* playful and men must be *unfailingly* industrious and competitive. Yet for a long, long while, women and men have been receiving just these messages. We can trace a direct lineage from the laws of Assyria governing the treatment of wives and female slaves to the following chart displayed at a kindergarten awards program in a progressive U.S. public school in an eastern academic community during the late 1980s.[1]

Girls' Awards	Boys' Awards
All-Around Sweetheart	Very Best Thinker
Sweetest Personality	Most Eager Learner
Cutest Personality	Most Imaginative
Best Sharer	Most Enthusiastic
Best Artist	Most Scientific
Biggest Heart	Best Friend
Best Manners	Mr. Personality
Best Helper	Hardest Worker
Most Creative	Best Sense of Humor

The components of a fully developed human being, whole and balanced, have been teased apart into two lists that barely overlap. If one were a girl possessed of a sharp wit—if she were adventurous or loved to figure out how things work—how would she locate herself on this chart? Suppose one were a boy who loved to be helpful, a boy of great empathy and sensitivity who drew beautifully—where would he go?

At least today we're asking these questions.

Puzzling over how such a simplistic and damaging arrangement fell into place so easily, all I can conclude is that for the time being, the effects of placing humanity in two separate spheres, "sexed" like chicks or kittens, were just not sufficiently catastrophic to have been noticed by anyone who also had the will or power to challenge the idea. And the effect of releasing men from the old constraints, which Enterprise in effect did, was dazzlingly productive.

The Decline and Fall of Women

Nobody would have experienced the disruptions of change brought on by the adoption of agriculture more keenly or directly than women. They had entered the transition to agriculture as free-ranging, self-supporting, resourceful individuals who participated fully and vocally in their community's life, forming with practiced ease the sort of alliance that helped them raise their children. And after an extraordinarily brief transition, they found themselves to be enclosed, dependent, silenced, isolated from one another, and in fact pitted against one another for the support and protection of powerful men.

How could that have happened?

It happened, though swiftly, in stages. As I mentioned earlier, a horticultural phase preceded agriculture in most places, and this small-scale subsistence model suited women's needs fairly well.

But before the first city-states began to spring up in the third and fourth millennia B.C., the horticultural pattern was giving way to full-scale agriculture. The invention of the bronze plow around 3000 B.C. would have made a critical difference in how much land could be cultivated by one person, but also in the kind of strength it took to do the work—strength that very few women would likely have possessed. And of course the same metallurgists who invented plows that wouldn't bend or break in hard soil made weapons too—weapons that were far more lethal than any had been in the past.

Agriculture, war, and the formation of city-states were all of a piece; and, in the new reality they composed, *men,* who had rarely united in any sort of formal alliance that pointedly excluded women, began to do so with a vengeance.

There's a tragic dimension to this development. To plow its fields, build its temples, and fight its wars, the nascent state needed a vast number of people who could be persuaded to give over their humanity—the satisfactions of sustained, intimate relationships, for example, and the ample leisure time that hunter-gatherers had used in a thousand "nonproductive" ways: ceremony, music, art, laughter. And it would find these individuals among the half of humanity—the male half—that had always understood itself to be expendable.[2] For even male primates appear to know that females can give birth and nurture, while they cannot. Whenever men could be persuaded that the state itself was in peril, and therefore the women and children within it, they could be enlisted.

Under agriculture, the world of women would narrow and deteriorate. Given the increased likelihood of death due to the diseases of propinquity as well as war, and given the need for more offspring to help in the fields and fight the wars, women were under intense pressure now to reproduce as often as possible. But in addition to these external pressures, the facts of agricultural life were implacable and determinative.

First, now that a dependable food supply was available, a woman didn't have to traipse around the countryside for food. She could wean her infants as soon as they could eat gruel, meaning that she could get pregnant again immediately. As a result, her fertility typically doubled.

Pregnancy itself would confine her now as she had never been confined before—particularly given that if she did want to walk about, she had not only "one in the oven" but one to carry as well. And with the general increase in wealth and population density, new dangers arose. It was no longer necessarily safe for a woman to leave her courtyard. She could well spend most of her life within its walls—pregnant, spinning, weaving, grinding, and baking.

Hard as these changes would have been on women, they took as great a toll on the infants themselves. Contemporary anthropologists have watched the impact on hunter-gatherers who have finally been compelled to give up their nomadic, foraging lives. When the !Kung of the Kalahari were forced off their ancestral lands and began to grow their own food, the greater availability of weaning food meant that babies did indeed begin to arrive twice as frequently, and this very fact produced a new subgroup of displaced persons: infants a year and a half old who in the old days would still have been on their mother's hip, but who wandered about the camp alone now, disconsolate, because their mothers had just borne another child.

As agriculture replaced horticulture, the fields that had belonged to women came swiftly to be owned and managed by men. Matrilocality having faded, the courtyard in which our Neolithic foremother lived out her days probably belonged to her husband's family. With families more isolated, she had lost the support of her network of kin as well, and without it, she was newly vulnerable. Under Assyrian law, for instance, a woman could be sold into slavery for as long as three years to pay off her husband's debts.

If there was a tipping point in human history, a time when women's fortunes turned definitively for the worse, the onset of agriculture was surely it. To convey the chilling reality of what took place, historian Gerda Lerner employs the phrase "the commodification of women's sexual and reproductive capacity."[3] Not just slaves, but *all* women, were effectively alienated now from any real say in their own reproductive life. They were valued primarily for the children they could bear, and their very fertility had become a thing that could be bought and sold.

And once women were confined to the courtyard, so visibly defined by their reproductivity, what would have been more natural than for a man to look out across his corrals at his sheep and goats and cattle (noting happily which were pregnant and which nursing) and half consciously count his own wife, pregnant now for the sixth time, among them?

In war as well as in agriculture, men had the chance to prove to themselves that they were no longer prey, but predator. Women did not. Did women of this period think of themselves as prey? It's hard to imagine that they wouldn't have.

In this changed world, all of the conditions identified by Peggy Sanday as "risk factors" for aggressive male dominance (see Chapter Six) were present:

1. *A culture of separation* had begun to establish itself. Men and women alike were above all else workers now, in large, complex economies; and as women's work confined females increasingly to the courtyard and men's work confined males to the fields or battlefields, the two genders saw less and less of one another.

2. *A feeling of high-stakes risk and anxiety* developed as men worked the plow—a feeling implicit, always, in agriculture. Even a relatively fertile region can begin to feel hostile (or at the very least fickle and resistant to human effort) once the task of mastering it has become imperative.

3. *Creation stories based on male symbolism* displaced traditional, more lighthearted tales that focused on the earth's generative and regenerative powers. The myths of the newly agricultural peoples were rewritten to reflect a new cosmology, and in the process the very idea of positive female energy was expunged— or at least severely marginalized. What the elevation of Marduk was in Mesopotamia, the emergence of Yahweh was in the Middle East—likewise the emergence of Zeus in Greece and of Vishnu in India.

Once men had committed themselves to cultivating the earth, the metaphoric identity between women and the earth took on fateful new significance. Until the earth was plowed—until there *were* plows—the imagery of the phallus couldn't possibly have the same kind of significance it would from then on. To mark off a piece of the earth as one's own, which was in itself unprecedented in indigenous cultures, and lay claim to everything that grew there, to defend it with the sword, work it with the plow, and keep everyone inside it subdued with the sword (the phallus) . . .

No, we were definitely in new territory, and the difference must have had a profound effect on how it *felt* to be male or female.

Much has been made of the endless toggle by which swords would be beaten into plowshares, and plowshares back into swords. Where conventional history is concerned, it's of course monumentally important whether, at any given moment, swords or plowshares were being deployed. But where the local ecosystem is concerned, and where the well-being of women is concerned, war and agriculture have been remarkably similar in their effects.

A DOUBLE BANISHMENT

By defining the values of Belonging as feminine, and declaring them applicable only to the home, the first agriculturists preserved the two paradigms of Belonging and Enterprise. But they achieved this at the price of wholeness, in what amounted to a *double banishment*. Actual women were whisked away out of sight, but so was a constellation of ideals that would have impeded Enterprise every step of the way. Assigned to women, the values of Belonging could have only a limited and circumscribed validity. By not disputing them—by merely walking away from them and labeling them "feminine"—our ancestors set things up, however unconsciously, so that any man who did embrace the values of Belonging would risk being seen as "womanish" (a perception that was no longer favorable).

The logic of specialization was inarguable. Women had always had the babies and had always taken care of them: Why should the basic arrangement change now that they were having babies twice as often? And homes built around courtyards weren't built just to keep women in, they were there to protect them as well, along with food surpluses, tools, supplies, and toddlers.

But once women were confined within, barefoot and perennially pregnant—so visibly immobilized and excluded from Enterprise, so very *prey*—it would have felt like the most natural thing in the world to locate the abandoned values of Belonging there as well. Like spinning wheels in an attic and washboards in the cellar.

The deal, then, was done.

Within the walls of the home, embeddedness, muted distinctions, and even the more innocuous forms of religiosity could be honored, as they certainly needed to be if children were to thrive there. Thus the values could be preserved, in a kind of symbiotic relationship with women. Women would be expected to believe in the values of Belonging and live them out in their homes, families, and (up to a point) communities. Men would protect the home and could have recourse to it and avail themselves of everything and everybody there "as needed," though for the most part surreptitiously, dipping into it hungrily on the run.

Fully and systematically disempowered, women would through their own permanently secondary status confirm that the values they were assigned to cherish were also secondary. Women had ceased to be the subjects of their own life-stories. They had become, rather—like water, soil, plants, and animals—a natural resource.

So it happened that a division that had been developing within human consciousness, between one set of values and another—

indeed, one reading of reality and another—became instead a split between human beings, along gender lines.

The challenge of figuring out how to integrate the two very different kinds of claims that Belonging and Enterprise made on us wouldn't have to be met after all. The individual wouldn't have to live by two seemingly contradictory laws at once—wouldn't have to learn the great developmental hat trick of holding in tension truths that seem contradictory.

Instead, we would separate onto two tracks.

Which is to say (if we were to think in anthropomorphic terms and picture the whole human race, poised at that crucial juncture, as a single being) that under the threat of tremendous losses, humanity devised for herself a way of being in the world—an identity structure, to use the language of psychology—that would allow her to soldier on. She would honor the various parts of herself, but in so highly compartmentalized a fashion that they wouldn't be in touch with one another. The right hand would have very little idea what the left hand was up to.

She would develop, in short, a neurosis. And of course the well-built neurosis has its legitimate place in the scheme of things, even if in the fullness of time it has to be dismantled. Like the tough carapace of a turtle or a snail or a dormant butterfly, a neurosis protects the parts of oneself that are too tender and too fragile to be exposed.

WE GET RELIGION

But there was another twist, and this one is of paramount importance in determining what kind of world we were moving into once we'd subscribed to the values of Enterprise. The simile of tectonic shift works well enough as a description of the way in which the values of Belonging slid underground along with women, but it's misleading too. Because, in a sense, the plate that constituted the values of Belonging didn't remain intact when it slid under the one that I've called Enterprise. Or rather, it did, but no one was permitted to *know* that it did. Under cultures of Enterprise, the values of Belonging would be represented as two different (though overlapping) sets of values—that is, "the feminine" and "the religious."

In pre-agricultural societies, "religiousness" had permeated the whole of life, suffusing the simplest everyday activities with enlarged meaning and beauty. The values of Belonging presumed a deep interconnectedness among all things that was, for the people who honored those values, synonymous with Spirit. This is why that complex of values was both resilient and potentially subversive. Whole, it was far more than the sum of its parts. When an individual embraced all the values of Belonging, or a community did, those values could threaten existing authority structures and society's whole commitment to Enterprise.

And that's of course why, if the values of Belonging were to be handed over to women, their spiritual content would have to be sheared off and placed elsewhere.

Certain of the values of Belonging could be entrusted to women without consequence. It would make for harmonious homes if women were self-restrained and empathetic, for example; or if they were noncompetitive and nurturant; artistic within reason, and devout; playful, within reason, and so inherently softhearted as to be lovingly disposed to everyone in their household. As long as such values were clearly labeled as womanish, and as long as growing boys understood that such values were "childish things," to be put away well before they started shaving, they posed no threat to the emerging Enterprise ethos and the institutions it built.

In other words, as long as women didn't take themselves too seriously, things would go along smoothly.

But in fact, cultures of Belonging, past and present, do encourage individuals of *both* genders to take themselves quite seriously. Foragers know that their actions will ripple on out, for better or worse, across the whole web of life. More than that, aboriginal peoples everywhere know that one can experience the sacred firsthand. Learning how to so dispose oneself that one is able to move at will into the deep Ground of Being—alone, through prayer, fasting, and soul journeys, or collectively, in ceremony—is for such people a very real possibility.

Visions confer authority. Visionaries tend to be a law unto themselves, and to inspire something of that disposition in others. So an emerging patriarchal state would certainly not want women developing visionary gifts. Particularly not if they were embracing other potentially subversive qualities as well, such as mutuality and irreverence toward authority. If women were to be consistently manageable and docile, they would need to be kept off-center and ungrounded. For that reason, it would be important for them not to engage in any nontrivial religious activities, and it would be just as important that they not be encouraged to imagine that home and domestic work might have any deeper meaning or spiritual *charge*.

In fact, an emerging patriarchal state wouldn't want much of *any-body* experiencing the potentially disruptive states of consciousness associated with direct religious experience.

It also wouldn't want the earth-centeredness of pre-agricultural spirituality to be part of people's religious repertoire anymore. Among the defining qualities of the pre-agricultural world had been its refusal to make hard-and-fast distinctions between the material and the sacred realms. The lives of Stone Age people had been shot through with awe and wonder. The small, recurring miracles—of moonlight and childbirth and blackberries, of rivers thunderous with snowmelt, of deer streaming across a hillside—had told them all that they'd needed to know about God (had all but *been* God for them).

But a watershed that's believed to be the body of the Mother can't be exploited and can't be owned. For agriculture to flourish, this attitude would have to change. Earth would need to be understood now as inert and bereft of consciousness, there to serve man as man was there to serve God. And in fact God would be effectively remade now in the image of man. Of the *new* man, in fact—violent, tyrannical, and yet curiously needy. These changes were accomplished brilliantly by the development of a whole new mythology that reduced the earth from protagonist to background.

So it was that a third domain carved itself out, a domain that was neither private nor public sphere but "religion"—construed now not as a personally cultivated, ongoing openness to Spirit, ritually centered in home or immediate community and embracing all of one's activities, but as a discrete category of experience, impersonal, institutionalized, and thoroughly governed.

There was another category of relatively marginal human beings who were more than willing to take charge of the new domain, a fact that facilitated this tremendous change. That category was made up of men who by temperament, circumstances, and/or conviction weren't well suited for Enterprise. As priests, clergymen, and religious functionaries of all kinds, these men would specialize in ceremony and doctrine. They would bring under strict scrutiny the more troublesome components of "religiousness"—mysticism, in particular. There would be no place in the new scheme of things for the idea that ordinary folk could experience God firsthand. The one God would be worshiped now as Lord, King, and Master, from a great distance, and worshiped through appointed intermediaries.

Understanding this dynamic helps us see why misogyny is so perennial a theme in institutional religion, expressed *directly* as hostility toward actual women, but *indirectly* too, in the fear revealed by male religious leaders on occasion that they themselves might be seen as effeminate for embracing values that fall outside the ordinary masculine code. During the Middle Ages, and again in nineteenth-century American denominations, "effeminacy" in religion was a particularly sensitive issue. One thinks of the anxiety that's surely implicit in the prayer Jewish men offer up regularly, thanking God that they're not women—a concern they might well feel that they have to address before humbling themselves in worship and prayer.

Hunter-gatherer cultures, and societies that are somewhat more complex, vary in their religious practices and beliefs. At one end of the spectrum—the end where women tend to receive better treatment—are those whose religious orientation is more interior.[4] These cultures honor female creation symbols and the natural regenerative forces of the earth and plants, and they support fathers who spend time comfortably with their children. At the other end, where women endure aggressive male domination, religious beliefs change dramatically, focusing much more on the external world. Deities are male now, and they live in the heavens and perform magic tricks; and animals eclipse plants in the ontological scale. In these societies, fathers tend to be aloof from their offspring. Societies of the first kind arise within environments that are relatively unstressed. Societies of the second kind emerge when the environment is experienced as capricious or threatening, and in them women's reproductivity is also seen as threatening.

It's useful to recall that distinction here, because it describes exactly what happened as the shift toward agriculture took place, and it makes sense of the precipitous fall in women's standing that took place at the same time—in Mesopotamia, in Egypt, and later in Israel.

When the Hebrews first came to Canaan in about 1350 B.C., there was an interim period during which they were decidedly pluralistic, incorporating many of the indigenous religious practices and outlooks—notably, a belief in fertility cults and female deities. But as soon as the Hebrews came under external threat, they adopted the sort of monotheistic and male-centered models that are more compatible with militarism—and agriculture.

In Israel as in other consolidating nation-states, the exclusion of women and the natural world from the serious business of religion was consonant with a growing inclination to draw sharp distinctions everywhere—between good and evil, heaven and earth, light and dark, reason and emotion, body and spirit. Dichotomous thinking was consistent with the "above and below" imagery that distinguished God from humanity, humanity from animals, man from woman.

Canaanite rituals had been intended to make the participant "like God," and that intention is consistent with the beliefs of pre-agricultural people everywhere. Whether in collective worship (such as the ceremonies through which a tribe might seek to "fix" the world) or in individual vision quests, the intent was, unapologetically, to experience the sacred firsthand. For the Hebrews, however, the idea of being "like God" was blasphemous. It would have to go, replaced by the ideal of "serving God."[5]

The state religions of Mesopotamia and Egypt had little to offer humanity by way of consolation or hope and a great deal to tell them about lines of authority. Did the common people of Mesopotamia get the feeling sometimes that their lives meant nothing to the gods? It would be understandable if they did, because as their religious leaders explained to them, the gods had molded them out of clay because they needed slaves. And those gods were notably harsh. If a person brought enough grain to the temples, though, and demonstrated satisfactorily enough his obedience to the temple priests, he and his family might just make it through the next flood or famine or war.

Egypt's religion, which was considerably more benevolent in its emphasis on truth, justice, righteousness, and the pharaoh's responsibility to embrace those ideals, was also a huge and complicated bureaucracy. Its focal point was death and a complicated model of the afterlife that was at least mercifully free of flood, famine, and war.

In Mesopotamia and Egypt, organized religion served the emerging state well, as it would the Roman Empire. By sanctioning certain values, such as honesty in business dealings, it would make for stability and allow an increasingly complex economy to evolve. Its teachings on moral responsibility would merge with the laws of the state. Once certain individuals had been invested with religious authority, they could in turn bless the undertakings of rulers: crown rulers king, declare their wars just, annul their marriages, and christen their children, all the while enjoying their protection and support.

The basic components of those first state religions are so familiar—the elaborate temples, the white-robed celibate priests, the payment of tributes, and the carefully constructed atmosphere of mystery and even glamour—that in a sense we don't question them for a moment. To many of us, this is more or less what religions still look like. But when we locate these components in the context of what we know of religious life among pre-agricultural peoples, the contrast is dizzying.

These early state religions were religions of intimidation and secrecy, meant to make the individual human being feel small, poor, and vulnerable. They materialized Spirit and then externalized it. Contemporary critic bell hooks, wanting to convey the dangers that today's media pose to our children, argues that they "colonize" the imagination.[6] The images that pass across television screens are banal; and yet, in their cumulative effect, they're very powerful, for they gradually render the individual incapable of generating her own images—in particular, the powerfully transformative images that precede revolution (personal or social and economic). The priests of Mesopotamia and Egypt, then, were consummate "colonizers" of imagination.

Fortunately, the spiritual aridity of those first religions wouldn't characterize the historic religions that evolved in their wake. There's an extraordinary period extending from about 800 to 200 B.C. that some historians of religion call the Axial Age.[7] Marking as it does the simultaneous emergence—in India, China, Greece, and the Niles-to-Oxus area—of a "high culture," it encompasses the sages of the Bhagavad Gita and the Upanishads, the Compassionate Buddha, Lao-tzu, Confucius, the Greek tragedians, Muhammad, and the prophets of the Old Testament. The Axial Age constituted what we might imagine as an explosion in consciousness itself, as pivotal and as multifocal as the Agricultural Revolution had been.

The Axial Age is also commonly described as the period when individualism and self-consciousness first became apparent. But on the face of things, the notion that individualism could have simply appeared out of nowhere two or three thousand years ago seems curious. The clearer picture one has now of the transition from foraging to agriculture and its probable effects on human beings makes another scenario seem plausible.

That is, one wants to draw a connection between the explosion in consciousness that brought us the Book of Job, *Oedipus Rex,* and the Koran, and the massive spiritual injuries that human beings had incurred with the rise of agriculture. A delayed reaction, yes, but perhaps it took that long for what was initially a wordless, overwhelming grief and confusion to finally find its way into words and into voice. Consider, from that perspective, the searing lament of Job: "He hath fenced up my way that I cannot pass, and he hath set darkness in my paths. He hath stripped me of my glory, and taken the crown from my head. He hath destroyed me on every side, and I am gone: and mine hope hath he removed like a tree" (Job 19:8–10).

Something was stirring, and it had everything to do with the values of Belonging. Perhaps the Axial Age didn't so much mark the *birth* as the *rebirth* of individualism—for hunter-gatherers are fierce individualists, determinedly resistant to authority. And insofar as it affirmed the dignity and value of the individual human being (male, free, and propertied) it initiated a revolution in consciousness that would have both religious and political consequences. Athenian democracy, the slave revolt led by Spartacus, and the signing of the Magna Carta were of a piece with the Sermon on the Mount and the Protestant Reformation, and when eventually the Woman Suffrage Movement and the American Civil Rights Movement came along, they were in that same tradition.

It might be important to emphasize that the illegitimate forms of authority against which people began to rebel in the latter part of the first millennium B.C. were jointly political and religious. The resistance that then began to coalesce, therefore, has to be understood as having been religious as well as political, even though it hasn't normally been described as such. The belief in the dignity of the individual in which the tradition of resistance was grounded derives ultimately from a pre-agricultural religiousness that attributed dignity to all living things. The paradigm of Enterprise values really doesn't honor that concept. For all its positive elements, Enterprise allows for the exploitation of human beings as resources in ways that the values of Belonging do not. To be sure, this isn't a hard-and-fast distinction, but it seems to me a legitimate one.

In the major historic religions—Islam, Judaism, Christianity, Buddhism, Confucianism, Zoroastrianism—the cultures of Enterprise and Belonging have coexisted, sometimes happily, sometimes with swords drawn. That's what has made those religions so eternally problematic for the individual seeker. The great teachings are there, enshrined in scripture and liturgy and elaborated upon by devout followers. But because Enterprise has always been in the mix as well, there have always been other more problematic elements.

By designating times and places for worship, by declaring temporal and local what had been timeless and diffused through all of reality, by assigning gatekeepers and discrediting the idea that one could know God directly, historic religions would pull in the immense transformative power of religiousness; separate it sharply from the world of women, from personal experience, and from the natural world; and claim it as their own. They would take control over it in exactly the way Egyptian pharaohs would dam the Nile to irrigate the vast plain of the delta, and for exactly the same reason: the religious longings of a people are a tremendously useful natural resource.

To be fair, the time-streams of the historic religions carry along in their depths a wealth of testimony to the accessibility of Spirit. But the central religious truth of the primal world—that God can be known directly—is anathema to the spirit of delayed gratification that built Western civilization. And to the extent that organized religions have aligned themselves with "earthly powers," it's anathema to them as well.

God-consciousness is by all reports synonymous with wholeness and utter satisfaction—is, in the words of Saint Bernard of Clairvaux, "honey in the mouth, a glad cry in the heart." But the building of great nations needs workers and soldiers who know little of honey and less of glad cries, so it has served Enterprise well for religion to be reduced as effectively as possible to a clutch of questions about what to eat, what sort of building to pray in, how to honor the dead, and which other religions to abhor.

One working definition that social scientists offer for the word "culture" is "a shared system of meanings." And in fact we see that with the advent of agri-culture, the *meanings* of everything—time, place, work, leisure, man, woman, the sacred, art, knowledge, and identity—would all change. We can look now at how this immense transition declared itself—how we passed from a culture of Belonging to a culture of Enterprise—in terms of the values upon which Western civilization would rest.

CHAPTER 8

A Changed World:
The Values of Enterprise

When I outlined the values of Belonging, I began with certain observations that can be rephrased now as questions regarding the values of Enterprise.

What values will I embrace if I envision myself as a single fragment seeking a niche in a continuously changing world whose laws I can't begin to fathom?

What ideals arise out of the habit of making sharp distinctions that seek to establish not only difference but relative superiority and even viability?

How does a literal and material vision of life determine which forces in consciousness will shape one's decisions?

What are the watchwords of an existence that places the supernatural at a considerable distance from oneself and one's deeds—indeed, sees it as a reality one encounters, in fear and trembling, only after death?

The points on this new circle—the values of Enterprise—are as different as they could possibly be from the values of Belonging. We'll take them up more closely now, looking at each briefly with reference either to fully established agricultural economies or (what I find even more interesting) societies that have moved away only in some regards from the foraging model. But this might be the right moment to emphasize something:

The purpose of elucidating these two paradigms isn't to exalt one over the other. It is, rather, to suggest that much of the confusion we're experiencing in Western society right now, and particularly in the United States, is the result, first, of our having responded so unrestrainedly to one value system as opposed to the other, and, second, of our having declared one set of values to be masculine and the other feminine.

CONTROL AND OWNERSHIP OF LAND

Hand in hand with agriculture came the idea of ownership. With this change toward possessiveness, the reverential "soul connection" that hunter-gatherers had had with the particular piece of the earth they inhabited gave way to other impulses. Intense speculative curiosity was one: Why *was* it (for example) that barley grew so well on one hillside and so badly on another?

Early farmers were, as we've seen, sedentary—in the short run. In the longer run and the bigger picture, though, they weren't: in fact, they were forever on the move. Even when they did settle down on a piece of land, their relationship to it was radically different from what a hunter-gatherer's would have been—appreciative, but exploitative and even calculating, wondering always whether the acreage next door wouldn't be more fertile. A farmer might well have argued that he didn't have the *luxury* his foraging grandparents had had of experiencing a spiritual connection with the earth, because he was too consumed by the labor of cultivating it.

CONTROL AND OWNERSHIP OF ANIMALS

Many an American Indian aligned himself naturally enough with Wolf or Mountain Lion, and Congo Pygmies often felt the spirit of the leopard breathing in their lineage. In the pre-agricultural world, human beings and animals were all hunter-gatherers: they were in a real sense kin. As a child of Bear or Eagle, moreover, a man could hope to reach the parts of his own nature to which he didn't always have access: courage, strength, wisdom, freedom, and beauty.

But to men committed to bringing forests and grasslands under control, the wildness of wild animals wasn't so dear. Wild animals preyed on their cattle and sheep and devoured their barley before it could head. In taking up agriculture, moreover, men had domesticated *themselves,* and the sight of an eagle soaring or a boar crashing through brush could always have the disturbing effect of reminding them of what they'd lost in the process.

Once a man had begun, on account of his culture's ethos, to feel ambivalent about his own animal nature, as well as actual animals, his approach to hunting would necessarily be affected too. The respect, verging on tenderness, of the hunter-gatherer—the Bushman, say, who poured a little fresh water in the mouth of an antelope he had killed—would fall away swiftly.

Just as certain plants emerged as supportive of the human population in its new growth spurt, so did certain animals. With the domestication of cows, sheep, goats, dogs, and pigs, a line was drawn. On the one hand, there were the "friends to man," and on the other, *wild animals,* of whom one might not have a lot of reason to feel appreciative.

EXTRAVAGANCE AND EXPLOITATION

Self-restraint was the hallmark of hunter-gatherers' lives, and it expressed itself most obviously in the prudence with which they tried to balance their own needs against the limitations of their traditional environment. Hunter-gatherers did not, of course, stay absolutely within their inherited territories; they gradually spread all over the world. But they did so very slowly, because their way of life required intimate and hard-won knowledge of a particular piece of land. The spread of agriculture took place far more quickly, because the methods that allow one to farm are much more portable and universally applicable.

Farmers didn't typically have to force foragers to leave: destruction of the foraging habitat sufficed. For a long while, agriculturalists must have felt that they could go on expanding indefinitely the land they were bringing under cultivation. Extending their reach just kept paying off.

Belief in hunter-gatherers' inherent restraint has been shaken in recent decades by the discovery that the great dying-off of fifty-seven large mammal species in the Americas at the end of the last Ice Age wasn't climate-induced at all, as had been thought. The Pleistocene Overkill is widely believed now to have been the work of human beings, acting in flagrant disregard of the environmental sensitivity we tend to attribute to them.

Similar stories have come in from several parts of the world, including New Zealand. Except for bats, New Zealand had never had mammals. Birds and insects filled the niches mammals would have elsewhere. It also hadn't been host to human beings until just a thousand years ago, and now it looks as if the people who first settled there—the Maoris, from the Polynesian Islands—managed in their short residency to kill off about half of the islands' species, among them a flightless bird, the giant moa, which could be up to ten feet tall and weigh 530 pounds. Archaeological evidence suggests that these birds were slaughtered, for their meat and eggs, for several generations before they became extinct. Again, how could hunter-gatherers have been so profligate?

The probable answer has two parts. One is that in both cases, the animals in question had evolved in the absence of human beings: they had neither the instinctive fear of humans nor the behaviors that would protect against them—fears and behaviors that animals had developed in places like Africa, where human beings had been around for much longer. The other part of the answer is that in both cases the human perpetrators were themselves new to the territory. The incredibly bountiful ecosystem into which they moved wasn't their own. The Maoris, as I mentioned, had barely landed in New Zealand when they did in the moas. The Clovis People, moreover, named after the site in New Mexico where their characteristic projectile points were first found (arrowheads that have also been found in the skeletons of many of the large mammals who were extinguished during the Pleistocene Overkill), only began to arrive in North America about 11,500 years ago. That period marks the commencement of the time of the great dying-off.

In other words, neither the Maoris nor the Clovis People had any idea what the ecological parameters of their new homes were. Which is to reiterate that the prudent self-restraint hunter-gatherers typically display toward their land isn't an innate quality; it's the product of their living within the constraints of a local ecosystem. It's *adaptive* to that life. The migrants into the Americas and New Zealand had left the environments they knew well; and in this sense they were more typical (and their extravagance was more typical) of agriculturists than foragers.[1] Their interest in change was already outweighing the conservatism of their ancestors.

THE NEW PASSION FOR CHANGE

Foragers are conservative for a variety of reasons, but cultures of Enterprise actively require that their members love innovation. That's because the expanding economies associated with Enterprise need consumers who are always on the lookout for what's new. That was as true for the Mesopotamians and Egyptians as it is for us today. Our orientation, therefore, isn't to the past, but to the future. If an innovation we've adopted turns out to have been destructive, we don't rue the day we acquired it; we trust in our ingenuity to fix things after the fact.

There are brahmin families in South India to whom certain sacred texts are said to have been entrusted thousands of years ago. The male children of these families memorize these texts so well that they can recite them backwards as well as forwards, lest a single precious syllable be lost, and they recite them regularly throughout their lives.

Today we count on computers to do our remembering for us (computers that have been developed and upgraded in significant part by South Indian brahmins who've emigrated to Silicon Valley!), and it isn't only because we trust their memories more than our own. Nothing from the past has the sacred importance for us that the contents of the memory banks of preliterate people did for them.

RECKLESSNESS AND SPEED

Because they're fundamentally competitive, cultures of Enterprise have always valued productivity, profit, and speed. The ability to do several things at once, and swiftly—automatically, in fact—was valued by agriculturists now more than the habitual deliberateness typical of hunter-gatherers.

The hallmark of acting automatically, of course, is that one isn't really present: abstractedness is thus a recurring feature of Enterprise.

Among foragers, time had typically been experienced as circular: spring gave way to summer, autumn to winter, and each month the moon passed through its phases. But with the advent of calendars and scribes and accounting records, time became relentlessly linear—an arrow. For the first time, things were happening *for the first time.* A new sense of urgency arose. Once human beings began to measure time, they couldn't help noticing how swiftly it moves, and with that realization came the need to somehow memorialize one's own brief span. With the first great city-states came the first massive memorial statues.

In traditional cultures, periods of deliberate inaction were undertaken regularly, accompanied often by fasting or vigils, precisely to discern and redress whatever kinds of imbalance one might have fallen into—with regard to health, relationships, or spiritual well-being. Under Enterprise, almost any action is preferable to inaction, because everything comes down to oneself: the earth itself can no longer be trusted to support you and your family because it's seen as inert.

MOMENTUM AND HIGH RISK

Moving away from the Belonging ideal of balance, Enterprise societies take a completely different attitude toward life's evident dualities. In the Enterprise model, one member of any pair is understood to be inferior—weak, deformed, "dark," and chaotic—and the other superior—strong, whole, bright, coherent. Thus the imagery that guides community and family life reflects not the need to establish equilibrium or harmony between contending forces, but rather the belief that "reason" or "strong leadership" must conquer and hold down the forces of darkness in a battle that never stops.

In "dynamic" Enterprise cultures such as Mesopotamia, the imagery of heroic mastery over turbulent passions becomes more and more prominent, and with it a love of momentum itself. Events are seen as a rapid, swollen river or a team of strong horses: the great leader rides the dangerous river, tames the powerful horses.

SECRETIVENESS

"Can you keep a secret?"

The hunter-gatherer typically couldn't—or wouldn't—because deep down he knew it would only make trouble. Expressiveness is useful within a small group, where secrets and slow-burning resentments can otherwise flare up suddenly into destructive rage. Hunter-gatherers are typically described as extremely talkative.

But that habit changed, and probably had to, when life-ways became more complicated.

The nomadic Bororos of sub-Saharan Africa are an interesting case in point. A people who are neither hunter-gatherers nor, properly speaking, agriculturalists, these pastoralists sell milk and buttermilk to villagers along the far-flung, arduous route they cover each year. But their relationship to the zebus that they milk is in certain ways more companionable than proprietary. They call them by name, for example, and let most of them die of old age. One observer reflects that, like the Laplanders and their reindeer, the Bororos don't so much *herd* their cattle, as *follow* them. The zebus need to move, and the Bororos follow, "like the white cattle egrets."[2]

Among themselves, the Bororos are highly expressive. But because their territory is under pressure from both the north and the south, they've come to feel threatened, and their first line of defense is elusiveness itself. They keep their children's names secret, and they're extremely cautious about receiving outsiders. They know that as a nomadic people, whose cattle graze on a vast commons, they're already to a very real extent under attack and must behave that way.

Secrecy is a perennially sensitive issue within Enterprise cultures, because its constant presence reminds one that such cultures are always of two minds. Insofar as Enterprise is about inventiveness and the free play of inquiring intellects, secrecy only gets in the way. But because Enterprise has also to do with the desire for mastery, it attaches considerable importance to keeping one's secrets one's own. Knowledge is power.

ACQUISITIVENESS

Generosity is second nature to hunter-gatherers: having more possessions than one needs isn't worth the energy it takes to haul them around, and envy is death to relationships in subsistence conditions. When an anthropologist settles in with a band of indigenous people with the intent of studying their life-ways, she'll typically work her way into their trust by the judicious dispensation of gifts. The gifts are received with such delight that visitors are surprised at how quickly many of them are given away, until they realize that in the intimate confines of a small society, being the only guy in camp with a flashlight, a jackknife, or a cigarette lighter can be more trouble than it's worth.

As long as our pre-agricultural ancestors were nomadic, they probably felt the same way. But with the advent of permanent dwellings and (later) forms of government that restricted thievery, the acquisitive impulses that are certainly intrinsic to human nature could be given full rein. And again, with the new capacity to *measure* that developed along with agriculture, one could describe the extent of one's possessions in terms that were meaningful even at a distance. One could *boast* (to use the vivid Anglo-Saxon term) of one's *hoard* (to use another). To have a great many things marked one out as enjoying the favor of powerful gods; and of course, conversely, the power of one's local gods was conveyed by the treasures amassed in their honor.

HIERARCHY

When noncentralized and egalitarian life-ways vanish, replaced by centralized and nonegalitarian structures, it's typically necessary to rationalize that change—particularly since the change is to the form of rule that Jared Diamond calls "kleptocracy."

To access the kind of authority that the ruling classes of the new cities and city-states felt they needed, they turned, invariably, to the religious domain. But, as Diamond notes, the religious beliefs of hunter-gatherers weren't set up to justify centralized authority or transfer of wealth. Therefore, the religious domain had to be reconfigured.[3]

In cities and city-states, religion would not be, as it had been for hunter-gatherers, the lifelong effort to align oneself with the forces of balance and beauty inherent in the natural world; it would be, rather, the worshipful service of powerful gods who could make or break the people who followed them. Earthly rulers were the window through which ordinary people could glimpse and honor those gods.

Until roughly 2800 B.C. a council of elders made the important decisions in the cities of Sumer. Whenever a war broke out, the council would appoint a "big man" to lead the city through its crisis. As the wars became more frequent, though, such men often ended up staying in office for long periods of time; and finally, the "big men" became kings who appointed their own successors.

By the second millennium B.C., in Assyria, the king, a "god-king" by now, ruled absolutely. Ordinary people were blindfolded before being led into his presence, and not even the crown prince had open access to him. The understanding was that he was the representative of the gods on earth, and to keep that channel open, he fasted regularly and made retreats in a reed hut.

In Babylon, during the next millennium, the king had the personal responsibility, during the New Year's festival, of winning the blessing of the god Marduk on his city. To accomplish this end, he had to remove his royal regalia and humble himself utterly, swearing that for the past year he hadn't offended the gods. After a fertility rite that included his making love with a priestess, who represented the goddess of fertility, Inanna, the king and the statue of Marduk, each in its own chariot, led a parade through the city of Babylon. The people of the city had left meanwhile, unworthy to be in the presence of king or god, and reentered after the parade, rejoicing that Marduk was on their side, the king was secure on his throne, and the crops would do well the next year.

Marduk had in fact been a minor deity among many until Babylon needed a divine patron, whereupon his status was steadily upgraded. At some point someone "realized" that it had been he, Marduk, who had more or less single-handedly defeated Chaos itself when creation began. A Babylonian statue in his likeness, Herodotus noted, was fifteen feet high and was made of twenty-two tons of gold.

The pattern by which hierarchy replaced egalitarian rule in Mesopotamia would repeat itself in the development of most other great city-states.

COMPETITIVENESS

In line with the newly hierarchic institutions that dominated the lives of ordinary folk, a model of human relationships emerged that was also hierarchical. Mutuality had little value in this new scheme of things. In any situation involving two people—even, absurdly, husband and wife—the driving question was, "Which of us is stronger? Smarter? Better connected?"

The concept of personal identity was relatively undeveloped among hunter-gatherers, who derived their sense of selfhood from their relationships to one another and the land they lived on. In the denser populations of cities, where those connections were loose if not gone altogether, identity was a serious matter. In fact—and this is one of those telling bits of what anthropologists call "material culture" that make their field of study so satisfying—Mesopotamian men began almost seven thousand years ago to use small incised pebbles (later these would evolve into tiny, intricately carved cylinder seals), unique to each individual, to "sign" their work. By stamping a lump of clay with their pebble-seal and attaching the clay to goods in transit, for example, they could guarantee that the goods would be recognized as their own. These seals symbolized their identities as surely as a signature would today.

Accumulation mattered, and extraordinary achievement: *glory*. In fact, the very idea of the hero—as demigod, as immortal—emerged at this time, with the cities and their perennial need for young men willing to die in their defense.

Competitiveness is intrinsic to the militarism that infused the great-city states, and so is oppositional thinking. And wherever oppositional thinking takes root, gender becomes polarized. The Assyrian laws were coolly explicit on the position of women. In fact, there's something eerie about looking, on the one hand, at photographs of magnificent gold jewelry found at excavations in what's now Iraq—jewelry that was made for women—and reading, on the other hand, that "a man may flog his wife, he may pull out her hair, he may damage and split her ears, with no liability attaching to him." Or that if a woman expressed even a desire for divorce, she could be thrown out of her home penniless and naked. Or that women who caused themselves to miscarry were to be impaled on sticks.[4]

RATIONALITY

Among the several modes of knowing favored by hunter-gatherers, rationality was always in the mix. But with the rise of agriculture, it simply took off, displacing intuition, "dreaming," whole-body knowing, the knowledge that came from the Trance Dance, and the like. The triumphs of reason were so palpable, and have continued to be, that for many people it's still the only interesting mode of knowing. The lunar calendar, the alphabet, accounting systems, and the early findings of astronomers were tremendously powerful in their implications: human beings would be tens of thousands of years working through those implications.

Other modes of knowing involve a temporary suspension of the rational intellect—a yielding to other sources of insight. Enterprise can accept art, dance, sweat bath, vigorous exercise, massage, and even meditation as relaxation or catharsis, but rarely as an avenue toward deeper insight. Disembodied, abstract thinking is the preferred mode.

Symbols of sacred powers would be manipulated shamelessly in the new milieu of city-states and armies on the move, and soothsayers would read the livers of sacrificial animals to predict the future. But all of this is at a real remove from the "symbolist mentality" with which hunter-gatherers looked out upon their world, and through their world, into its deeper, radiant reality.

A rising commitment to rationality discouraged symbolic readings of the natural world and found the material world to be increasingly interesting in its own right. For some, interpreting the bumps on a sheep's liver probably felt as pragmatic and scientific as growing cultures in a petri dish.

BUSINESSLIKE SOBRIETY

The playfulness that had gotten hunter-gatherers through their darkest hours had no real place in the rising city-states of the ancient world. The stakes were too high now. In taking over the job of keeping great numbers of people fed, human beings—especially men, especially leaders—assumed responsibilities that in the old view of things the earth itself had carried, as a living, spiritually charged entity. Over time, with the building of cities, the establishment of elaborate social structures, and the increasing threat of war, the weight of those responsibilities only increased. The mien of perpetual solemnity that one sees on the busts of distinguished Greek and Roman figures became the preferred affect—a mien implying one's essential seriousness and suggesting that one was privy to deep state secrets. In a very real sense, these men were demigods.

EXCLUSIVENESS

Before agriculture, population densities worldwide were so low that members of a particular band or even tribe had the option of keeping themselves to themselves. This meant that one could spend one's whole life interacting only with people of one's own band (and maybe the band over the hill with whom it was traditional to trade brides for bridegrooms).

Despite that relative isolation, cultural difference hadn't assumed much importance yet. If on a hunting expedition one did run into other hunters, one could assume, and probably did, that these "others" were much like oneself. A certain careful protocol governed those encounters, but that protocol wouldn't have presumed an adversarial relationship.

The globe got steadily more crowded, though, and agriculturists embraced the idea of ownership, putting more pressure on everyone. As a result, encounters at the edge of one's territory involved greater and greater tension.

In addition, the mechanisms of cultural evolution (as opposed to biological evolution) came into play more and more, because more people were in closer contact with one another. Cultural evolution allows *behaviors* to be transmitted from one generation to another—behaviors that are entirely specific to one group and that then come to define that group *as* a group. One generation of Pomo basket-makers might begin weaving clockwise, for example; they would teach their daughters to weave clockwise, and pretty soon all Pomo baskets would be woven clockwise even though a few miles south the Miwoks were weaving them counterclockwise.

As populations increase, members of different cultures come into more and more regular contact with one another; and when they do, their feelings about difference can sometimes turn sour. The members of one group can begin to believe that the members of another group belong, quite literally, to another species (a phenomenon primatologists call *pseudo-speciation* when they see it among chimpanzees). If this phenomenon occurs, the inhibitions against intraspecies violence that normally govern hunter–gatherer life can start to fall away.

Social exclusiveness has its intellectual counterpart in oppositional thinking: the First Farmer's dictum—"This is a plant; this is a weed." Basic to the trajectory of Western civilization is the understanding that in encountering any duality—high roads and low roads, East and West, Toyota and Plymouth—*one must choose.* There can be no middle ground, and compromise is cowardice. Zero-sum thinking, in short—the winner takes all.

Within the new frame of reference, where difference itself matters in ways it never did before, the idea that individuals might be particularly valued by the community because they stand outside ordinary recognized categories—they're blind or their sexuality is ambiguous or their skin is without pigment—is an "unavailable concept."

AGGRESSIVENESS AND VIOLENCE

The way of life emerging with agriculture was decidedly more violence-prone than earlier life had been. As it became apparent to human beings that they were living in a world where there were a great many people who felt distinctly "other," and that the old ways, which presumed intimacy, weren't effective, they realized that a new kind of mechanism would have to be developed to keep that violence in check within cities and city-states—systems of law, police forces, and so on. The way of life emerging with agriculture was decidedly more violence-prone.

Although hunter-gatherers were typically egalitarian, there were exceptions. Among the nonegalitarian groups—certain Indians of the Pacific Northwest Coast and California, for example—the level of violence was considerably higher than among egalitarians. However, these groups were also atypical in ways other than their nonegalitarianism: given that they were also characterized by sedentism and high population densities, and that they had food storage, prestige goods, and occupational specialization and currency, it's clear that they were well on their way toward agriculture.

Among egalitarian hunter-gatherers, aggressiveness is counterproductive. The aggressive individual is typically defused by a combination of avoidance, ridicule, and teasing that barely qualifies as nonviolent conflict resolution. But as bands enlarge into tribes, and tribes into villages and cities, even those very rudimentary techniques aren't as workable: members of larger groups lack the base of intimacy they presume.

As we saw in Chapter Six, agriculture is by its very nature aggressive. Farming is always *somewhat* like war; it pits one man against another in competition for limited resources—land, water, labor, and "market share" for one's crops. Farming is inherently expansive: as the size of a farming family grows, so does its desire for more land (so that each son and grandson can have his own parcel). The commercial institutions that have come along in the wake of agriculture—institutions wherein if we're lucky, we "make a killing"—are also involved in activities that are *somewhat* like war.

MATERIALISM

In arguing that with the rise of agriculture, materialism substantially eclipsed spirituality, I don't mean to suggest that the religious sensibilities of pre-agricultural peoples or even later hunter-gatherers were uniformly superior—"better" or "deeper"—than those of all religious peoples to come. In fact, one could just as reasonably argue—and many theologians have—that spiritual heroism can emerge only when individuals actively choose to live by values such as mutuality, generosity, and nonviolence in contexts that permit, or even encourage, people to choose otherwise.

I'm not even entirely comfortable with the idea of contrasting "materialism" and "spirituality," given the multiple meanings both words have—particularly because that distinction wasn't one that had a great deal of meaning for pre-agricultural people: matter and Spirit hadn't been pulled apart in people's minds to the extent that they would be later. One's relationship with the sacred wasn't a category of experience sharply distinct from other relationships or activities.

Furthermore, in the relatively slow pace of pre-agricultural life, there was always time—a commodity without which nobody has ever cultivated religious depth. Again, then, the individual who embraces the values of Belonging in Enterprise cultures is perhaps more to be admired insofar as she has to actively resist the "pressure to produce" that such cultures impose, aggressively carving out the time that an active interior life requires.

What I want to emphasize in contrasting the spirituality of the pre-agricultural world with the materialism of our own is that with the perfecting of the technologies that made agriculture possible, the material possibilities of the material world opened out as they never had before and simply crowded out the continuous engagement with Spirit that had characterized foraging life. The field of human attention would be so taken up now by the tremendously interesting task of figuring that world out and dispelling its mysteries that everything else would take a backseat.

In addition (recalling once again the two-phase nature of Enterprise), the sudden expansion in technologies made possible an unprecedented degree of control over nature and other people. The very idea of control took on a luster now that it couldn't have in the past, and humanity's image of itself shifted accordingly. Pre-agricultural peoples may well have seen themselves as grateful children of a bountiful, Spirit-filled natural world, but their agriculturist descendants saw themselves, quite understandably, in a very different light. If human beings could redirect rivers and make deserts fertile, if they could forge invincible weapons of bronze and steel, if they could navigate by the stars and build virtually indestructible monuments to themselves and their gods—as plainly they *could*—then surely, the reasoning must have gone, that was how they should be spending their time. In a world that appeared to be coming more and more completely under human control, there was less and less room for Spirit.

The state religions of Mesopotamia, Egypt, and (later) Rome were all shaped by this drive for control. Perhaps the most direct way to recognize how fully Enterprise cultures redefined "religiousness" is to look at the massive and opulent temples that sprang up in the first city-states. The strategy is so transparent it takes one's breath away. The human being's inborn response to beauty, the capacity for awe and wonder that had taught us to look out upon the natural world and find it holy, were taken firmly in hand now and redirected: averting our gaze from the earth, we were to look instead—in wonder and awe—at statues larger than life-size, covered with jewels and draped with silk, placed in massive temples that fairly dwarfed the ordinary human being. God was a king, and the king was God, victorious over all challengers, in this world and all other realms, surrounded by His spoils. Material wealth quite literally became the outward, visible sign of a deity's power.

This model of religiousness was deeply flawed in exactly the same way that the corresponding model of humanity's relationship to the natural world was flawed, but it would take a long time for those flaws to be recognized. Thousands of years would have to pass before human beings wedded to Enterprise values would begin to see what kind of problems arise when the ideal of perfect mastery over nature shapes individual and collective aspirations. In fact, that "awakening" is in many regards barely starting to surface. The inadequacies of the Enterprise model of religion are also becoming more apparent.

Paradoxically, the effort made in early city-states to endow images of God with greater power and authority served also to impose limitations on deity. Once God was "He" and "Father," the divine could no longer be She and Mother. Once He was in heaven and the breast of the faithful adherent, He couldn't be everywhere. Once He was One, He couldn't be many. Once He was king, He couldn't be you and me. And the glaring fact was, and is, that this new, sharply defined version of God, anthropomorphized and linked inextricably to the Enterprise ideal of absolute mastery, has proven Himself to be no more capable of routing evil from this world than human beings themselves have. "God" has failed to keep the promises that, from the perspective of Belonging cultures, "He" may never have made in the first place.

To the extent that they managed to redefine religiousness in material terms and co-opt religious impulses to serve the state, Enterprise cultures have to an impressive degree shut out the potentially disruptive forces inherent in pre-agricultural spirituality. However, as we will see in Part Three, they could never exclude it altogether.

PART III

Cultures That Never Stop Clashing

Years ago I saw a documentary film on the life of the late Corita, whose bright serigraph posters graced so many Berkeley apartment walls in the 1960s and 70s. While Corita was Sister Mary Corita, an Immaculate Heart nun living in Los Angeles, she taught art at the college run by her order, and the documentary I watched included footage of a field trip her class took to a neighborhood carwash.

The scene couldn't have held less aesthetic promise, but Corita seemed undaunted. She gave the students each a small cardboard frame and told them to walk around, crouch, come close or move back—whatever they wanted—in an effort to define, with their frame, any number of different perspectives on the place and the people there. Then the students were to briefly sketch what they saw, with the idea of turning the sketch into a painting later.

The results were remarkable—sharply dramatic, angled visions that made palpable art out of the dreariest sort of urban blight.

Corita had shown her students how to *look*. And she'd taught them that the same chunk of ordinary reality can yield as many meanings as the various perspectives one might bring to bear on it.

At some point a few years ago I realized that the perspectives that were available to me then on the issues that mattered to me most—religiousness, gender, social change—weren't serving me well enough. They just kept generating the same old dead-ended storylines. My conclusion that the "gender wars" weren't really about gender at all, but values, and my resultant attempts to look hard at a long-running unresolved conflict between two very different sets of values (those of Belonging and Enterprise), has shattered the old storylines and relocated my whole standpoint.

Acknowledging that no one lens will ever do justice to the complexities of human history (Corita's frames were cardboard, many, and disposable), I've nevertheless found this particular lens to have enormous explanatory power.

The cultures of Belonging and Enterprise—intertwined and mutually adversarial—have operated as powerful forces in history. In this third part of the book I want to consider, in necessarily broad terms, what the span of the past ten thousand years looks like from the perspective of that relationship. I fully believe that many of the problems that plague us most relentlessly today—including racism, gender imbalance, environmental degradation, and religious fundamentalism (with the violence that arises from it)—can begin to be alleviated only when the complex ongoing interplay of Belonging and Enterprise is better understood.

Certain of the values intrinsic to Western civilization—expansion, invention, and competitiveness—are essentially the values of Enterprise. So most of our history books are, in fact, histories of the culture of Enterprise, and that in itself is a good reason not to linger long over the actual progression of events. That reporting has already been done in spades. What hasn't been done, and I'll try to do in Chapter Nine, is to consider what Marxists might call the internal contradictions of the culture of Enterprise, and the effects of those contradictions on contemporary institutions.

Chapter Ten will focus on the values of Belonging as they struggle (and sometimes flourish) within the larger culture of Enterprise. We'll look in particular at the heroes and heroines of contemporary Belonging, seeking to determine what unites them.

With Chapter Eleven I want to come into the present and outline four reasons why I believe we may be poised *right now* to accomplish the reconciliation of Belonging and Enterprise that our ancestors could not.

CHAPTER 9

Falling Forward:
Cultures of Enterprise

If one were looking around for a distilled description of what went on between the cultures of Belonging and Enterprise as agriculture spread outward from its several points of origin, a passage that appears in Ursula K. LeGuin's recent novel *The Telling* might fill the bill nicely.

The Telling is set sometime in the future on a planet called Aka, which has been taken over by a zealous reform movement. LeGuin refuses to be pinned down, but Aka is presumed by many of her readers to symbolize Tibet and its transformation under Chinese rule. Here's how LeGuin describes the reformers' efforts:

> From a great consensual social pattern within which each individual sought physical and spiritual satisfaction, they had made it a great hierarchy in which each individual served the indefinite growth of the society's material wealth and complexity. From an active homeostatic balance they had turned it to an active forward-thrusting imbalance.[1]

Tibet, yes, but not *only* Tibet. Ursula LeGuin is the daughter of Alfred Kroeber, one of the founders of modern cultural anthropology, and Theodora Kroeber, whose beautiful *Ishi in Two Worlds* tells the story of the last of the Yahi Indians of central California, a man whom her husband had befriended. One guesses that by the time she knew much of anything about anything, LeGuin knew what had happened to California's native people. Several of her earlier books reveal that she understands in intimate detail the difference between the "active homeostatic balance" of California's Indian societies and the "active forward-thrusting imbalance" of the settlers who destroyed them, but she clearly also understands that destructive act to be just one enactment of a perennial scenario: cultures of Belonging have been getting annihilated by cultures of Enterprise for at least ten thousand years.

One notes that LeGuin doesn't describe the one culture as passive and the other as active. She sees both as decidedly active, which is to remind us that, as we've seen, pre-agricultural societies weren't static or stagnant. Changes did take place—but gradually, and in so profoundly stable a context that they rarely swept the very context away.

That phrase "an active forward-thrusting imbalance" captures perfectly the very different energy of Enterprise and the near-inevitability with which it overran cultures of Belonging. The earlier paradigm was, in many important regards, vulnerable. There were sound reasons why it lost its hold on human will and imagination when it did. But by the same token, once we understand the inner workings of Enterprise cultures, we can see the faultlines along which they're most susceptible to breakage.

OF GENES AND MEMES

I spoke about the values of Belonging as having been "adaptive" to the conditions under which human beings lived for their first few hundred thousand years. Just so, the values of Enterprise could be said to be adaptive to the world that unfolded after agriculture developed, but in a rather different sense.

During that first long stretch of human evolution, adaptations were still taking place at the genetic level, and the rate of change was accordingly slow. Well before the past ten thousand years, though—hundreds of thousands of years earlier, by some tallies—the engine of naturally occurring genetic evolution had stopped. For the mechanism of natural selection to operate, there have to be isolated environments where a specific adaptation can develop over long reaches of time, and (legends of Shangri-la notwithstanding) those environments are long gone. So, outside of human manipulation, nothing more is expected to happen with respect to human genes. We continue to evolve, but culturally rather than genetically, and that's a very different process indeed.

What the *gene* is to biological evolution, the *meme* is to cultural evolution.[2] A meme is a "bit" or a "megabit" of information that's transmitted by teaching or imitation, rather than being inherited, as genes are. Memes can be as small as a song or as big as a theory of governance, but whatever their magnitude, they're understood to be very powerful. Ideas, as we all know, are infectious: they can jump from one mind to another, like a virus.

Cultural evolution had been taking place all along, but until the rise of agriculture, population density was so low that neither ideas nor inventions could spread swiftly. As populations began to expand, however, the rate of change accelerated, and it has kept on accelerating.

Cultural evolution is a far more slippery business than biological evolution, because its "adaptations" can come and go. The values of Belonging, coalescing as early as they did into a coherent system or ethos, would seem to be more deeply rooted in our evolutionary past than the values of Enterprise are. Enterprise values are certainly linked to ancient human impulses, but collectively, as an ethos, they're a "cultural construct" to a much greater degree than the values of Belonging are.

As we try to imagine the transition from foraging to farming, it's helpful to think of a "meme-tic" explosion. It's appropriate to think about Enterprise itself as a meme, but one that at its very core is *dual:* as we saw earlier, inventiveness and dominance are two sides of the Enterprise coin. They are themselves both memes. Reviewing briefly the steps by which Enterprise edged out the cultures of Belonging, we can see how symbiotic the relationship is between invention and the desire for control—control over circumstances, other people, resources, and territory.

Initially, there was that simple hankering after one another's company, which may have had something to do with the bigger, more complicated brains human beings were developing. Villages formed where food was ample, and nomadic life-ways were abandoned.

As population density increased in these areas, so did the rate of technological innovation, and soon cereal grains could be cultivated, stored, and transported. With dependable food supplies, population began to increase even more, concentrating in particular areas. In those more densely populated locales, it gave rise to still more inventiveness and greater cultural richness, more crowding, and subsequent expansion into new regions.

Each new technology opened the door to others, and because all these innovations were being made in the context of populations competing for space, water, access to harbors, and other benefits, each "new, new thing" was welcomed not only in its own right but for the survival edge it might give one group over another.

New technologies altered the way people lived, and social structures that had held firm for thousands of years began to loosen. The old intersecting affiliations with land, clan, and immanent Spirit that had all but defined the individual fell away now. Acquisitions, social status, and connections with the emerging state would rush into the vacuum; and in Mesopotamia, Egypt, Mesoamerica, and China, the heads of state would be declared embodiments or earthly deputies of divine authority.

With increasing work specialization, new sources of identity would be available—for example, membership in professional societies and workers' guilds. But these affiliations could also divide a community, making neighbors strangers to one another.

Anxiety levels rose: life was richer and riskier at once, and by all accounts much, much *faster*. Competitiveness made it so. And in an increasingly combative and accelerated atmosphere, perceptions of difference turned easily into struggles for dominance.

So there it is. The very idea of dominance had become a meme, and a highly contagious one at that. In addition, the capacity to see other human beings as belonging to a species different than one's own had also made it easier to start looking upon other people as *things*—natural resources to be exploited, like water or soil, or annoying obstacles to the achievement of one's own ends.

We can see how inexorably each change led to the next, and how rare the moments must have been when someone could have looked around and said, "Oh, wait, stop—we're getting in over our heads!" and been heard. It's this recurring cycle—invention, anxiety, expansion, and control, then more invention, more anxiety, etc.—that drives the chronic societal instability LeGuin describes in Aka: a continuous "falling forward."

Reflecting on how swiftly the values of Enterprise declared themselves, coalesced into a system of meanings and an ethos, and became the core values of Western civilization, we're tempted to speculate that an idea, or a complex of ideas, can have a life of its own. To take that position would be to take very literally the comparison that evolutionary theorists make, playfully, between genes and memes.

Because genes do, in effect, have a life of their own. From a biological point of view, you and I are really only vehicles—unwitting tools, and disposable tools at that—for our DNA, whose drive to replicate itself is so powerful that it shapes our behavior in all kinds of ways. But memes are very different. No piece of information, no song, no scientific theory is in fact alive. Just as the moon borrows its light from the sun, a meme has only the borrowed force of human desire. An idea survives because of human commitment to it. The values of Enterprise are alive and well because a great many people embrace them—people who see themselves, and their own identities, in the light of those values.

The Enterprise Two-Step

I've tried to convey how cyclic the process was by which agriculture brought villages, then cities, then city-states into being, altering people's life-ways fundamentally as it unfolded. As city-states jostled with one another, their consolidation into empires was the inevitable next step, and it has been an abiding passion of historians to trace out the rise and fall of various empires: How did they get there? Why did they collapse?

The dual nature of Enterprise goes a long way toward answering those questions, but so does a phenomenon that archaeologists call "island fever."

Island fever breaks out when an isolated culture hits upon an exciting new technology before travel to their land has become easy. Easter Island is a case in point. Archaeologists have figured out how those mysterious stone figures were moved from the quarry where they'd presumably been carved to their present locations near the sea. Clearing that mystery up has also explained why there are no trees on the island, (though the fossil makes it clear there had been) and no people either.

Once the ten-ton figures were carved, researchers have determined, they were placed on sleds made by strapping logs together in the same basic technology with which Pacific Islanders built canoes. The wooden sleds were then placed on logs that rolled along on tracks made of parallel lines of still more logs: as soon as a sled had moved across a log, a couple of people would quickly take it to the front, and so on, across the island. Taxing as it was, the project has to have been terrific fun. It probably took on a competitive edge too, as different families sought to memorialize their ancestors in this remarkable fashion. At some point, someone may have looked around and said, "You know, we'd better stop or we're going to have no trees left—none to bear fruit, none to build houses with . . . "; but if someone did, nobody listened, because in fact the Easter Islanders apparently didn't stop until they'd cut down every last tree.

In the grip of "island fever" a people can get so carried away that they override longstanding patterns of resource conservation. But island fever can take place only when a society doesn't have to employ a significant part of its resources or energy defending itself against outsiders.[3] Very few societies have ever had that luxury, but quite a few have behaved as if they did.

The sequence is so familiar, and so timeless: In the aftermath of a successful military campaign, or maybe just successful migration into a relatively unpopulated frontier, an emergent nation-state consolidates its power, feels its muscle, and wants to unleash the inventiveness of its own people—their "native genius." Huge communal works are carried out on a grand scale and with enormous ingenuity—pyramids, cathedrals, tabernacles, palaces, stadiums, theaters—the sort of undertaking that fuels civic pride, solidifies national identity, and incites envy in the heads of other states.

But the architects for these projects draw upon the same treasuries that support the military, which is out on the nation's boundaries, fighting off would-be invaders, collecting tribute, and allowing the rulers (who've come to believe, many of them, that they're gods or demigods) to behave as if they lived on a remote island.

Which, of course, they do not. As the wealth, power, and "national genius" of this emergent nation-state becomes more and more visible, leaders of other nations become envious, and the heavily levied peasants within its own borders grow restive. The military guardians of the state come under increasing pressure: they need more weapons and more ingeniously constructed weapons. They need spies, counterspies, and surveillance technologies. They need, in fact, the same inventive minds that are engaged in building those fabulous communal works.

The tug of war begins, and the tug *toward* war begins, and more and more of the nation's resources, human and nonhuman, are diverted away from Research and Development and into National Defense. The mood of the nation shifts: the ebullience of that first creative period is over—the national objective now is to preserve and defend, and enemies are understood to be both within and without. The meme for inventiveness has given way to the meme for dominance.

And there you have it: the "forward-thrusting imbalance" of Enterprise is off and running. Meanwhile, in some small nation that has happily escaped everyone's notice, a place that really *is* something of an "island" (or, to bring us into the present context, in somebody's garage), another round of inventiveness is getting underway.

That basic template serves well enough to map out the rise and fall of imperial governments down through time. In one empire after another, the wildest dreams of Enterprise have been incarnated, and always that shippage from invention to dominance repeats itself.

Still, the history of Enterprise is every bit as interesting as chroniclers have told us it is, because each time its two phases are most visible—in they were in Mesopotamia, Egypt, Rome; as the Holy Roman Empire, the British Empire, the USSR; and most recently in the United States—there are new twists.

There was, for example, the so-called Constantine Donation of 324, when Emperor Constantine, head of the Roman Empire, decided to banish the pagan gods who'd watched over Rome since she was a village and declare Christianity the official state religion of the empire. (The event was probably real, but the document long believed to have spelled out the details has been known to be a forgery since the fifteenth century.) It was a brilliant move, in that it "capped" the potentially disruptive energy of the infant church— known for its informality, its disregard for social class, its inclusion of women, and the palpable affection its members demonstrated for one another—much as Texas oilmen cap a "gusher," and rerouted the energy of its adherents toward the state. Whereupon Christianity itself became increasingly ceremonial, developing its own priestly hierarchy, subordinating and silencing women, and moving its services out of the home and into cathedrals that looked remarkably like Roman temples.

The builders of the British Empire studied Rome's successes and failures assiduously and then added their own to the list. The Industrial Revolution reprised in many ways the dazzling inventiveness of the Neolithic Transition and the genius for engineering of the Roman Empire, and in the process kicked off a double thirst—for more raw materials and for new markets for the products it made out of them. England probably outdid any state in history for the genius with which its industrial and colonial projects were dovetailed: cotton grown by poor Indians for their British "landlords" was sent to England to be milled and woven, and then sent back to India again and sold to the Indian people as cloth (which most of them could barely afford) for their saris and dhotis.

Kleptocracy had been raised to a high art.

The British Empire was of course nobody's Mesopotamia: The artistic and intellectual traditions of Great Britain bore the stamp of the Axial Age. Belief in the dignity of the individual and a penchant for social justice (neither of which appear to have kept the rulers of

Uruk or Ur up late at night) made for an ongoing state of deep con-flictedness on the part of those who benefited most from the empire itself. In fact, one is tempted to see something like a multiple person-ality disorder running through the whole of British colonial history: very, very good these people were, and very bad indeed. Good, above all else, at compartmentalizing.

The American Revolution brought a new nation-state into exis-tence, and appropriately enough the brilliant inventor and philoso-pher Benjamin Franklin was one of its most prominent founders. Buckskin against redcoat, guerrilla improvisations against regimental discipline, native wit against haughty arrogance: the clever American colonists made their British oppressors look spectacularly foolish. So foolish, in fact, that several hundred years later we *still* fail to remem-ber that those brave colonists were themselves colonialists—"settlers" of a land that until their arrival had been remarkably placid.

Looking at human history from the point of view of the relation-ship between the values of Belonging and those of Enterprise, we see how the values clash. But if we recognize in addition the inherent dis-sonance between the two phases of Enterprise, the picture gets at once clearer and more complicated.

This isn't the place to trace the steps by which a scrappy band of freedom-fighters evolved in just two and a half centuries into a world power that is in many regards *the* world power and a close approxima-tion to a world empire. The swiftness with which the United States has come this far has to do with the innovative and risk-taking spirit of its citizens, yes—but it has at least as much to do with fertile soil, rich mineral deposits, vast forestlands, and broad rivers that no one had previously exploited—and, for that matter, with men and women kidnapped from their homes in Africa and sold to Americans to work in the fields. Like the British, Americans have been of two minds all along, and not merely because of their commitment to the highest ideals of Western spiritual and philosophical teachings.

The dilemma is inherent in the values of Enterprise itself. Paradoxical as it might seem, Enterprise has a strong commitment to inclusiveness. Basic to any technological revolution is the recognition that when everyone is brought on board and included in the information flow, good things happen. The exuberant, innovative phase of Enterprise is inherently democratic. But the ensuing phase, the exploitation of invention to exert control over others—competitors, a market, or another country—closes doors, closes ranks, and keeps secrets.

In talking about the cultures of Belonging and Enterprise, it's easy to slide into the very sort of dualism I've criticized in other contexts: good model, bad model; good values, bad values. In fact, of course, the relationship between them isn't that simple. Whatever objections one might have to the values of Enterprise and their impact on our lives, those objections can't be rooted in any sense of moral superiority you and I might feel in regard to the "empire-builders" of the past. In our own lifetimes we've seen how seductively new technologies can take us over and move us down tracks we haven't consciously chosen. We've watched our domestic and working lives change profoundly with the arrival of televisions, cell-phones, computers, and even microwave ovens. We also know how inevitable it is that powerful new technologies fall into the hands of those who would tyrannize, and we know how easily ordinary human beings can become tyrannical—or at least disastrously bloody-minded—when, for any number of reasons, they're "ripped untimely" from the matrix of human connection.

Had Enterprise been about curiosity, cleverness, and nothing more, it would be one thing; but it's been a hybrid all along: competitiveness, exploitation, and pure greed have always kept coming into the mix. Shortly before his death in 1980, anthropologist and cybernetics pioneer Gregory Bateson summarized with considerable bitterness the relationship between science, technology, and commerce, on the one hand, and the environment on the other, tracing to the Industrial Revolution the ideas he believed dominate contemporary Western civilization. Advocates of applied science and the "free enterprise system," in particular, Bateson believed, argue as follows:

It's us against the environment.

It's the individual (or the individual company, or the individual nation) that matters.

We *can* have unilateral control over the environment and must strive for that control.

We live within an infinitely expanding "frontier."

Economic determinism is common sense.

Technology will do it for us.[4]

In another context, Bateson characterized the ethos of applied science in the late twentieth century as arising out of a "deep epistemological panic."[5]

It's tempting to see in the intersecting political, economic, and social forces that define us today a culmination of Enterprise itself—as though its logical conclusions were very close to being reached. What inclines me most to that opinion is that the inherent contradictions of Enterprise are pulling at it—at us as a society—to an unprecedented degree, giving rise to something it doesn't seem at all exaggerated to call a *deep epistemological panic*.

The intersecting forces of Enterprise now affect virtually everyone on the planet. The degree of interdependency has never been higher, and that's why we're running into large and intractable problems.

Some of the most thorny problems have to do with education. Who should receive an education, and what kind of education should it be?

Administrators of the British Raj saw early on how helpful it would be to create a class of educated (or at least trained) Indians to help run the enormous bureaucracy by which the British governed India—individuals who would be so thoroughly identified with colonial rulers as an educated class that they would have little interest in fomenting revolution. In the hope, then, of raising up an army of efficient clerks, the British opened schools all over India and even sent some Indian students to England.

There was a risk, of course, that literacy alone—never mind studying at university—would expose Indian students to dangerous memes such as the alluring concept of citizenship in a free nation. They might change allegiances, after all.

Just so, in the United States, it had become clear in the nineteenth century that educated workers would build a stronger economy, and educated women would preside over homes wherein children would be healthier and better prepared for school. Besides, the ideals expressed in our founding documents made it impossible to withhold forever from women and other excluded populations the right to be educated.

In both cases, a mix of ideals and pragmatic good sense won out. A considerable number of Indian students received an English education; and in the United States, schools and universities were opened to women. The result in the first case was a determined, nonviolent, and ultimately successful campaign against British rule led by an Indian lawyer trained at London's Inns of Court. In the second case, simultaneous with women's entry into colleges and universities, a long, protracted struggle got underway for women's rights across the board—a struggle that even now may really be just beginning.

A Culture of Imbalance

Had the values of Belonging and Enterprise been able to coexist in something like a real equilibrium, the story of the last several thousand years would have been very different. Economies and social structures might have evolved that balanced human beings' needs for complexity and outward exploration with their needs for connection and interiority. Who knows? Given enough time, we might have developed as a species some sort of inner gyroscope—an intuitive alarm that would go off when we were about to go too far in one direction or the other.

But in fact the very idea of balance is foreign to Enterprise.

It's the nature of Enterprise to lean hungrily into the future, borrowing from today to fund its next great adventure and trusting in the ingenuity of tomorrow to remedy the mess it's making today. Magnificent as its achievements have been, there has never been anything in this "forward-thrusting imbalance" like a good set of brakes—nothing to prevent its evolving finally into its own caricature.

One thinks of Toad, in *Wind in the Willows,* and his motorcar:

> As if in a dream he found himself, somehow, seated in the driver's seat; as if in a dream, he pulled the lever and swung the car round the yard and out through the archway; and, as if in a dream, all sense of right and wrong, all fear of obvious consequences, seemed temporarily suspended.[6]

The culture of Enterprise has never thought it needed brakes, because it has never had any plan to stop. In fact, as an infinitely expanding economic model, it's probably well served by having workers and consumers alike exist in a state of chronic dither, so perpetually destabilized by change and speed that they don't organize to resist it, and they buy a great many products in the hope that they'll simply feel better.

"As if in a dream," indeed. Because what else but a dream could we call the belief that on a planet with finite resources, an economy can go on expanding indefinitely—employing more workers, developing new products, finding new markets for them, breaking ground for new factories, and hiring still more workers?

A Culture of Separation

At the last census, it was learned that for the first time more Americans are living by themselves than are living with even one other person. That trend is in close keeping with the unfolding culture of Enterprise.

If connectedness was the central motif of the pre-agricultural world, fragmentation has defined us ever since. After all, it made sense to specialize as we undertook big collective projects. The trade-off has rarely been questioned: one analyzes to understand, one separates (squabbling children, striking workers, rioting prisoners) to control. Interestingly, those lines of separation have regularly been reinforced under the pretense that they have to do with gender.

The British Raj applied the Roman idea of divide-and-rule to remarkable effect: one hundred thousand British residents controlling something like four hundred million Indians. For nearly three hundred years the British were able to curb the growth of an Indian national spirit, and they did it in several ways. One was to use an elaborate system of awards and "perks" to ally the educated, well-to-do classes with the colonial rulers, over against the poorer masses. Another was to emphasize, with the help of gendered imagery, the differences between India's various populations. Comparing so-called martial and nonmartial races, for example, they described the martial races as masculine—strong, virile, and aggressive—and the nonmartial races as "effeminate"—passive, weak, and impotent.[7]

One sees the same pattern in the white settlers' view of the American Indians. While the Plains Indians hunted the buffalo, settlers maintained, California's Indians were "vegetarians" who ate roots and were little more than animals themselves, "too lazy and effeminate to make good hunters."[8]

This kind of rhetoric, encountered in so many different contexts, has raised for me a recurring, disturbing question: Is contempt for women a kind of epistemological prerequisite to the culture of separation, and therefore for Enterprise itself? Do other kinds of exclusion from power and basic human rights—exclusion by race, class, age, religion, and ethnicity, for example—find their ultimate justification in the "natural" exclusion of women?

Anthropologist Claude Lévi-Strauss believed that it was. Before slavery or class domination existed, he maintained, "men built an approach to women that would serve one day to introduce differences among us all."[9]

There's a bright side to that admittedly bleak perspective, and that's that contempt for women may not be as deeply rooted as it can sometimes seem. That phrase "built an approach to women" is very interesting. It suggests, as I've been arguing, that women (and, I would add, the values with which they'd been linked) were first subordinated almost pragmatically, as a rationale for a great many other subordinations that needed to take place in order for a particular kind of civilization to be built.

Contempt for girls and women doesn't in fact come naturally to boys; it has to be transmitted anew with each generation, and Enterprise cultures are set up to do that.

Sociologist Barrie Thorne has spent years observing playground behavior, and one of the questions she seeks to answer is how it is that children learn, and teach one another, that *real* boys don't play with girls.

Much of what she's observed has an almost comic innocence: a second-grade boy teaches a kindergarten girl how to chase him by slowly running backward, beckoning her to pursue him, and calling, "Help, a girl's after me." But of course these almost ritualized behaviors are only the first steps: entwined with episodes of chasing are rituals of pollution—games of "cooties," or "cootie tag," for example—and the ultimate source of such contamination is inevitably girls (though a low-status boy will sometimes be called a girl).[10]

A boy who's called a girl knows exactly where he stands in the playground hierarchy. As long as a culture embraces the model of separation—opting for exclusiveness, hierarchy, and secretiveness, for example—insistence on women's basic inferiority is useful and, one might even say, adaptive. Only, therefore, when a society chooses egalitarianism and inclusiveness instead, across the board in all its institutions—and not one minute sooner—will its female members be fully voiced and fully respected.

A CULTURE OF EXTERNALITIES

A culture defined by imbalance and fragmentation perpetuates itself—keeps us buying—by directing our attention outward. The single greatest threat to the corporate-consumer complex is that on our way to the mall, we might get distracted.

We might sit down instead in a quiet park, close our eyes, listen to the wind in the trees, and stumble before we know it into . . .

Balance.

Coherence.

Stillness.

Relatedness.

And in that unfamiliar state, pointed questions could begin to arise. Questions such as, "Why should I run around trying to buy happiness when I can sit down somewhere and experience this gentle inrush of joy and fulfillment?"

If the culture of Enterprise is held in place by the force of human desires—by the belief that it will fulfill us—then it's the task of Enterprise to engage the senses so fully that we never fall into the deep rabbit hole of self-awareness. No one thing poses a greater danger to the values of Enterprise than inwardness, unless it's the closely allied faculty of imagination. Both are intrinsic to the values of Belonging and their earth-centeredness. In the words of contemporary "eco-theologist" Father Thomas Berry, "When we destroy the natural world, we destroy the ground of our religious imagination."[11]

A Culture of Hierarchies

As a meme, dominion has proven to have tremendous vitality. Many Americans are troubled today by the degree to which corporate privilege is encroaching on constitutional democracy and by the emergence of a disproportionately wealthy upper class. We *should* be troubled, but probably not surprised, because however strong our national commitment is to democracy, we're also committed to the values of Enterprise; and the idea of hierarchy—the *belief* in hierarchy—is of a piece with those values.

When foraging gave way to farming, women lost a measure of their humanity. The difference between women and cattle was blurred as both acquired docility and became "domesticated." But over time, men as well have undergone the same kind of loss.

In the 1930s, many factory workers worked inhumanly long hours, but it took men with guns to keep them there. Today, curiously, no external prodding seems to be needed to keep workers on the job sixty and eighty hours a week. I've asked people about this and gotten a lot of different answers.

"Actually, I work *two* jobs, because neither of them pays enough to live on."

"I think it's something that got going with the startup companies, and everybody else just picked it up. It got to be one of those things where if you *weren't* working sixty, eighty hours a week, you weren't trying hard enough."

"The downsizing of the 1980s just scared the socks off people."

"At my company, as soon as you earn a hundred thousand dollars or more, you belong to them. You feel so good when they give you your cell-phone, your beeper, your Palm Pilot—but soon you realize that you can't take those things off. The company has you by the electronic tether."

A CULTURE OF VIOLENCE

My friend Annie was at a school fair not long ago with her thirteen-year-old son. Nick is popular, so kids were finding all kinds of reasons and ways to catch his attention. One boy had what seemed to her a very peculiar gambit: he pulled up his sleeve, held out his forearm, and shouted, "Hey, Nick! Look at my *guns!*"

What is it about Americans and violence?

It may be intrinsic to the zero-sum logic that drives Enterprise cultures that it isn't enough to simply steer clear of the individual or group that feels uncomfortably foreign—that it's much better to eliminate them altogether, or at the very least warn them off with a display of one's superior firepower. As we've already seen, militarism was a close sibling to agriculture from the very beginning, and when commerce replaced agriculture as the primary carrier of Enterprise values, it became the "warrior culture" that it's understood to be today. Warriors everywhere share the traditional belief that when you eliminate an enemy, you absorb his ferocity into your own.

Thirty years ago a report was issued by the Milton S. Eisenhower Foundation, a nonprofit research group that grew out of a commission President Johnson created in 1968, which said that crime and poverty were tearing away at the nation's social fabric. That report was updated at the end of 1999, and it concluded that with respect to both crime and poverty the United States has in fact moved backward.

Unusually high levels of prosperity during the 1990s, and very low unemployment, had led to declines in crime rates, as was widely reported. But those were declines as compared to the unusually *high* crime rates of the 1980s. Today, the situation is very close to what it was in the late 1960s, and violence is in fact much more prevalent today. The odds of dying in a violent crime remain much higher in the United States than in most other industrialized nations. One reason is that the number of firearms has doubled to nearly two hundred million in this country.

Our policymakers could have made the right social investments, said one of the commissioners, but instead they made "a lot of wrong choices," including hard-line policies such as "zero-tolerance" laws, the building of more prisons, and the so-called "war on drugs."[12] Those "wrong choices" were all profoundly reflective of the warrior mentality that runs deep in Enterprise cultures.

As I've suggested already, there are certain contradictions within the constellation of values associated with Enterprise. Inventiveness and creativity thrive in social milieus that are egalitarian and inclusive. The rigid social stratifications that tend to develop in very competitive and materialistic societies can stifle the spirit of innovation. So, for that matter, can the top-down militaristic assumptions that often shape the governments of Enterprise societies—particularly those that have a lot to protect. So between the inventive aspect of the culture of Enterprise, and its desire for control, there's always been a palpable tension. A little bit of the Belonging ethos has therefore always had to be in the mix.

It may be that these internal contradictions, visible all along in the great civilizations of the past, are becoming more acute today, and in the United States in particular. A list I saw recently of "the values Americans live by" gave me reason to think that they are.

This particular list was included in a pamphlet my son's college sent him a few weeks before he was to leave for a semester in Europe. To communicate effectively across cultural differences, it advised, one should be aware that certain values dear to most American would strike an Italian or a Tahitian as exotic in the extreme.

The very first value was, sure enough, "personal control over the environment"—and I loved seeing that, because it confirmed my sense that the fundamental difference between the culture of Belonging and the culture of Enterprise is the difference between intimate knowledge of the natural world and the will to control it: all the other differences flow from that one. Among the other values cited in the list were materialism, competition, an orientation to the future rather than the past, and efficiency. For Americans, the writer observed, change is synonymous with progress and improvement.

The quintessentially "American" values turned out to be almost identical with those I'd already identified as the values of Enterprise. The exceptions, therefore, fairly leaped off the page: Americans value egalitarianism, this pamphlet said, and they love informality, directness, openness, and honesty—classic hunter-gatherer traits.

Between the desire to be inclusive, though, and the desire to be wealthy (wealthier, ideally, than one's neighbors), between the desire to be egalitarian and the desire to compete uninhibitedly, between the desire to be honest and the desire to get the upper hand in business dealings—between all these pairings a sizable fissure can open up; and perhaps the anxiety associated with that fissure marks Americans as definitively as their values.

CHAPTER 10

Staying Power:
The Culture of Belonging over Time

The clash that I've described between the cultures of Belonging and Enterprise didn't end in a complete rout of Belonging values at all. That's what makes the arrangement that did fall into place so very interesting. The values we lived by for our first few million years are so intrinsic to *being* human that we carry them along with us whether we choose to or not.

It's as if the values of Belonging had been placed in a trust. One thinks of fairytales about treasures hidden until some prince or princess solves the riddle, finds the magic sword, or just wakes up.

The culture of Belonging isn't merely resilient; it's resilience itself.

It's like the Gundestrup Cauldron.

More than a hundred years ago, a mysteriously beautiful object was found, in pieces, in a bog in Jutland. Assembled, its thirteen silver plates form a deep bowl, sixty-nine centimeters across and forty-two deep. Each of the plates is decorated, in a style most of us would call "bas-relief" but art historians call "repoussé," with a great many wild creatures: elephants, a dolphin, lions, a hyena. All these and a man with antlers who is very probably the Celtic god Cernunnos, who was associated with life, death, birth, rebirth, and transformation.

The cauldron is believed to have been made in Eastern Europe around the second century A.D., and it was probably used in sacrificial rites of some kind. The figures that dance along the side and bottom, inside and out, are, in any case, magical and arresting.

Judging from the way its silver plates were disposed, archaeologists believe that the Gundestrup Cauldron was taken apart deliberately so that the pieces could be buried separately. In fact, one of the outer plates has never been found. Whoever possessed the cauldron, and had to hide it, wanted to make very certain that its power didn't fall into the wrong hands. In pieces, it would be innocuous.

When the values of Belonging are seen in relationship to one another—when it's understood what a coherent and unified ethos they comprise, and how differently life unfolds when those values are honored—something in us stirs.

Cernunnos, perhaps. Radiant god of life and death, birth, rebirth, and transformation.

The values of Belonging have always had a powerful hold—imaginative, spiritual, maybe even neurological—on men and women alike. In order for the culture of Enterprise to supplant the culture of Belonging, therefore, it needed to loosen that hold. Representing the values of Belonging as separate, unrelated pieces—some of them "feminine," some of them "religious," some of them "artistic," and none of them truly "manly"—would go a long way toward accomplishing that end, provided those representations got reinforced regularly down through time. As long as the values of Belonging were kept apart from each other, their full transformative force would be annulled and the swift unfolding of Enterprise culture could proceed uninterruptedly.

The persistence of this arrangement makes all the more impressive the regular "outbreaks" of Belonging culture that take place in certain areas of human experience. I'd like to look at some of these now, excluding for the moment the most obvious: the fact that women have never stopped creating cultures of Belonging within their homes and workplaces. This simple fact may well be the single most important reason that the values in question still have such a strong claim on us, but it also serves to reinforce the argument that those values are, in the final analysis, feminine.

Indeed, most of the individuals that I bring into this chapter are male. That they were men and *nonetheless* embraced values such as inclusiveness, playfulness, and intuition—and made their mark in history anyway—is, in a certain sense, the whole point of what I want to say about gender and the values of Belonging. Francis of Assisi could have been a wealthy merchant: he chose not to be. Gandhi was a successful lawyer: he chose not to remain so. When a woman embraces the values of Belonging, it's only what we expect of her; no one thinks more of the values themselves on account of her choice. But when a *man* embraces them, it's news—man bites dog!—and his biography is a perennial bestseller.

By the logic I've just trotted out, it would of course have made sense, in the preceding chapter, to illustrate my discussion of Enterprise culture by drawing on the lives of women who embraced the values of Enterprise. Not so easy, that. There are only so many Margaret Thatchers.

Three sorts of individuals have made particularly strong contributions toward keeping the values of Belonging alive and attractive: artists, mystics, and social or political reformers. That those three categories tend to collapse into one another—that the artists have visions, the mystics demand social justice, and the revolutionaries write poetry—only confirms what we've already learned: these values are as absolutely of a piece as the life-ways they reflect.

It became apparent to me only after I'd assembled the content of this chapter that all the individuals I was writing about were engaged during their lifetime in an active critique of the "dominant culture," the culture of Enterprise. And I don't mean that in a broad, general sense, either. As we'll see, these people took issue very pointedly with the whole complex of Enterprise values.

LOOSE CANNONS: LITERARY ARTISTS AND THE VALUES OF BELONGING

Imaginative works that celebrate the culture of Belonging matter tremendously, because they nourish and expand our sense of what's possible; they keep it alive. Few are as unforgettable in that regard as the epics of Homer.

Homer was blind, tradition says. Undistracted by the surface of things, he saw into the depths—saw the wholeness that had been, and reassembled the scattered fragments in the epics he sang.

Homer's *Iliad* and *Odyssey* are, of course, not "pre-agricultural"; they reflect the warrior culture of Greece in the eighth and ninth centuries B.C. But they retain something of a pre-agricultural sensibility. Sometimes the poems feel like a long, drawn-out collision between the ethos of warriors and the ethos of farmers. The values of Belonging are all the more manifest in these poems because they're embattled. Greed and imperial ambition, the Enterprise values that launched the Trojan War, threaten, in Homer's account, to tear apart the whole fabric of life—specifically, human interconnectedness.

Like the Hindu *Ramayana* and *Mahabharata,* the Homeric epics were composed orally. Long before these epics were given a more or less final form and put in writing, the poet "sang" them—chunks of them at a time, anyway—before listeners whose specific concerns (the occasion might be a wedding, a funeral, a reunion, for example) would influence the particular shape the stories took on a specific occasion. Thus the epics, which never came out exactly the same, were in a very real sense "collective," reflecting of necessity the desires and convictions of the people themselves—both men and women, young and old, wealthy and poor. Descriptions of the coastline and sea, the olive trees and beehives, were descriptions of the world that the people themselves knew and loved.

The values of Belonging shine out between the lines of both of Homer's epics. The beauty of the earth and waters and animals is always there, as is the very real possibility that Aphrodite or Pallas Athena might suddenly materialize next to you and the certainty that the gods will be "at your back" whenever you're in danger. Kinship bonds hold firm, and for all the urgency of battle, there's at every turn time to do what is seemly. At key moments, time simply stops. Self-restraint is here (though only intermittently), along with a sense of balance and deep skepticism about change.

Still, Odysseus is the very embodiment of ingenuity, restlessness, and expansiveness—Enterprise values, all. He's clever, and yet his cleverness gets him in trouble; then he has to be cleverer still to get out of trouble. Indeed, one way of reading his story is as a meditation on being clever, self-reliant, and enterprising (and on the consequences of being so).

Odysseus loves his island home: it's an extension of himself. But at the same time, the Trojan War has been over for ten years before he finds his way back. When he does return to his home and wife, retrieving them is no small matter, and everyone in Homer's audience would have known why: Odysseus has played fast and loose with what's supposed to be most precious, and everyone knows what you risk when you do that. Still, everything is held in a remarkable balance—and perhaps that's why we go on loving these stories so. Nothing real about who we are has been discredited or left out of the picture.

Few moments in the literature of romantic love compare with the famous homecoming episode. The reason it's so magnificent is that it's a delicate and perfect celebration of mutuality. For Penelope is every bit as clever, self-reliant, and enterprising as her mate, and just as unsentimental—though, in fact, decidedly more chaste. (Inexcusably late as Odysseus is in getting back from Troy, having dallied for romantic as well as adventurous reasons, he has nonetheless disguised himself—for strategic reasons, yes, but in part, to learn whether his wife has been faithful!)

The homecoming episode is clearly what it is and where it is in the *Odyssey* because the poem's audience included *everyone*—women as well as men. Its scenes are intercut with Odysseus's preparations for ferocious combat with the Suitors, so that even as male listeners were fully engaged, the women weren't forgotten. As the battle looms, tension mounts all the more effectively for the delays that are created by the intimate domestic conversations between Penelope and Odysseus—long, quiet conversations by firelight. These are among the moments in the poem when time seems to be suspended.

Seeing through his disguise, and pretending not to, Penelope defeats her husband finally in a maneuver that's the relational equivalent of a fiercely played hand of poker. It's a short leap indeed from the ingenuity of Penelope to the cleverness of Shakespeare's comedic heroines; and the whole lineage of strong, witty, resourceful women of which they're all part is probably one of the best things Western civilization can say about itself.

Mutuality is just as pervasive a theme in the *Iliad,* but there the poet isn't as concerned with the distance between men and women, as he is with the distance between warriors, and how that distance can be bridged. In the crush of battle, one human being after another, over and over again, ceases to be human and becomes, as Simone Weil observed, a *thing*—and that's as true of the Greeks as it is of the Trojans. The poem is so brilliantly constructed that one is simply not able to take sides. There's no triumph in this war: we grieve with Achilles over Patroclus, we grieve with Andromache and Priam over Hector, and we come away knowing—as pre-agricultural people did—that there's no enemy as cruel or destructive as war itself.

The best artists can't help but remind us of our losses, because they feel and see those losses so vividly; and this of course makes artists the subversive loose cannons of every society. Almost cursed to tell the truth, they have a way of going right to what *is,* ferreting out without even planning to, the truths that established power most want to have left dormant. The relationship between artists and the state has therefore always been dicey, as we see right away when we look at what happens to the epic tradition under the emergent state.

Caesar Augustus commissioned Virgil to write the *Aeneid* to celebrate the greatness of imperial Rome, and Virgil accepted the commission. He was way too good a poet to play it straight, however. He worked from the Homeric epics, as he was surely supposed to, drawing in elements of both, but to dramatically different effect.

What Virgil's epic evokes for readers even now is not so much the grandeur of Rome, but its terrible cost. Aeneas is no Odysseus, and he's no Achilles either. He's a man who has lost just about everything, and we're never allowed to forget his sorrow. Virgil summed up in the single phrase *lacrimae rerum* (literally, "the tears of events") the unspeakable human losses that constitute the real price of empire— *any* empire.

Virgil got his commission, his ambivalence about empire being sufficiently concealed, even from himself. Shakespeare got the royal patronage he needed to stage his plays too, despite their complex insights into the moral dilemmas of kingship. But it's always been touch and go between artists and the state. No one has stated the dilemma more eloquently than Adrienne Rich in July 1997, when she refused the National Medal for the Arts:

> There is no simple formula for the relationship of art to justice. But I do know that art—in my own case the art of poetry— means nothing if it simply decorates the dinner table of power that holds it hostage.[1]

Imagination is one of the most powerful links we have to the submerged Atlantis of Belonging, but our response to beauty is another. That response is intimately related to the values of Belonging, and just as central to them as imagination is. The late Iris Murdoch, novelist and philosopher, conjectured that "anything which alters consciousness in the direction of unselfishness, objectivity and realism is to be connected with virtue," and from that premise she went on to ask what it is in our own surroundings that most typically "unselfs" us.

She found it to be beauty.

Describing a kestrel she'd seen hovering, Murdoch reflected that the sight had indeed unselfed her insofar as it banished "a cluster of feelings that normally promote the self." Prior to seeing the kestrel, she admits, she had been anxious, resentful—sensitive, perhaps, to a professional slight. But afterward, it was as if the space that had been taken up guarding or advancing her self—or her prestige—was now freed up for "some more capacious mental act."[2] One is reminded of the Trance Dance, Dreaming, and the hunter-gatherer's readiness to cast aside, by any means possible, the narrower, more contracted forms of thought that persuade us we're in the company of enemies.

Something very like Murdoch's "unselfing" happened, when he was just a child, to the man who would become the great Bengali saint known as Sri Ramakrishna.

Mystics: The Culture of Belonging Embodied

A small boy walking across a rice paddy in Bengal looked up to see a crane flying overhead. The beauty of the white bird silhouetted against the dark monsoon cloud was more than he could bear, and for an hour or two he lost consciousness altogether. Years later, Sri Ramakrishna told his biographer that this was the beginning of his life in God.

There's probably no more direct track into the archaic paradigm than the one laid down by the mystics. Women and men have turned up in all religious traditions who have needed no mediator, and no particular knowledge of religious doctrine, to experience God directly. The lives of the Compassionate Buddha, Ba'al Shem Tov, Teresa of Avila, and William Blake mirror the whole complex of Belonging values almost systematically.

And so, of course, does the story of Saint Francis of Assisi, who talked to sparrows and taught a lamb to genuflect before sending it as a gift to his young follower, Clare, and her community, the Poor Ladies. Francis found his own fastidiousness so repellent that he sought out a leper, embraced him, and kissed him on both decaying cheeks.

He danced, he sang, he rejoiced in every living thing.

Repudiating the hierarchical structures of existing monastic orders, Francis created a brotherhood instead, and then a sisterhood as well, headed up by Clare, the one among all his disciples who was most faithful to his teachings. Francis established what has come to be known as the Third Order, composed of women and men who, on entering the order, returned all ill-gotten goods (which in many cases meant everything they had), made a commitment not to bear arms or take oaths except under extraordinary conditions, and agreed to live in such a way as to preserve peace among themselves and with others.

The altered states of consciousness that play such a crucial role in the life of American Indians and Australian Aborigines were a regular occurrence for Francis; and for him, as for them, the world was "transparent" to deeper meanings. His magnificent Poem of the Creatures, "Brother Sun, Sister Moon," embraces not only all living creatures, but water, wind, and the earth itself. So profoundly inclusive was his vision of things that toward the end of his life he welcomed even "Sister Bodily Death, whom no living man can escape."

When our ancestors turned themselves from prey into predator, they made an axial shift, and the zero-sum logic that evolved out of that experience is still very much with us. But Francis transcended the grim terms of that logic. By accepting the stigmata—indeed, by asking for them—he took upon himself the outward signs of being prey. He asked God to let him experience all of the pain Christ had endured on the cross, but he also asked to feel the full measure of Christ's love. Like Jesus Christ, and for that matter like every woman who has given birth, he let himself be reduced to bleeding, anguished flesh.

Only it wasn't, in fact, Francis him*self* that was so reduced—and he emphasizes this—but his *body*. He had already worked out for himself a relationship between himself and his body that allowed him to feel both detached and affectionately custodial: "Brother Ass," he called it, pledging to care for his body and keep it fed, but never for a moment to confuse it with himself.

Francis wasn't prey, and on the other hand, he was determinedly not to be a predator either. It's tempting to read one of the best-loved stories from the famous collection *The Little Flowers* in the light of that triumph. The villagers of Gubbio send a message to Francis: Can he help them deal with a ferocious wolf that's been terrorizing the town? And of course he does. But he doesn't ride into town and *destroy* the wolf. Instead, he goes to the village, calls Brother Wolf to him, and reduces him to a quivering mass of remorse, converting him before he leaves to a life of nonviolence and penitence not awfully unlike his own.

In the light of what I've said about the extent to which the historic religions have been almost haunted by ideas about control—in particular, the control of nature—one might be tempted to make much of the fact that individuals like Francis did, in their asceticism, go against their own very human desires for sleep, good food, sex, and a great deal else besides. But to see the disciplines they imposed on themselves as attempts to thwart or dominate nature misses the real point of what they were doing. By unifying their desires, they sought to unify attention itself into a kind of laser beam powerful enough to penetrate the veil of ordinary life and reveal the presence they believed to be hidden behind it. What one senses, reading the mystics' own accounts of these struggles, isn't a dogged, bitter struggle for self-mastery, but rather a joyful recklessness—that of a lover throwing off every encumbrance as she rushes toward her Beloved.

Fasting, thirsting, keeping vigil, abstaining from sex—in indigenous cultures everywhere, all of these are accepted practices for one who would experience the sacred. They're undertaken not as a show of individual strength or self-mastery, but as ways of emptying oneself, the better to be filled by God.

Each time someone like a Francis or a Gandhi walks onto the historical stage, everyone gets an alternative reading of the human condition itself. As their lives unfold, we see how powerfully disruptive the constellation of Belonging values is to Enterprise—the more so, depending on how fully that constellation becomes manifest.

And we don't have to look only at spiritual giants to understand this. Most history books, distracted by the rise and fall of governments and empires, pass over certain individuals who turned whole regions around in absolutely crucial regards. Most Americans believe that the Abolition Movement didn't get underway until the early nineteenth century, and names such as John Brown and Frederick Douglass are the ones that come to mind as its initiators. But John Woolman, who persuaded the Quakers of eighteenth-century America that slaveholding was incompatible with their faith, and who is all but unknown outside Quaker circles, carried out his work between 1745 and 1772.

How much impact on the eventual abolition of slavery did John Woolman's itinerant ministry have, conducted as it was a hundred years before the Civil War? It would be difficult to quantify, but he laid solid groundwork for slavery's rejection by the Quakers, and Quakers such as William Lloyd Garrison were at the center of the fledgling Abolition Movement of the 1800s (as they would be of the Civil Rights Movement in the twentieth century).

Early in his journal, Woolman sums up his understanding of religion. I want to cite his words here, because he's so obviously speaking of something that transcends institutionalized faith altogether.

> [I was] early convinced in my mind that true religion consisted in an inward life, wherein the heart doth love and reverence God the Creator, and learns to exercise true justice and goodness, not only toward all men, but also toward the brute creatures; that, as the mind was moved by an inward principle to love God as an invisible, incomprehensible Being, so, by the same principle, it was moved to love him in all his manifestations in the visible world.[3]

The practice of slaveholding was far more common in the northern colonies than most of us realize. (As late as 1800 there were 12,442 slaves in New Jersey.) Woolman's own objections to slavery appear to have taken shape gradually.

Woolman was, among other things, a scrivener, and it was in this context that he first felt a scruple. Asked to write a will that entailed the bequeathing of slaves, he simply expressed his belief that the practice was incompatible with Christian faith before carrying out the task. But as he learned more about slavery, his resistance solidified, and he became an active, vocal opponent. Traveling through the South in 1746, and again in 1757, he saw slavery as a "dark gloominess hanging over the land" and predicted that its consequences would be grievous to later generations of white as well as black people.

Woolman's analysis of the root causes of slavery illuminated for him the situation of the Indians of his region as well. The Indians who lived adjacent to the land taken over by white settlers followed a way of life, he observed, formed by "the custom of a great many ages," and one that required "much room."[4] It would be wrong, he believed, to seize still more of their land until newcomers had done everything they could to make do with what they already had. White settlers should curb their desires and live simply.

In 1763, Woolman set out unarmed to visit the Indians living on the western frontier of Pennsylvania—a region still seething in the aftermath of the French and Indian Wars. He had no particular design: "Love was the first motion, and thence a concern arose to spend some time with the Indians, that I might feel and understand their life."[5]

As we trace his course in and around the "colonies," and thence to England (where he would die of smallpox), noting his anguish at the working conditions of the sailors on the way over, and the postboys in England itself, we get the feeling that his very skin was growing thinner and thinner. Near the end of his life, he seems to corroborate that impression. Recalling a period of severe illness a couple of years prior, he maintained that he had come so near death that he forgot his own name:

Being then desirous to know who I was, I saw a mass of matter of a dull gloomy color between the south and the east, and was informed that this mass was human beings in as great misery as they could be, and live, *and that I was mixed with them,* and that henceforth I might not consider myself as a distinct or separate being.[6]

The empathy and the mutuality of feeling that are so intrinsic to the culture of Belonging were driving passions in the life of John Woolman, as they had been in that of Francis of Assisi—and that brings us to the question of gender.

Gender empathy is perhaps the single most reliable marker of the culture of Belonging. It turns up only if most or all of the other values are already in place. If in a particular historical setting we find that women are visible, audible, and generally unmolested, we know that we're likely to run across other anomalies as well. Woolman's story tells us little in this regard (unless you want to count the fact that in his journal he refers several times to "my dear wife"), but Quaker women were fully voiced within their community, and Woolman himself, without dwelling on the fact, mentions working with several other itinerant Quaker preachers who were women.

The importance to women in particular of Saint Francis of Assisi and John Woolman (and others like them) doesn't lie, though, in any direct contribution they may or may not have made to women's emancipation. It lies, rather, in the fact that both of them walked away from conventional male scripts. They would *not* pile up fortunes, they would *not* take up arms, and both were known to cry in public unashamedly. By all their actions, they rejected the logic that makes each of us either predator or prey; and there may be no better thing one *could* do to make the world safe for women, and for everybody else, than to repudiate that logic.

Reflecting on the lives of Francis of Assisi and John Woolman, one wonders whether deep prayer and meditation aren't the ultimate "wormhole" down and back into the realm of Belonging. Both men are regarded as religious figures, but in truth, their lives obliterated the lines that the culture of Enterprise so resolutely draws (and Belonging cultures refused to) between religion, politics, and economics. Whenever that happens—whenever the whole constellation of Belonging values begins to reassemble itself—it's as if an alarm were going off somewhere in the depths of Enterprise culture, triggering a massive retaliatory response. It isn't *always* that someone is publicly discredited—called a heretic, or a traitor or a communist, depending on the context. And it certainly isn't *always* that someone is killed. Sometimes a concession is made which can be retracted quietly at a later date. Most effective of all is the outbreak of war.

Some of the best-known advocates of social and economic reform to grace the past couple of hundred years challenged the culture of Enterprise openly and energetically. What happened to them when they challenged more than they were supposed to is quite interesting.

REFORMERS AND REVOLUTIONARIES

Besides artists and mystics, there's a third category of individuals who have consistently upheld and embodied the values of Belonging within cultures of Enterprise. In the United States, for example, many have fought to extend to all women and men the civil rights outlined in our nation's founding documents.

The decision Elizabeth Cady Stanton made in 1895 to publish the *Woman's Bible* was in effect an attack on the culture of Enterprise—

specifically, on the role that religion played in perpetuating sharply defined gender stereotypes.

Stanton's fellow suffragists believed at the time that they were very close to winning the long, drawn-out struggle for women's right to vote, and they'd received considerable support from certain Protestant clergymen. They were appalled, therefore, at the thought of alienating the religious establishment; and the *Woman's Bible,* a pungent screed against conventional misogynist interpretation of scripture, was bound to do just that. Shortly after the first volume of the *Woman's Bible* was published, the National American Woman Suffrage Association, which Stanton had cofounded in 1869, issued a public censure, denying any official connection between the book and the association. It was the beginning of the end of Stanton's long connection with that group.

Stanton's vision of what was really at stake for women had enlarged steadily all along, alienating her permanently from many of her long-time companions in the struggle. She had come to see how meaningless the right to vote would be if the attitudes that had rationalized denying women the vote in the first place weren't addressed and changed, and she saw how deeply embedded those attitudes were in institutionalized religion. (Indeed, some historians argue plausibly that the only reason women got the vote when they did was that southern males wanted to check the power of the black vote—black men having won the vote during Reconstruction. Southern white men were confident that "their women" would vote as instructed.)

Many clergymen endorsed enthusiastically the notion that women should be given the vote, on the grounds that their special maternal qualities would benefit society. The nineteenth-century doctrine of True Womanhood, linked to a Bible-based Christianity interpreted by male clergy, presumed that women would go on playing the one role they had been assigned to play all along—the role of "carrying" the values of care and connection—while men went on waging war and capitalism. The doctrine further presumed that women were to perform their acts of care and connection under the guidance and protection of . . . male clergy.

Stanton saw right through that, and she wasn't having any of it. Women were fully selves in their own right, she argued, and that was the only acceptable basis for their being given full citizenship. She had seen through the religious arguments for keeping women silent. She understood that as long as the values of Belonging—of care and connection—weren't fully honored (which they certainly weren't in late-nineteenth-century America!), then women who tied their selfhood to those values would remain marginal.

The great sin that Elizabeth Cady Stanton committed against the movement she herself had led was to choose what she believed to be true over political expediency. The wrath she stirred up by doing so was considerable, and it was a foretaste of what another heroine of progressive thought would undergo not long afterward.

As long as Jane Addams confined her attentions to the immigrant poor in Chicago and other American cities, she was what we would today call a "media darling." Indeed, during the period just before World War I, she was regarded as "a blend of the saint and the statesman."[7]

With the onset of the war, however, and Addams's outspoken opposition to it—opposition grounded in the values of Belonging and perfectly consonant with everything else she believed and had stated—her public image changed. She had dared to apply the kind of reasoning that arises out of the values of Belonging *outside* the narrowly defined niche where the "dominant culture" had placed her, and that was not to be borne.

"Jane Addams is a silly, vain, impertinent old maid," read a representative editorial, "who may have done good charity work at Hull House, Chicago, but is now meddling with matters far beyond her capacity."[8]

That same sharp reversal of public acceptance prefigures the last days of Martin Luther King, Jr., as well. King's name was all but synonymous with the Civil Rights Movement from the time of the 1955 bus boycotts in Montgomery, Alabama. By the spring of 1968, though, King was distancing himself publicly from "Project Breadbasket," Jesse Jackson's effort to stimulate black capitalism. Confessing to a growing distaste for capitalism of any color, he alienated many of his supporters.

King spoke his mind on other issues as well, heedless of the effects on his popularity. In reiterating his unqualified commitment to non-violence, he distanced himself from young black militants such as Stokeley Carmichael and H. Rap Brown; in urging withdrawal of American troops from Vietnam, he lost the support of members of the liberal political establishment that still supported the war; and in calling for a multiracial Poor People's March on Washington, D.C., he antagonized a wide range of followers by appearing to shift his focus from racial to class injustice.

Like Elizabeth Cady Stanton and Jane Addams, King rejected the merely expedient. His real allegiance was not to specific programs but to the ideals that had drawn him into political life in the first place—ideals such as inclusiveness, egalitarianism, nonviolence, and mutuality. And those very ideals kept leading nearer and nearer to the realization that the *whole* society was off track: racism, violence, and poverty were different symptoms of a single illness. He was moving closer by the day to the recognition that a great many feminists have reached today: until the entire constellation of Belonging values is rehabilitated and placed on an equal footing with the values of Enterprise, there will be no authentic or sustainable progress toward racial equality *or* gender equality *or* nonviolence *or* the redress of poverty.

Environmental awareness is basic to cultures of Belonging, but not many of the great nineteenth- and early-twentieth-century reformers attached the importance to it that we do today. An exception was the extraordinary John Muir. A transcendentalist who memorized the whole of the New Testament, and an environmentalist (before there was such a thing) who persuaded Theodore Roosevelt to set aside national parks, John Muir was at once literary artist, mystic, and reformer.

No one who is even a little familiar with the life and writings of John Muir can hike the trails of Yosemite without imagining him there in 1869—thin, bearded, his eyes strangely bright, scrambling tirelessly up vertical granite cliffs, overcome with joy at everything he saw. Muir kept a diary of his first trip into the Sierras, and with each entry he sounds more like a visionary. His descriptions of Yosemite Creek suggest to some that he saw in the creek itself something that was more than metaphor for his own spiritual quest—something like ego-death:

Emerging from its last gorge, it glides in wide, lace-like rapids down a smooth incline into a pool where it seems to rest and compose its gray, agitated waters before taking the grand plunge, then slowly slipping over the lip of the pool basin, it descends another glossy slope with rapidly accelerated speed to the brink of the tremendous cliff, and with sublime, fateful confidence springs out free in the air.[9]

As if compelled to get as close to the creek and its freefall as he could without falling himself, Muir crept out onto a shelf three inches wide, at the creek's very edge, where he could look "down into the heart of the snowy, chanting throng of comet-like streamers." Later, realizing the danger of his position, he couldn't remember how long he'd stayed there, or how he'd gotten down. Soon afterward, in a diary entry that reminds me of Pascal's famous fragment, he wrote, "No pain here. No sense of dead stone, all spiritualized. . . . No fear of the past, no fear of the future. . . . Gift of good God."[10]

Mystic that he clearly was, Muir felt no call to an enclosed contemplative life. Trained well in the science of his day—botany and geology, in particular—he had an intimate knowledge of lily, stream, and redwood that was neither analytic nor objective. Unitive, rather, and ecstatic. Contemporary environmentalists who recognize him as the founder of their movement try to downplay his religiosity, but it's there on every page of his diary.

When a literary artist depicts the culture of Belonging, he or she looks to the past, tapping into buried collective memories.

The social reformer looks to the future and asks us to think it possible that the culture of Belonging can be reborn, as William Blake prophesied, "on England's green and pleasant land."

The mystic, though, exists in the permanently present tense. She doesn't merely talk about the values or culture of Belonging; she embodies it.

CHAPTER 11

The Quickening Spirit of Change

Theoretically, the cultures of Belonging and Enterprise could go on as they have indefinitely, wrangling publicly, often, and inconclusively like certain married couples everyone really wishes would break up. But there are several reasons for thinking that the relationship between these two very different ways of being in the world may be about to shift dramatically.

One reason I've touched on already is that a great many of the individuals most alarmed about the state of the global ecosystem see the several environmental crises facing us today as a result of exactly those blind spots I've associated here with the values of Enterprise. They note that exploding populations in particular, and the excessive use of natural resources and destruction of ecosystems that come in their wake, have everything to do with expansiveness, acquisitiveness, materialism, and chronic disconnection from the earth.

But the reasons for thinking change is in the air that will be explored in this chapter all have to do with a shift in perception that's been growing steadily over the last hundred years or so. One might characterize that shift as a slow, sober, and very thoughtful awakening to the several ways in which contemporary Western civilization disappoints.

Certain crucial insights into the culture of Enterprise are available only now, for the first time ever. Some have arisen out of a lively critique of liberal democratic theory that's been gathering steam for the last forty years, some out of the study of other cultures (led by anthropologists, in particular) over the past hundred years and more, some out of a vigorous discussion of gender that began in the early 1970s and is in important regards just hitting its stride, and still others, finally, out of a new willingness of the leaders and practitioners of various religions to look more objectively at their own and one another's histories.

The fact that these insights converge—and emphatically, coming as they do from so many quarters—is allowing a new kind of question to be raised, and raised persistently.

Inside and outside of academic settings, these separate inquiries are illuminating one another, resulting in, if not a solidly united front, a growing consensus around exactly the issues that this book has been raising. It has gotten increasingly difficult to treat them as separate inquiries, as if they had no real bearing on one another.

I would like in this chapter to touch on the most important developments in each of these four "discourses"—political theory, anthropology, gender, and religion—and make it clear how and where they're converging. Gender is in fact a prominent issue in all these areas, and that shouldn't be surprising if indeed the "assignment" of Belonging values to women was as basic to Western civilization—to its political theory, its social structures, its religious institutions—as it appears to have been.

LIBERAL–DEMOCRATIC THEORY UNDER FIRE

As we noted earlier, Enterprise cultures are often at odds with themselves with respect to political inclusiveness. An open, democratic society is inherently more creative than one that's highly stratified and heavily controlled, but because that very creativity can feel threatening to the hierarchical social and political structures that often typify Enterprise, new groups are rarely welcomed unreservedly.

In the United States, political theory is further complicated by our rich mix of ideologies. American political ideals represent a confluence of several streams, including Judeo-Christian religious beliefs and the Enlightenment philosophies of eighteenth-century England and Europe: brotherly love, on the one hand, and on the other, a strong faith in rationality—both expected to lead humanity steadily forward into more and more just and equitable relationships.

Over long reaches of time, and for many reasons, various groups of Americans awoke to the extent of their exclusion from full citizenship and began pressing for change—notably, in the nineteenth and twentieth centuries, women and African Americans. I've already mentioned Elizabeth Cady Stanton, but I want to cite in particular the remarkable speech she made in 1892, her seventy-eighth year, called "The Solitude of Self."

Stanton was addressing the Senate Committee on Woman Suffrage, as she had many times in the past. She had given the same speech two days earlier before the National American Association for Woman Suffrage and received a standing ovation. But now she was speaking to an audience of men—politically powerful men who weren't notably well disposed to her message.

Still, they were men of her own social class and religious background. Daughter of a prominent judge herself, she knew them very well. Her opening words reminded them that she was one of them by noting that the linchpin of liberal democratic theory as well as of Protestantism ("our protestant idea," she called it, and "our republican idea") was the idea of individualism. And individualism, she insisted, was also the basis for women's right to vote.

There wasn't a hint in her remarks of cajolery or flutter. She and other women had been coming before this committee for sixteen years, she reminded them, to plead the cause of women's suffrage. There was no need to reiterate their arguments. So she did something else. Dropping swiftly down into a place of such undiluted seriousness that it must surely have drawn everyone in the room along with her, she began to talk about isolation.

Gently, but persistently, Stanton dismantled the conventional objection to suffrage for women. "We know that you would be glad to protect us," she said (I'm paraphrasing here), "and we are grateful, and often we would like to lean on you. But given what life is, and given what its real exigencies are, you cannot protect us in any meaningful way, because at the definitive moments in our lives, every human being is alone. Since we must face life's crises alone, we must be permitted to develop all the resources we need to do this."

Far from appealing to male gallantry, far from promising that when women had the vote a new civility would spread across the land, she summoned up the same vision of life that a Buddhist monk might have—stark and unrelieved.

"The strongest reason why we ask for woman a voice in the government under which she lives; in the religion she is asked to believe ... is because of her birth-right to self-sovereignty; because, as an individual, she must rely on herself."[1]

Denying that men can actually do for women what they've been brought up to think they must—support and protect in all circumstances—Stanton hinted pointedly at the possibility that behind the political questions raised by the disempowerment of women in Western civilization lie substantive religious questions as well—questions that Protestants in particular were obliged to weigh in their heart of hearts about what it means to play at being God. She concluded on a note of stern indignation: "Who can take, who dare take, on himself, the rights, the duties, the responsibilities, of another human soul?"[2]

Elizabeth Cady Stanton was anticipating by eighty years or so the work of feminist theorists and civil rights activists who would argue—and still argue—that the chink in the edifice of American liberal democratic theory *as practiced* is the idea that only some of us have selves. And it seems important to note (as we did in the preceding chapter) that the concept of selfhood is historically both philosophic and religious. No contemporary figure has grounded that concept more firmly in both the Judeo-Christian tradition and the tradition of American constitutional law than the Reverend Martin Luther King, Jr. In his famous "Letter from a Birmingham Jail," King wrote to fellow clergymen, explaining to them why he and other African Americans were no longer willing to wait, and referring to the anguish of "forever fighting a degenerating sense of 'nobodiness.'"[3]

At the core of a vigorous, ongoing assault on American political theory is the argument that it values liberty and independence almost as absolutes, pretending that "all men are created equal" and attributing to all citizens a degree of personal autonomy that only a few enjoy—not the disabled, for example, or the caretakers of the disabled, to say nothing of the caretakers of infants and small children. The several groups who have been excluded from full enjoyment of what they believe to be their constitutional rights have articulated their discontent plainly: "No, we are *not* all created equal. And no amount of sacrifice or hard work will necessarily cover the distance between us that my gender, my color, my ethnicity, my religion, my sexual orientation, or my disability has created *in your minds.*"

Perhaps, some argue, it's time to recognize that many people lead lives of meaning and dignity who are nonetheless dependent on others for their entire lives, and that in fact *all* of us are intermittently dependent, particularly in infancy, old age, illness, and pregnancy, and that we're no less fully human, or less "selfed," for that fact. Perhaps it's time to rethink American political theory accordingly, placing interdependence at the center. Security and well-being are ultimately as important, surely, as the unrestricted license to roam, armed and dangerous, that some will always insist was the Founding Fathers' intention.

THE ANTHROPOLOGICAL PERSPECTIVE

Ethnographic studies amassed by cultural anthropologists and archaeologists this past hundred-plus years demonstrate irrefutably, as we've seen, that societies have indeed existed, sustainably and gracefully, for which interdependence was the core value. Merely knowing that, and carrying around vivid mental pictures of what life can be like when personal liberty is *not* everyone's ultimate ideal, can jumpstart the imagination. What *would* American society look like, we start to wonder, if that fundamental shift were to begin taking place?

We've come to understand now that there was nothing sacred about the trajectory by which Western civilization established itself. Agriculture got started in six or seven different places about the same time, and the city-states that came along in its wake weren't all like the Egyptian and Sumerian cities that hover in the background of the Roman Empire (and therefore in "our" background). In what's now Pakistan, for example, the cities of Mohenjo-Daro and Harappa were beautifully laid out—highly "civilized" by any reasonable standard— though they included no large temples and no palaces. Remains of household shrines demonstrate that religious life was essentially home-centered. And in what's now Thailand, a "rice culture" flourished for thousands of years, beginning before 5000 B.C., that produced magnificent ceramics and bronzework but no cities at all, and no temples: just a network of villages that clearly had a very high standard of living and no bureaucratic overlay.

In other words, the pattern of highly centralized political/religious authority and sharp social stratification that marks Western civilization wasn't universally associated with the rise of agriculture. It looks as if the "first phase" of Enterprise, involving inventiveness and industry, was in some places able to unfold without bringing on the aggressive will to control that typically characterizes the second phase. That kind of insight can move us today to look searchingly at places like Kerala State, in India, which (though it has one of the lowest per-capita incomes in the world) has no shortfall in food, extremely low infant and child mortality rates, and almost a hundred percent literacy.

As the findings of anthropologists percolate out, they alert us to the strengths of very different societal models. They also equip us with certain conceptual tools that open out the inner workings of our own society to remarkable effect.

The term "warrior culture," for example, is used regularly now to describe the worlds not only of the military, professional athletics, and syndicated crime, but business as well—particularly at the highest levels—and government. I'm not sure how common that usage was before anthropologist Patricia McBroom published her important book *The Third Sex: The New Professional Woman* in 1986, but it's certainly part of ordinary parlance today.

When McBroom began interviewing men and the exceedingly small number of women who held the highest positions in corporate America two decades ago, it was because she wanted to figure out why women had made so few inroads into that world. Her first eye-opening discovery was that the world the men described to her was one that anthropologists would call a "warrior culture."[4]

It's important to bear in mind that despite the popular tendency to lump hunters and warriors together and trace all of "masculinity" to that conjunction, warrior cultures aren't identical with hunting cultures at all. In pre-agricultural societies, hunters hunt within an earth-centered frame of reference that's essentially that of Belonging. A warrior culture, on the other hand—with its emphasis on exclusively male alliances, control over women, and generalized anxiety about the environment—is based on the values of Enterprise. It defines masculinity not in a fundamental way, but as it enacts itself under certain conditions.

Outside of his professional status, McBroom saw, the corporate "warrior" has very little sense of self. His identity is bound up not just with his professional status, but with his performance. He'll typically say that he's doing it all for his family; and yet insofar as relationships, home, family, and play make inroads into his capacity to give his all at work, he often experiences them as threats to his very identity.

The heroes of the corporate world—men and women alike—are those who work too long and too hard to do anything else. They don't kid themselves that they're valued in their professional capacity for being a particular kind of person; rather, they're valued for what they can *do*. Love, sex, and appreciation are the rewards to which they feel entitled in exchange for leading lives of flat-out self-sacrifice.

Under the warrior ethos, performance is what matters: one doesn't expect to enjoy the work, McBroom's subjects told her, or to be comfortable in the workplace. So when women coworkers express concern for justice, comfort, and kindness, they sound almost laughably naïve, or even whiney. Most of the misgivings these men expressed about women entering that world reflected their belief that women don't grasp the centrality of performance.

"Professional women don't know how to take abuse the way men do," one of them said. "Women get bent out of shape emotionally when they have to deal with injustices."[5]

Why are women experiencing so much difficulty getting and keeping positions at the managerial level—especially considering how much legislation has been passed to clear the way, and how much "consciousness-raising" has gone on over the past few decades?

While recent Census Bureau figures show that more women are indeed making their way into managerial positions, the pay gap between men and women managers has widened considerably. In January 2002, the General Accounting Office released a study of the ten industries that together employ seventy-one percent of the female workers and seventy-three percent of the female managers in the United States. The study revealed that in 1995, full-time female managers earned less than male managers in all ten fields, and they still did in 2000. In seven of the fields the earnings gap actually grew during that time. In 1995, for instance, female managers in the communications industry made eighty-six cents for every dollar earned by male managers. Five years later, women managers made only seventy-three cents of the dollar that male managers did.[6] Of the three industries in which women had made small gains, all were either heavily regulated or were in the public sector.

New York State Representative Carolyn Maloney said of the study, "I don't find one line of good news in the report. Yet I think people believe women are doing better."[7]

Most people *do* believe that women are doing better, because by the logic we imbided in high school civics classes, they *must* be. Enshrined in our national monuments, and in the stories we tell ourselves about ourselves, is the confidence that as a nation we're becoming ever more just and inclusive. It may take some time, but we're getting there, and we *want* to get there. Given that confidence, regressive situations such as the one I've just outlined—and they're just as visible with respect to other excluded groups—confuse us. Especially when the individuals who make the decisions that keep women working for lower pay are our most privileged and best educated.

The Enlightenment philosophy that permeates our founding documents would presume that these leaders—men, for the most part— would be moved to act justly. But we shouldn't be confused, the cultural anthropologists remind us. Cultures have their own inner dynamics, and ours is a culture that honors inclusiveness only up to a point—to the point, for example, where it runs up against other of the values I've associated with Enterprise (competitiveness, say, or a passion for hierarchy).

It's interesting that the men questioned by McBroom didn't say that women should be excluded because the Bible says they should keep their heads covered and be quiet, and they didn't say that women are fundamentally irrational. All they really said was that women didn't know how to behave as a warrior must. Women couldn't do business "as if it were a game," as the men themselves claimed they were doing. These men might have majored in philosophy or literature at Dartmouth—might even have taken a gender studies class—but their commitment to the warrior code (wordless, for the most part, and even unconscious) ran much deeper than their liberal arts education.

If that commitment seems to have a stronger grip at the very highest levels of American society—if women are finding it harder to break into the highest paid and most powerful positions—that shouldn't surprise us, because the highest positions in government, law, finance, entertainment, and related fields are held by people who've been the most willing to compete hardest, and to set everything else aside, to get to the top.

And what can we learn from the women who *do* manage to manage? Susan Estrich, first woman president of the *Harvard Law Review* and currently the Robert Kingsley Professor of Law and Political Science at the University of Southern California, wrote her 2000 book *Sex and Power* to ask why it is that so few women have made their way to the most powerful positions—not only in law, business, and politics, but in academia, medicine, and entertainment.

"Ask successful corporate women what the key to their success is," says Estrich, "and first and foremost, they cite a record of always exceeding expectations. Because less is expected, more is required." Yet, she notes, these same women must appear to be so lighthearted, so *feminine,* that nobody feels threatened. The attempt to honor both modalities at once constitutes, says Estrich, a vise. "In seeking to make men comfortable," she adds, "women end up tightening that vise."[8]

In discussions of body image among adolescent girls and the related problems of anorexia and bulimia, the imagery of a vise is also frequently evoked. Young girls appear to be squeezed in the "vise" of drastically mixed messages where their personal appearance is concerned—messages that reflect exactly the same contradiction that their mothers and aunts are encountering in the workplace. The media give them unequivocal cues—look alluring, playful, and deliciously vulnerable. But that advice doesn't work well at all if they want to be taken seriously.

What's at stake in both instances is "social power"—not the power that comes from connection and internal grounding, but the influence that one can have over others just by approximating a certain highly desirable *look*. It seems significant in this regard that one of the risk factors for anorexia is being a member of a family that values achievement. High-achieving girls are the ones who tend to feel that vise most acutely when they're barely teenagers.

Once we recognize the dynamic of the supposed influx of women into professional worlds, it becomes much easier to understand why the formula "Add women and stir" has made so little difference. I've come to rephrase that formula, in fact, as the "false resurrection." Women are indeed brought into previously all-male environs, as law and good sense dictate, but once there they're pummeled with signals telling them that they absolutely do not belong. Women may enter the law firm, the Senate, the theological seminary, or the firehouse, but only if they set aside the very qualities and values they've been trained to embody. If they *don't* set them aside—if they wonder aloud about daycare, or worker morale, or low-grade communication skills—how seriously will they be taken, as lawyers, senators, theologians, or firefighters?

It's almost as if somebody who was in charge of keeping Enterprise culture in place realized that excluding women from all positions of influence wasn't necessary after all. As long as the basic structures of institutions didn't have to change, and as long as the values of Belonging were still understood to be too "womanish" to have relevance in the professional world, *actual* women need not be excluded—just the values traditionally associated with them. And the very process by which women make their way into that professional world is set up to disabuse them of the values associated with care and connection. They learn to act as if they despised them too.

And if, once they *have* arrived, they should have second thoughts—if once they've been initiated into "hardball" and "the real world" they should begin to wonder whether good law, good business, good medicine, or good theology is even possible in an environment dominated by zero-sum logic and unto-the-death competitiveness—what can they do?

Because even to raise such questions is to commit the worst of sins: it's to think "like a woman." Each step in that direction is a step toward being unseen and unheard—toward vanishing into the archetype "woman." Under the warrior code, women are barely perceived, except as the spoils of war.

Fortunately, a growing number of individuals are coming to see that the warrior culture isn't intrinsic to masculinity—that in fact it's just one way among many of *performing* masculinity. The maturation of anthropology as a field of study has strengthened immeasurably the work of those who would better understand the role that gender plays in our collective life. And as we'll see in the next section, a great many people who've never heard of the term "warrior culture" are nonetheless shaking free of that pervasive paradigm by building, within the web of their own most intimate relationships, their own kind of culture—quite literally a counterculture, however small.

Peeling Off Gender Straitjackets

In the course of trying to figure out what the underlying habits of thought are that keep women silenced and marginal, feminists came to realize how harmful those habits of thought are, ultimately, to everyone.

What began about forty years ago as the "women's liberation movement" and evolved into the "women's movement," and "feminism" would eventually give rise to "gender work" and "gender studies" carried out in almost every field from art history to wilderness management, and finally to "men's studies," the "men's movement," and the "study of masculinities."

With that gradual change a powerful truth has emerged: however much privilege men might enjoy within this culture of Enterprise, and however much power they wield in public spaces, they're not, as a group, faring well. Peering back now at that crucial period ten thousand years ago when women incurred such massive losses, we're able to make out that what happened to women happened also to men. The effects were different in form, but equally damaging.

My nephew Ben was probably five years old the afternoon something went seriously wrong at the neighborhood Boys and Girls Club, and he burst into tears.

"Hey, Ben," said one of the counselors (affectionately, it was later conceded), "boys don't cry!"

Ben stopped sobbing—briefly—gave him a long, leveling look, and said, "That's not true. My mom says boys *do* cry. And it's okay."

It isn't easy to intimidate someone who is whole—who isn't haunted by a sense of insufficiency or shame or need, and who can therefore listen politely to what's offered (or threatened) and pass. Ben is comfortable in his skin. Such people are notoriously hard to recruit.

It's fortunate for the brisk, forward march of Western civilization that the Bens of this world are rare. There have been ways all along to take ordinary people and persuade them, without putting it in so many words, that wholeness—simply being the person you are—isn't an option. Promoting highly contrastive models of gender—boys don't cry, girls don't yell—has been one of the more spectacularly effective means to do this. That's because while gender straitjackets don't actually fit much of anybody (they pinch in the shoulders, the sleeves are too long), no other kind of garment is generally available, so almost everybody is walking around feeling self-conscious, awkward, and inadequate, and that makes us all exceedingly malleable.

The working vocabulary of those who study gender can be arcane, but some of the terminology is apt and useful. Getting back to the question we asked above—for example, Why in this supposedly most liberal nation in the world are women still excluded from positions of real authority?—sociologist Sandra Bem offers much the same answer that anthropologists do; but by using the term "gender schemas," she helps us feel the full impact of rigid gender stereotypes on individuals.

By the time we reach adulthood, Bem believes, we've internalized from the surrounding culture narrowly defined ideas about what a man and a woman *ought to be*. She calls these definitions "gender schemas"[9]—lenses through which our impressions of the world and ourselves are filtered, lenses that show the world to be male-centered and, with respect to gender, absolutely polarized. (Remember "All-Around Sweetheart" versus "Very Best Thinker"?) Gender schemas lie so close to the core of personal identity, Bem believes, that they shape our most basic thoughts and feelings about "what is alien to the self and what is not alien."[10] In other words, great whole regions of ourselves might as well not even be there. A real man doesn't go *there*, and a real woman wouldn't want *that*. It doesn't matter if "there" or "that" constitutes the object of your deepest yearning; if it falls on the wrong side of the gender line, it's off-limits.

When we live in compliance with gender schemas, then, we live in disconnection from our selves, and that's painful enough in itself. But in doing that, we also deprive ourselves, as psychologist Judith V. Jordan warns us, of authentic connection with others. A sense of isolation can set in, along with "loss of clarity, loss of creativity, drop in self-worth and a deadening of the potential source of energy that can arise in real connection."[11]

Exactly. That's the beauty of gender straitjacketing with respect to the sort of institutions that fit the Enterprise paradigm. The energy that can arise in real connection, and the clarity and creativity that connection breeds, are the last things one would want people to experience in an economy that's set up to go on expanding indefinitely.

After all, people who feel isolated and disconnected from themselves and others are needy. Needy enough to accept sixty- to eighty-hour work weeks. Needy enough to believe that upgrading their sound system or computer or wardrobe will make them feel whole and adequate. As individuals, such people may be unhappy, but as dedicated consumers, they're the lifeblood of a growth economy. The gender empathy that Jordan advocates instead would pose a serious threat, because the energy that can rise in real connection is the stuff of revolution.

All of which is to say that gender schemas are intrinsic to the culture of Enterprise. They hold it in place.

So what exactly do gender schemas dictate for women and for men. What do those two generic garments look like?

No great surprises here.

At the core of the gender schema for women is the fact and idea of motherhood. Motherhood, or at the very least "motherliness," is the one form of identity that's unequivocally available to women *as* women. If one isn't born in a male body, one is already removed from "selfhood"; but if one is born female *and* doesn't become a mother, or at the very least act maternal in her relationships and demeanor, she may be very close indeed to the complete "nobodiness" to which Martin Luther King, Jr. referred.

Just as gender is fundamental to identity in Western culture, so too is motherhood fundamental to the reduced form of identity that's available for women. Even today, for all the progress women have made, it's tacitly understood that the intense mutuality associated with maternal relationships can make one unfit for full membership in the community of freestanding, individual selves. We're too easily bought, it would seem, and our judgment too easily influenced. All those hormone-laced feelings make patsies of us.

The core of the gender schema that dictates norms for masculinity in Enterprise culture would seem to be performance, but performance in a sense that makes it very close to combat. A man's identity has everything to do with his résumé: what he's done, what he can do, and even more to the point, what and whom he can master, beginning with himself. As young as four and five years old, boys learn that their own emotions are treacherous things that must be brought under strict control.

In the past this "armoring" hasn't introduced any serious contradictions in men's lives, because the script for boys and men has mirrored the script for society itself. In a nation that wants to be the single greatest world power, it's logically sound for its male citizens to want to be the most powerful or influential in their own sphere.

But today—and this is precisely because, as I said at the beginning of this chapter, our perceptions of our own tradition are changing—a great many men are feeling substantial pressure to move into the very areas they've been taught to shun like the plague. Asked as fathers especially, and partners too, to be more aware of what they're feeling, to express themselves more openly, to admit vulnerability, and to ask for directions, many men are declaring themselves to be in a double bind remarkably like the one women are in: "We can be the providers you want us to be; we can be strong—a wall against all contingencies. But we can't at the same time be 'in touch with our feelings.' The world isn't set up to let us be both."

Drawn as men might be to reclaiming "the missing half of who they are," each step they take in that direction threatens to awaken the fear of something very much like annihilation. Under Enterprise culture, mastery itself is so fundamental to male identity that the very idea of an ethos of mutuality and interdependence can prompt in men a kind of existential terror. I saw this terror clearly for the first time during a weekend workshop on gender and social change.

Sunlight filtered through old redwoods, warming the room where eighteen of us sat together feeling our way into some of the most sensitive issues we would be addressing. Darrell X, a therapist, had been complaining about what he saw as the separatism of feminists. Wasn't it time to move beyond the women's movement and start a new movement that would include both men and women and whose whole purpose would be to end "gender wars"?

Susan B, a prominent feminist educator and activist, well equipped to explain in concrete and vivid language why women are wary of appeals to set aside preoccupation with gender, and how easily "gender-free zones" can degenerate under the force of habit into the old, unquestioned, male-dominated hierarchies, took the question.

"Look, Darrell," she said. "We have a movement. It's called feminism, and men can belong. Men *do* belong. Women have never asked to dominate; they haven't wanted a 'gender war.' All they've ever asked for is equality in a context of social justice for everyone. Why don't you just join *our* movement?"

Darrell opened his mouth, but he didn't speak. He looked for a moment as if he were swallowing air; then finally (clearly stunned by what he heard himself admitting) he said, "I can't. I'm afraid that if I did I'd lose my voice. I'd . . . disappear."

For about a minute, nobody said a word. I know, though, that many of us were thinking the same thing, and with full sympathy—that the genuine fear Darrel had just expressed sounded and looked exactly like the fear so many women feel on the threshold of a professional enclave run by men: "I could vanish in there."

Seeing firsthand how threatened a man can feel at the idea of moving into territory that looks to be "female" didn't just tell us something about Darrell. It told us, too, why so few effective resistance movements have sprung up to fight the serious encroachments on democracy and community and agency that are taking place today. The values that underlie reform politics are all but identical with the values of Belonging. Concern with relationships, "both/and" thinking, sensitivity to the environment, voluntary simplicity, playfulness, nonviolence—these aren't the values of Enterprise culture, and the man who publicly identifies himself with them knows that he risks a great deal.

The loss of voice that Darrell feared, were he to "come over" to feminism and publicly advocate values such as inclusiveness and mutuality, was in fact a loss of the unequivocally masculine voice that he knows very well to be the only one that gets heard.

The double bind that excludes women and the values they're assigned to carry from corporate culture appears to work just as effectively to keep many men from playing a more active role than they do in progressive politics.

There's something almost diabolically clever about it. No wonder we're so immobilized; no wonder mutual accusations fly; no wonder it all feels so complicated.

RETHINKING RELIGION

In Chapter Seven, I suggested that when the values of Belonging lost the primary position they'd held while our ancestors were still hunter-gatherers, they were in effect parceled out: certain values would be in the custody of women, while others would be within the purview of priests, rabbis, and pastors. "Religion," as a separate category of human experience, came into existence at that time, and so did a whole new kind of institution.

Organized religions have mirrored, in many ways, the secular institutions that govern political, economic, diplomatic, and military affairs—especially insofar as, with a very few exceptions, they've been strongly hierarchic and run entirely by men. And they've been useful to secular institutions as well.

But there have always been crucial differences between the two kinds of institution—secular versus religious—and those differences have weighed as heavily on the men who have charge of the religious sphere as they have on the women who've been oppressed within it. Because from the Axial Age on, anyway, certain of the values intrinsic to the major Western religions—especially to Judaism and to Christianity in its various forms—aren't at all friendly to Enterprise. They're not the values that have driven Western civilization along its trajectory of expansion and exploitation. They're not the values of the heroes of Western civilization.

Such is the position of religion in the hierarchy of Western ideas that when we say that someone or something is religious, we commonly mean—or are taken to mean—that the person is religious *as opposed to rational,* or religious *as opposed to objective,* or religious *as opposed to scientific, practical,* or *pragmatic*—and therefore irrelevant to the chambers where political, military, or economic deliberations take place. So it is that values intrinsic to the Judeo-Christian tradition—among them, self-restraint, mutuality, nonviolence, and intuitive or mystical modes of knowing—are effectively quarantined.

Hence the anguish of men whose job description or conscience requires that they advocate these values publicly. Their own manliness comes into question when they do, and in a culture that values masculinity as highly as ours does, that's a serious matter. Priest, pastor, and rabbi can spend the better part of their lives in the double bind I described above, trapped between two value systems that seem almost mutually exclusive.

Every religion takes shape within a particular culture and invariably carries along in its current all kinds of detritus from that culture. The historic religions of the West took shape in a cultural context that valued certain kinds of relationships and certain roles almost exclusively. Those relationships and roles were idealized in the religions themselves.

I'm thinking in particular of the paternal relationship and the heroic mode here—and of a Sunday morning in the Midwest when the full poignancy of the male religious leader's position really came home to me.

I'd given a weekend workshop at a large, urban Protestant church in Ohio, and before leaving I attended the regular Sunday morning service. I hadn't met the pastor yet, but the members of his congregation were so open-minded, smart, and genuine that I was fully prepared to like him. And I did. At least, I very much liked the way he conducted the service.

This happened to be baptism Sunday, and the front row was filled with young parents holding babies in long white christening gowns. As each little cluster came to the front, Reverend W. took the baby and, with great tenderness, held her up and introduced her to the congregation, promising as he did so that her spiritual family would support and cherish her. He took his time, he had something a little bit different to say with each family, he was witty, and not a single baby cried. It was very impressive.

The baptisms took maybe half an hour, and when they were over Reverend W. went to a chair at the side and sat down while the choir came up to sing. He wasn't visible to the congregation at this point, but as a guest I'd been seated on a pew at the front from which I could see him clearly—could see him almost collapse into the chair (fatigued, it was obvious, down to his toenails).

He barely moved for the next fifteen minutes while a series of announcements were made. His eyes were closed and his jaw slack.

And I realized, finally, what should have been obvious. He'd been working hard up there, turning in the best performance he could in a state of utter exhaustion—a state that was probably the fruit of round-the-clock meetings: fundraising, membership drives, food drives, homeless advocacy, confirmation classes . . . the endless duties of the committed religious professional. Baptizing those babies had taken its toll, and he still had the sermon to give. When he *did* give the sermon, just a few minutes later, it had to do with stewardship and our responsibility to share what we have.

The sermon was lively, and while he spoke Reverend W. looked, again, as if he were enjoying himself. A couple of times I thought I glimpsed the boy he'd probably been, enthralled in his New Testament class, dazzled by the intricacies of patristic theology, concluding therefore that he was destined for the clergy.

For a few months I carried around the memory of this fine middle-aged man, slumped in his chair where his flock couldn't see him, and at last I realized what it was telling me:

The creation of a special enclave wherein religious values could be celebrated had indeed allowed the values of Belonging to be perpetuated. But at the same time, because the culture itself was shaped so pervasively by Enterprise values and assumptions, those enclaves can't help but mirror secular institutions, and the men who run them can't help but emulate the "warriors" that flourish in those institutions. They really *can't* help it, because they're working from the only model available. So if a man is assigned to a big neighborhood church, he works himself into the ground on its behalf in exactly the way his corporate counterpart does. He might think wistfully about the daily prayers he had time for in seminary, but that was then.

Another weekend, another workshop, this one with a group of ministers' wives. We weren't half an hour into our first conversation when someone asked whether anybody else's husband seemed to be overly anxious about the size of his congregation. They'd been transferred recently, she said, and her husband's new congregation was smaller than the old one. There was a silence, everyone looked at the floor, and then one of the older women asked gently, perfectly deadpan, "Are you talking about . . . parish envy?"

With so many of us having grown up thinking that religion is churches and food drives and hardworking clergy, the very real pathologies concealed in that model don't leap out at us. Maybe we begin to see them only when we've been exposed to radically different ideas about what it means to seek out the sacred. Today, as never before, we have access to such ideas.

For example, there's the testimony of certain great religious figures (Christian, Hindu, Buddhist, and otherwise) that it's possible to experience God directly, and without waiting for an afterlife; that God isn't angry with you and nobody needs to intercede with Him on your behalf; that certainly nobody needs to die for your sins. The great obstacle to seeing God, these individuals tell us, is the illusion of separateness, and there are time-tested ways in which one can dispel that illusion.

These arguments might not persuade us on their own, but something about the religious figures themselves, or accounts of their lives, might give their testimony weight. And once we hear their message— once their alternative ways of looking at things take hold of our imagination—we find it difficult in the extreme to grasp why God wouldn't want to show us His face until a heroic man whom He loved dearly had died on our behalf.

As we learned earlier, readiness to die in defense of one's kin is seen not only in human males, but in primate males as well. If there's any one quality that distinguishes "the male of the species" from the female, it might be this: two parts nobility, and one part (I speak as the mother of a son) goofball recklessness. Something in their very mitochondria knows that males are more expendable to the survival of the species than females, and they act accordingly.

But by seizing upon the motif of the dying hero and making it into the highest religious symbol—a relatively late development in early Christology—Christian theologians actually strengthened the hold of warrior imagery and made it seem sound, universal, and supremely good, when in fact neither sacrificial death nor sacrificial exhaustion resonates powerfully outside the framework of the warrior code that characterizes Enterprise culture.

For weeks after my Ohio epiphany I had exhausted men on the

brain. I saw them everywhere. I even remembered a related story about Francis of Assisi, who came late in his life to his beloved friend Clare, dead-weary, and asked her whether she thought he couldn't come in off the road now and spend his remaining years in contemplative prayer. He was increasingly troubled at what had become of his movement because it had ceased to be just a movement and was fast on its way to becoming an institution. (Membership drives. Fundraising. Homeless advocacy.)

Francis trusted Clare's intuition and the depth of her prayer. She withdrew for a while to think about his question, and when she came back she said no, it wasn't to be. His calling in this life was to go on being the itinerant preacher he'd been. And of course he did—but in his last months he had himself carried to a little hut outside her convent, and it was there that he composed those final verses to Sister Bodily Death.

And I thought of Michelangelo's *Pieta*. Of Mary holding across her lap the body of Christ crucified—her solidity and encompassing embrace, and his utter depletion.

And in those two images—Francis dying as near to Clare as their vows would permit, and Christ dying across Mary's lap—it seemed to me that at least the motif completed itself. The other half of the performing, heroic male, dying "on behalf" of others is woman as earth itself, receiving and containing her sons.

When certain patristic scholars placed the emphasis they did on Jesus' death by crucifixion, they must have known that men shaped by militarism would respond powerfully to the archetype of the dying warrior. But in evoking that archetype, they also evoked, tacitly, its other half. For with respect to the dying hero—friend, son, father, brother—all women would be, and always have been, *like Mary*. We're there—wordless, tender, sheltering, and (it goes almost without saying) absolutely uncritical—to catch them when they fall. Exactly what women are expected to be in cultures of Enterprise.

I love the stories of Francis and Clare and love the *Pieta*, and I embrace wholly the archetypal content of both. But there are so many more stories, so many more models, and in particular so many more ways to be male and female. The idea that men exist to perform—that they act tirelessly on behalf of their "flock," that they speak eloquently while women serve in silence, and that they die at their battle stations—is the stuff of stirring tales. But it's not the *only* model for spiritual awareness or for spiritual leadership. The archetype of the heroic male, dying for his people (or counting his life meaningless if he doesn't), is no longer one with which all of us feel entirely satisfied. We've seen too many of the side effects: depression, addiction, self-destructiveness, inability to sustain relationships, and perhaps worst of all, cycles of abuse and predation passed down through the father-line and beyond.

The image of the spiritual teacher as compelling speaker can be problematic, too: the orator seated on a raised platform, faces upturned expectantly while he utters memorable words. A fine preacher is a joy to hear. Yet one guesses that the most memorable times Jesus's disciples spent with him were filled with deep, companionable silence. Extrapolating from what we know now about other great spiritual teachers, we suspect that Jesus spoke rather sparingly, reluctant (as the Balinese are) to "hold forth" at great length, and just as inclined to teach by osmosis—*not* so much through what he said *or* did, but by who he was: tender, and sheltering. Solid, like the earth.

If he *did* favor the more indirect sort of teaching—if he believed that spiritual wisdom is contagious and is not so much taught as caught—would that have made him "feminine?"

Collectively, we're ready for other storylines, other kinds of hero, better images of God—and they're all beginning to surface.

The models of religious life and thought that have been most compatible with Enterprise culture are breaking down, not so much under the pressure of external criticism as by displacement. Vibrant new models are pushing upward—models that reflect with amazing consistency the full constellation of Belonging values. One of these models is emerging in the writings of Sister Ivone Gebara.

Sister Gebara is a nun of the Brazilian Sisters of Our Lady (Canonesses of St. Augustine), and by her own designation she's an ecofeminist. She's also a prominent theologian who lives and works among Brazil's urban poor. Her unusual theological positions won her an official two-year silencing by the Vatican—a measure that clearly didn't alter her course substantially, because in her latest book, *Longing for Running Water,* she writes that "God is relatedness."[12] In effect, she does for religion what others have proposed should be done for political theory: place interdependence at its center. More than that, she quietly walks away from the language and imagery of an anthropomorphic God.

Confidently, drawing as heavily upon the life she shares with Brazil's most destitute as on her own extensive training as a Catholic theologian, Ivone Gebara maintains that relatedness is the primary reality. "It is constitutive of all beings. It is more elementary than awareness of differences or than autonomy, individuality, or freedom."[13]

One minute she writes in the abstract language dear to scholars, and in the next, glowingly, and echoing indigenous mythologies, she invokes the imagery of weaving: "It is the underlying fabric that is continually brought forth within the vital process in which we are immersed. Its interwoven fibers do not exist separately, but only in perfect reciprocity with one another—in space, in time, in origin and into the future."

Relatedness, she insists, shouldn't be confused with moral goodness. "Rather, it points to *the vital power of the interconnection among all things,* independent of any anthropological or ethical judgment we might make about them" (italics added).

What is being rediscovered and reclaimed, by Gebara and a great many others, is the vital power of relatedness—a reading of power itself that challenges the model of dominion and celebrates instead the magnificence of living systems, of all beings as conduits through which the life-force can pass, gathering strength as it goes.

IN CONCLUSION

As one traces out across time the complicated relationship between the values of Belonging and the values of Enterprise, certain patterns emerge. In particular, we see the effective ways in which the yeasty, transformative powers inherent in the values of Belonging are checked and capped by deeply ingrained definitions—not just gender schemas, but religious and philosophical and political schemas as well. These would include the insistence that full selfhood presumes autonomy, that rationality is superior to all other modes of knowing, and that (for the most part, in most situations) there *is* no middle ground.

The persistence with which I've kept coming back in this chapter to considerations of gender might seem to fly in the face of my having argued earlier that the "gender wars" are more about values than gender. The fact is, though, that rigid gender stereotypes have been a bulwark of Enterprise culture since its beginning. They're of a piece with the values themselves, and not a day passes when one headline news story or another doesn't make that relationship abundantly clear. I want to offer just one recent example, because I think it will allow me to clarify the place of gender in this discussion of values.

In January 2002, over two hundred world religious leaders met in Assisi at the invitation of Pope John Paul II to discuss violence. The participants agreed, and stated forcefully, that invoking God's name to rationalize killing someone is absolutely not acceptable.

In fact, many of these same leaders have met on other occasions and issued impassioned statements condemning corporate greed, environmental degradation, racial and religious prejudice, and more.

And whenever they do, I always wish that I could be more buoyed. Because what I hear now in those proclamations is an immense, ringing hollowness—a determined refusal to take a systemic look at the ills in question. When we even begin to take that kind of look it becomes obvious that, like corporate greed and environmental irresponsibility, state violence finds its rationale in a particular set of values—Enterprise values such as disconnection from the earth and other living creatures, chronic abstractedness, acquisitiveness, and recklessness. It isn't an enormous leap from that recognition to the understanding that the "seed thought" for all of these values is the notion, or meme, of dominion. And it's an even shorter leap to the realization that the idea of dominion is validated everywhere with reference to the essential "rightness" of man's dominion over woman.

We can be unequivocal on this point: no institution whose governance excludes women can pretend that it's not perpetuating and even sanctifying the idea of dominion in all of its forms. No institution should dare call publicly for an end to poverty or violence or ecological insanity that hasn't first addressed the bedrock reality of sexism within its own structures. If world religious leaders want to be taken seriously in their opposition to state violence, they have to renounce the presumption that women aren't fully human.

They have to make sure, at the very least, that more women will be invited to the next conference than the two dozen that were present at the last one.

So yes, in a sense, we've come full circle. Even as we conclude that "it isn't about gender but about values," we're compelled to recognize that the values of Belonging can't be rehabilitated unless women are too.

The corollary of that recognition is the knowledge that if the values of Belonging don't come into favor, the best that women can hope for is the "false resurrection" described above: they may enter the innermost circles of professional privilege, but only on the condition that they check at the door certain values by which they may well have defined themselves.

Behind this symmetrical stalemate, though, we can catch glimpses of a thrilling new possibility or paradigm. It has to do with the emergence of "religiousness" stripped of the overlay of Enterprise culture. It has to do with women, fully included, fully voiced, fully honored. And it has to do with men walking away by choice from the myth of the sacrifial warrior.

When those three pieces are in hand, we will be looking at something very like the Gundestrup Cauldron, reassembled and charged with transformative power.

PART IV

All of a Piece

CHAPTER 12

Reclaiming Balance and Wholeness

In this final chapter I want to reflect on the possibility I raised at the very beginning of this book: that we might effectively revisit the period ten thousand years ago when the values of Belonging were set aside, and that we might rehabilitate them. Can we imagine, and then build, a civilization that doesn't occlude one of its two eyes?

It will be immeasurably more difficult to do this than it was to launch Western civilization in the first place, because that earlier process wasn't a matter of deliberate choice at all. My recurring use of words such as "decision" has of course been euphemistic, because while the Agricultural Revolution was gradual and spontaneous, the new revolution will have to happen at a good pace, quite deliberately, and it will have to draw on virtually everything that our inventive and inquisitive Enterprise past has taught us.

But suppose that we really are wise enough and brave and resourceful enough to accomplish the melding of our two value systems that our ancestors did not. What would an ethos look like that honored the exuberant, innovative impulses of Enterprise (even while curbing Enterprise's inclination toward dominance and exploitation) but never, ever lost sight of the deep, earth-centered wisdom of Belonging?

In certain respects, it would look very much like the combined agendas of a great many people who've never heard of either Belonging or Enterprise: environmentalists; advocates for children, the homeless, the disabled, and campaign finance reform; feminists; peace workers; artists, educators, and civil rights activists—at the very least. The specific programs that would arise out of our new paradigm are fairly predictable, in the light of everything that's already been said about the values of Belonging.

But I referred to "*combined* agendas" quite deliberately. Special-interest groups tend to focus on one Belonging value only: while environmentalists work to reinstate connection to the earth, for example, other activists focus on mutuality or nonviolent conflict resolution. And yet, once one has understood that the values of Belonging are more like atoms in a molecule than beads on a string, it's clear that none of them can be celebrated or reclaimed meaningfully independent of the others. These values don't make competing claims on us; and when we behave as if they did, we lose whatever gains we think we've made. Thus the capacity to understand the interconnectedness of these values is crucial to bringing about the changes at issue here.

The alliance of Belonging and Enterprise must part from progressive programs of the past in another crucial way: difference itself—and that includes the specific differences between advocates of Belonging values and advocates of Enterprise values—must not be seen as synonymous with division, nor can it be allowed to be a rationale for dominance. If this final chapter has a single theme, it's this: the intention this time out must be to acknowledge and balance the competing claims that the values of Belonging and Enterprise have on every one of us.

In other words, the absolutely all-important key to bringing Belonging and Enterprise into equilibrium is the spirit in which we approach difference itself and the particular issues that would seem to divide us.

One reason that the values of Belonging have been eclipsed so easily and regularly over time is that the advocates of those values, the people for whom they're second nature, don't tend to be comfortable or effective in highly combative situations. Strategic thinking and combat-readiness are foreign to Belonging cultures. Historically, hunter-gatherers simply lived out their values, without straining themselves tremendously to put them into words—let alone to turn them into ideologies that would then have to be promoted and/or defended. They could define their values through action alone precisely because their cultures existed at a certain comfortable distance from one another.

Unfortunately, therefore, those who are most instinctively affiliated with the values of Belonging tend to walk away when things heat up, handing over unresistingly whatever power they hold. If they do try to organize and stand their ground, their alliances are rarely strong enough to stand up under pressure. Formation of political alliances is, after all, quintessentially Enterprise. Divided against each other—cleverly, be it admitted, by people who are very good at this—they fall apart.

Ironically, compromise is often too much for the advocates of Belonging culture. Ordinary inexperience and a rigid hold on their ideals often combine to unfit them for the fine art of negotiation.

The life and work of Mahatma Gandhi is the best possible antidote to all these Belonging tendencies. Gandhi never confused spirituality with passivity. He tried never to let the Free India movement be divided by class or religious affiliation or gender. And he was not only an arch-idealist, he was also a master of compromise—not in the sense of cutting his losses and accepting whatever small advantage he could get by caving in, but in the sense of energetically and often very affectionately working *toward* his opponent, looking tirelessly for a way that the two could think and act "as one" in however limited a capacity (almost as if that fleeting experience of interpersonal unity were more important than the issue at hand).

If any one individual embodies the integration of Belonging values with the first-phase values of Enterprise (before the will to control kicks in), and is thus a useful point of reference for this inquiry, it's surely Gandhi: innovative, experimental, curious, unbelievably hard-working, and a risk-taker par excellence! Grounded as he was in India's timeless spiritual tradition, he was nonetheless altogether modern as well.

I want for the remainder of this chapter to reflect more tangibly on the look and feel of what we could appropriately call an entirely new paradigm. We'll identify certain programs that are already in the works and look at the entrenched habits of thought they challenge. We'll think about the difference between "top-down" and "bubble-up" models for change, and about the power of individuals and "dyads" of every kind. Along the way, we'll consider the rich reservoir of insight and inspiration that traditional cultures of Belonging make available to us—in ceremony, myth, and artistry.

Eating Our Cake, and Having It Too

As we've seen in looking at the values of Enterprise, the problem they pose lies less with the values themselves than with the habits of thought that give rise to them—specifically, dichotomous either-or thinking (which in turn leads to zero-sum styles of negotiation and rationalizes violence) and infatuation with hierarchies, abstractions, and dominance.

For example, under Enterprise logic the use of law to resolve differences tends to result in litigation. Each party hires the best lawyer it can afford, and they engage in something rather like a medieval tourney. One party leaves the courtroom satisfied; the other, defeated.

My friend Kate Nowell was a good litigator. But by and by she wearied of the process. She found it particularly unproductive where family law was concerned, and so she began to look for a better way to go about things. Mediation law was definitely a better way, and she did that for years, spending less and less of her time in courtrooms, vastly relieved that the divorces she handled were far less bitter and acrimonious.

But then she went a step further, to something called "collaborative law," and now she feels as if she's finally come home, both professionally and spiritually. Not a paragraph of her extensive knowledge of the law is wasted, but the human context around what she's doing is finally coherent.

In a divorce, for example, that's worked out through collaborative law, the two parties and their attorneys are committed to resolving their differences in a series of meetings without going to court. In fact, if the process should break down and go into litigation, both lawyers must withdraw. Thus neither of them stands to gain from litigating. The emphasis is on cooperative strategies instead of adversarial techniques and on the use of the sort of skills lawyers rarely get to use in litigation law, such as the imaginative generation of options and the creation of a positive atmosphere. Mutual respect and sensitivity to everyone's needs is the hallmark of the process.

Collaborative law can allow a marriage to be dissolved in a timely fashion, and with far less financial impact than a litigated divorce, but it still gives both parties the help of an attorney. Best of all, though, by sharply reducing levels of animosity, it places any children who are involved in a far better position. In fact, it was out of concern for the children of divorce that collaborative law was initiated in the first place.

"I can't begin to tell you the difference," Kate told me. "When one of these divorces is settled, you'll typically see everyone embracing everyone else (and we all *mean* it), and it isn't unusual for someone to open a bottle of champagne. That never happens in a litigated divorce!"

So all right, this brave new world we're designing can include lawyers. What about farmers? Are agriculturists always and necessarily "waging war" on the environment? Can they meet the food needs of all six billion people in the world without harming the biosphere irreparably?

Organic farmers insist that we can, and they have the data to prove it. The organic gardening and farming movement is alive and well.

I'm thinking, for example, of the two-acre garden my friend Steve manages (with the rest of us pitching in sporadically), whose diversity goes way beyond the kale, cauliflower, chard, green beans, and other produce it puts on our table almost year round. In and around the vegetable beds, flowers and herbs are planted that attract butterflies, repel gophers, ward off flu, strengthen the soil, gladden the eye, and infuse a headily fragrant moisturizing cream called Moonflowers. The garden is dense through spring and summer with life-forms, color, the hum of bees, and the low whistling of quail working their way along the raised beds eating insects. All the vegetable waste goes into a compost heap, and out of that heap comes heat and nourishment for the plants. Nearby is a pile of commingled sawdust and horse manure from a local stable. Strategic placement on that pile of a straw hat, gloves, ancient boots, and sunglasses startles for a split second: Manure Man?

Organic gardens generate meaning and metaphor as well as food, and they do wonders to break down Cartesian dualities. They teach us that species are interdependent, that there's no such thing as a "waste product," and that some years are just better than others—for tomatoes, peppers, sweet corn . . . and snails.

For some people, organic gardens are places to heal.

Just two hills over from Steve's garden is Saint Anthony Farm, an offshoot of the Franciscan Saint Anthony Foundation, whose soup kitchen in San Francisco serves more than two thousand meals a day. The farm is primarily a dairy operation, though it has a garden that provides vegetables and fruit for the people who live there. The men and women who work the farm—forty-three live there at a time— are participants in drug and alcohol recovery programs, and they typically stay for four to six months.

The garden has been organic since it was first planted, in 1993, but the dairy operation became completely organic only a couple of years ago, after some of the foundation directors decided that Saint Francis probably would have been pretty keen on biodynamic gardening.

What nobody anticipated was the impact that the adoption of organic farming methods would have on the men and women who live and work at Saint Anthony. Spending time outdoors, taking care of the cows, feeling productive, supporting one another—these benefits have been clear all along. But these days participants speak of something even more powerful. Working the land the way they are now, seeing the soil itself get richer and stronger, eating organic food themselves and knowing that the milk from the dairy is free of chemicals and growth hormones—all of this seems to deepen and amplify their own healing process, connecting them viscerally to the land itself.

Enterprise cultures keep things in boxes. They prefer to regard food production, environmental health, and education, for example, as separate concerns. So it is that we end up with factory farms that use limited resources irresponsibly; with vast wilderness areas set aside in certain states where we can camp in the summer; and with high schools dedicated single-mindedly to raising students' SAT scores.

But if one is inclined habitually to think in terms of whole systems, and of human beings embedded in local ecosystems, strikingly different arrangements fall into place—as they have at Casa Grande High School in Petaluma, California where students are simultaneously healing habitats, producing food, and learning life sciences in the most vivid, hands-on ways you can imagine.

Twenty years ago Adobe Creek, which had been the main source of drinking water when the Petaluma Valley was first settled, was seven miles of choked-up, lifeless desolation. The city had diverted one hundred percent of its water to city reservoirs, and the creek itself, an embarrassing nuisance by now, was about to be put underground in a cement pipe. The lower five miles of the creek had no riparian habitat whatsoever. The Adobe Creek steelhead trout that had spawned there in the past were almost extinct, and the Chinook salmon were only rarely spotted.

Enter the students of biology teacher Tom Furrer, stirred to do something, convinced that they could. As the United Anglers, they would over the next thirteen years restore the entire seven miles of Adobe Creek to its pristine state. They would plant 1,100 trees a year on the creek's banks, rebuilding a riparian environment supportive of all kinds of wildlife. And the wildlife would heed the invitation: in 1995, sixty-four steelhead returned to spawn. The students also raised over half a million dollars to build a state-of-the-art conservation hatchery and fisheries research facility on the Casa Grande campus, which they run entirely by themselves in consultation with scientists at nearby Bodega Marine Laboratories. The purpose of their work is to protect biodiversity and genetic variability.

During January 2002, heavy rainstorms raised the level of some of the local creeks so high that they flooded fields. A number of salmon that had been coming up the creeks to spawn were trapped in shallow puddles when the water receded. Someone spotted the fish flopping helplessly in the water and called Casa. The students showed up promptly, equipped to carry out a successful rescue operation, and a few weeks later stories appeared in local papers detailing the manner in which the eggs of the rescued salmon had been hatched and the care that the "fingerling" salmon were receiving now at the school facility.

Big dreams for high school kids—and the fact that they carried them through so brilliantly has been a huge inspiration for the town. Students who graduated ten and fifteen years ago come back every year to visit the hatchery, and they speak of their experience there as life-changing.

FIXING THE WORLD

The sobering truth about the far-reaching redirection of Western civilization that's proposed here is that it will draw anyone who cares about it into one protracted conflict after another. There's just no getting around it. I doubt whether Casa's fish hatchery got approved without a few acerbic school board meetings. As Ben Franklin said, democracy is an invitation to struggle.

The task is immense, and it's going to take more than computer simulations to complete it. Traditional societies have their own approach to "balancing" or "fixing" the world, and I suspect that they have something to teach us.

Jump Dance, for instance, is performed every two years in a village near the Klamath River in Northern California. It takes place over ten days following September's full moon, and it brings together the members of two tribes that have lived adjacent to one another for as long as anyone knows.

Jump Dance addresses the sort of differences that arise and accumulate between human beings wherever two or more of us gather together over time. But the reason it's so powerful, I believe, is that it also, more fundamentally, addresses difference itself.

The conflicts that the Yurok and Hupa dance to resolve aren't abstract; they're contemporary, raw, and complex. They concern land use, for instance, and water rights, preservation of native traditions, and religious differences (for some of them are Christian)—the issues that human beings have always come to blows over. And yet the singing and dancing don't address specific issues directly or explicitly.

The ceremony itself is extremely arduous. Male dancers representing two "sides"—seen to be both complementary and competing—take turns dancing in a partly subterranean pit. Many of the younger men fast and thirst and barely sleep the whole time. Two lead singers perform in the middle, "bound together," as anthropologist Thomas Buckley observes, "by a rock-steady chorus of men ranged symmetrically beside the singers, forming a line."[1]

The ceremony is carried out with the sense that it has to work. The various tensions that have divided people against one another must be transformed into a collective yearning for unity, and then, for even the briefest moment, that unity must be experienced by everyone present. No one expects it to go on forever—just a taste is considered enough.

While the dance is going on, hundreds and even thousands of people gather to participate and observe, and in the two camps the women of the two "sides" feed them all—and feed them well. Even as Jump Dance is going on, with no reference to the specific issues that might be of concern that year, the camps themselves are the sites of lively discussion. So it isn't that ceremony *replaces* debate: both modalities have their function.

As the ceremony enters its last days, the number of dancers and singers increases, and the most ancient and beautiful regalia are brought out and displayed in the dance.

On the last day, the men in the pit are joined by young women, and finally all of the dancers from both sides join together; and if the two lead singers are very, very good, the songs move from unison to perfect harmony. And for just that moment, everyone present feels a falling away of differences and a mysterious sense of wholeness and balance.

Through the intensity of their engagement and their longing, they have, however briefly, "fixed the world."

Buckley describes the climactic moment of the 1990 dance, on the tenth day, when the early September heat broke and both sides danced together, raising their medicine baskets in union: "Spectators said later a great spiritual force rose from the pit to hang in the sky above. People were happy (and perhaps relieved) as they went off to feast and talk in the two camps. 'If we can get through the dance we can get through the next two years,' they said."[2]

Politics is Jump Dance, one informant told Buckley. And Jump Dance is politics.

The beauty of Jump Dance, from what I can gather, is that it doesn't pretend that one side is right and the other wrong. The burning question is simply: How can we transcend separateness? And the answer appears to be that every one of us must want mutual understanding so much that we'll work as hard for it as we work to stay on our feet and keep singing during the ten days of the dance. That's why the ceremony seems to me to have such universal significance.

And because that desire for mutual understanding is so strong, Jump Dance participants carry their moment of unity with them for the next two years, knowing that difference itself—and the many tribal differences they face routinely—will never go away.

"The Seeds of the New Within in the Shell of the Old"

Sociologist, Quaker, peace activist, and feminist Elise Boulding has spent a considerable part of her life looking at conflict and conflict resolution, and in her recent book *Cultures of Peace,* she notes the existence of two fundamentally different approaches to bringing about social change. The two correspond so closely with the cultures of Enterprise and Belonging that I want to introduce them here by way of reminding us that even as one is trying to reinstate the values of Belonging, the methods and assumptions of Enterprise can take over and sabotage the whole project.

Boulding distinguishes "between the desire for central control and the recognition that locality has its own competence; between the desire to destroy all traces of oppressive structures and wipe the slate clean before beginning anew and the impulse to nurture the seeds of the new within the shell of the old, trusting that gentleness, not violence, will free the goodness in humans."[3]

It's clear enough what Boulding's own preference is, and everything we've learned about the culture of Belonging supports her. If the reader will recall, anthropologists have noted the presence in tribal societies of two very different spiritual orientations—one sacralizing the earth's natural regenerative forces, the other locating God in the heavens and attributing "magic tricks" to Him. Much would seem to hang on whether we're more interested in lasting transformation that takes place from the inside out, by slow degrees, or the kind that's wrought from outside, abruptly, via lightning bolts or celestial visitors in thin disguise. Contemporary cultures of Enterprise tend to prefer the "magic" of the techno-fix.

The scenario for change that's most in keeping with the values of Belonging is the kind that begins at the grass roots—or maybe "in the streambed" is the better metaphor—with the individual who takes responsibility for the quality of her own life and thoughts. It isn't all that different from restoring Adobe Creek.

IT BEGINS RIGHT HERE

"Feet hip-width apart," she'd said. But how wide was that, really?

As I struggled with the posture called "downward-facing dog," my yoga teacher came by and made a couple of simple adjustments. She moved my feet back a few inches, and then she had me spread my toes, grip the ground with them, push my palms *hard* into the mat ("Not the fingertips, the *palms!*"), and elongate my spine. And suddenly, *Wow!* Something was tingling in the soles of my feet, my palms, along the length of my spine—something that felt like nothing so much as intelligence. This had to be *whole-body knowing.*

The beauty of working with the whole catalog of Belonging values is that small epiphanies such as my yoga moment start to take place all the time. You begin to see them for what they are, and you begin to recognize all the junctures in your daily life where you can either embrace the values or sidle on past. The process isn't completely pleasant, because going along on automatic is no longer an option. To make things harder still, the connections *between* the values can no longer be ignored. I no longer get to pretend I'm nonviolent and still drive my car into town every time I feel like it.

But I love working with the full repertoire of Belonging values. It gives shape and substance to my vaguer good intentions. For instance, I've always thought in a general way that it would be a good thing to know more about the wildlife in my area, but I've never been motivated enough to start. But I understand now that the knowledge that each of us has of the particular place where we live (or where we feel most solidly embedded, if you will) is our point of entry into our relationship to the whole of the earth and its welfare.

I see my responsibility more and more now in terms of resistance. Can I become strong enough to resist the subtle, incessant pressures that Enterprise culture imposes on me—the pressure, for example, to move so fast that I don't have time for relationships? That kind of resistance begins with deciding what kind of thoughts I'm willing to entertain. And to resist at that level one really has to get serious about a meditative practice.

AWOL FROM THE WARRIOR CULTURE

To be held in the matrix of a sound relationship—lover, spouse, friend, parent, child (*any* solid trusting connection, really)—is to have a powerful measure of resistance to the memes of Enterprise.

My friends Paul and Sarah are British citizens who've lived and worked for decades in Belgium, she with a consulting firm, he with an oil company. His company was bought out a while back, and in the restructuring Paul lost the exceedingly demanding position that he'd held for maybe twenty years. He began almost immediately to send out his résumé, but Sarah stopped him.

They're both in their fifties, their two kids are nearly through university, Sarah's job pays very well, and Paul's severance package had been generous.

"Do you really want to do this?" she asked him. "Because you know, you don't *have* to. We've got plenty of money. I could cut back too, and I'd like to. Why don't you take some time?"

He looked at her a little blankly, she recalls, and then excused himself and went to bed. He slept for the better part of several days; and when they finally sat down together again over tea, he looked over at her and said almost wonderingly, "You know, I've never liked my work."

That was about a year ago, and by now Paul is beginning to get a feel for what he *does* like to do. His future is looking rather bright after all.

But imagine—here was this guy, immensely gifted and relational, who'd given himself over body and soul to a job he'd never enjoyed, a job that had had very little value for him, and he'd never even allowed himself to *acknowledge* that mismatch before.

Such is the hold of the warrior ethos. But my reason for recalling Paul's story now isn't to again belabor my thoughts on exhausted men, but to say that it was because he was safely held in the transformative space of a deeply loving relationship that he could finally start to unwind. (We might note, too, that Sarah's being well paid for what she does is part of why this whole thing worked. Paradoxically, the most liberating thing that could happen for a great many men would be for women to start receiving the wages they deserve.)

It may be a long, long while before we see lasting, healthy change in either politics or the professional world. But at the more intimate level, there *is* movement, and there's room for even more. "Every important relationship," writes psychiatrist Jean Shinoda Bolen, "is a universe of two. Even though there are two people in it, you are either in a circle or a hierarchy."[4] It's in our personal relationships, then, that we can most effectively begin to unlearn the habit of dominating or of allowing ourselves to be dominated—controlled not just by other people, but by other people's ideas of who we ought to be. There are ways of going about being a family that give rise to a kind of alternative reality, within which the unspoken rules of an Enterprise-driven society get suspended—a space where the near-desperate attachment to material success (which makes for gender hostility) can be nudged aside by another kind of desire.

In her recent book *Flux: Living in a Half-Changed World,* Peggy Orenstein interviewed married couples in their early thirties to see how they were doing in a world where, as many have put it, "half a revolution" has taken place. The couples Orenstein interviewed who were most satisfied with the overall balance of their lives had certain things in common. The wives earned at least half of their family's income. The husbands had jobs that were flexible enough to let them do the same things women typically do (handle emergencies, stay home with sick kids, and in general devote more time to family life); and because they were able to take on these family responsibilities, the husbands developed—this was perhaps the real watershed—their own parental style and authority.[5]

Often such arrangements fall into place because something unexpected happens. One good friend of mine had waited until her sons were well launched in school before she went back to work, and when she did, she landed a job that was full of promise and perfectly tailored to her gifts. The only downside was that it required her to travel across country once or twice a month. Apprehensive still about how this was going to impact her family, unsure how (or even if) she was going to pull it off, Rachel had been working for only a few weeks when her husband's company imploded suddenly, leaving him jobless.

This was one of those moments that define a marriage and a family. Instead of looking for full-time work right away, Zack decided to take on the role of primary caretaker. Almost overnight, this brilliant laser physicist became a Cub Scout pack leader, a painter of sets for high school drama productions, and a force on the local school board. (He also made himself available for part-time consulting work.)

Today the boys are both in college, and Zack is once again up to his ears in exciting research. Was his choice an act of heroic self-sacrifice? It was . . . but again, it really wasn't. At the end of the day, all four of them are flourishing, and Zack himself has had the luxury few men have of intimate, daily connection with his sons. His marriage with Rachel exemplifies the balance and the mutuality that are hallmarks of Belonging cultures. Observing their relationship over the years, as I've had the privilege of doing, has confirmed my belief that the trust and mutual respect that exist in a good marriage form an ideal context for learning to live "off-script" with regard to gender roles. The same thing could be said for a good friendship, or a good relationship with a sibling, child, or parent.

As a footnote to Zack and Rachel's story, I would recall one conclusion that anthropologist Peggy Sanday reached with respect to aggressive male dominance: it rarely occurs in cultures where men are intimately involved in the rearing of their sons.

WHAT THEY SAW IN ISÀNÀKLÈSH

The questions that arise when we begin to envision a rapprochement between Belonging and Enterprise can be overwhelming. But if we approach these questions with nothing but the rational intellect, we're confining ourselves within the limited paradigm of Enterprise. Native American tradition provides a glimpse of how else we might proceed.

There's a story from the Mescalero Apache tradition that serves as the basis—the narrative frame—for the ceremony that marks a young girl's coming into womanhood in that tradition.[6] It's often disorienting to read such stories, because the form is so different from that which most of us are used to. This particular story reads like the description of someone's dream: time keeps turning back on itself, for example, and suddenly you get a vivid detail from a scene that's already taken place.

Floodwaters are receding, and the Holy People are walking about in what sounds like the dawn of time. At first light, they see something in the water—something lying there, mostly submerged. It looks like them, but it's different. They keep their distance at first, a little fearfully, but then draw near.

The creature's dark hair is matted from being so long in the water, and the lower half of its face is stained white with minerals, colored just the way a river bank is when the water level is low.

Then an eagle comes into the story, and it holds out its wing feathers to the creature—it's a girl, we learn—and the eagle slowly leads her out of the water, so slowly that it takes days. The men make moccasins for her and kill an antelope to feed her, and the story goes on . . .

The young girl is the goddess Isànàklèsh. She brings with her the knowledge of everything that will heal her people and bring them balance. She knows everything about minerals, grasses, and herbs.

Every time a young girl undergoes initiation and acquires that knowledge herself, she *becomes* Isànàklèsh—giving over her own youth in exchange, so that the goddess never grows old. The initiate must run long distances each day in heavy clothes so that she knows the cost of a strong body.

And each time a girl is initiated, says the Mescalero Apache tradition, the whole earth is recreated.

What haunts me about this story isn't only the reverence for girls and women that it reflects (as Indian myth and ceremony so often do), but the deliberate, painstaking way in which the men assist in her gradual epiphany. Their exquisite care for her, the songs they sing, help *draw forth* her divinity. One speaks of menarche as a kind of awakening, but the story of Isànàklèsh suggests to us that there are awakenings, and then there are *awakenings*.

I was seized by this story, too, because it hints at the way in which the values of Belonging exist dormant in our own culture—submerged, all but drowned—and it suggests that retrieving them, or reawakening them, is a collective act that requires every one of us.

There's something, too, about the sheer tenacity and dedication required of us if we're to see whole what comes to us in pieces.

In other words, it may be that the greatest challenge we have who would reclaim the whole complex of values I've associated with Belonging is not to confuse the part with the whole, or even settle for one or two parts in place of the whole. We must heal the environment *and* challenge gender schemas *and* relieve poverty *and* celebrate Spirit.

By drawing on a story that so clearly points toward the Sacred Feminine, I might seem to be contradicting my insistence that the values of Belonging aren't *feminine,* but ineluctably *human.* Only I think that the story is subtler than that. For Isànàklèsh to become who she is, and for her gifts to flow out into her people, the men themselves have to become utterly tender and solicitous themselves. The distance between men and women has to narrow almost to nothing.

The story is irreducibly mysterious. The very way in which it unfolds is so solemn and slow and otherworldly—making one think of the Aborigines and Dream-Time—that it suggests that we can only see Isànàklèsh when we have moved to a deeper state of consciousness ourselves.

Finally, beauty itself is central to the telling. "With beautiful language they described everything in great detail," the story says.[7] Mescalero Apache understood, as we must today, the transformative power of beauty itself, and our response to it.

What do we learn from Isànàklèsh's story? Whether the primal values can coalesce again into a radiant wholeness depends, if this tale is any indication, on our capacity to imagine. It depends on our response to beauty, too, and our ability to put something together collectively: for inherent in the story is the understanding that no one of the men saw everything that needed to be seen, and no one of them sang a song that said it all.

BUILT UP IN FRACTALS

This capacious Pomo gift basket is more than 150 years old, and with its pattern of rich brown triangles offset against a pale gold background, it's extraordinarily handsome.

But looking at it from outside doesn't begin to prepare you for what you see when you look down into it from above. It's like looking into a spiral nebula. Everything is wheeling away from the center. The sensation of movement is almost dizzying. And the eye keeps changing its mind: Are the triangles foreground or background? There's something almost playful going on here, in the way that light and dark require and define and inhabit one another.

I'm dazzled by what I see, and confounded by what it must have taken to create it. My friend Helen looks over my shoulder. An accomplished multimedia needle artist, she's appreciative, but not as dumbstruck as I am.

"It *is* wonderful," she agrees. "But look. See how she began it. Just focus for a minute there on the first few rings, and then trace around each successive ring, and you see that she did it the same way women knit really complicated Aran sweaters. Counting, and adding on. It's built up in *fractals*."

I look again, and for a split second I see. For all its rich density of design, the eye-of-the hurricane effect has been achieved by someone who simply worked her way around, one stitch at a time, counting and adding on. And the basket is no less magical for my knowing this.

Notes

INTRODUCTION

1. Niles Eldredge, *Dominion* (Berkeley: Univ. of California Press, 1997), 190.

2. A break in the pattern, called a "dau," is explained variously, but usually with reference to First People (the tribe's progenitors). These ancient ones have to be able to get in and out of the basket comfortably, goes one explanation—the presumption being that they tend to hang out in well-woven baskets. Another says that they have to be able to enter the basket and look all around and inspect the weaver's work.

   The appearance of a bit of reddish-brown something signifies the feather of a flicker, and it's inserted to mark the unexpected arrival of the weaver's period: one isn't supposed to weave when menstruating.

3. Greg Sarris, *Keeping Slug Woman Alive: A Holistic Approach to American Indian Texts* (Berkeley: Univ. of California Press, 1993), 181–183.

CHAPTER 2

1. Cited by Roger Lewin, *In the Age of Mankind,* Smithsonian Books, (Washington, D.C.: 1988), 190.

2. Richard A. Gould, *Yiwara Foragers: of the Australian Desert* (New York, Scribners, 1969), 75.

3. *Vanishing Peoples of the Earth* (Washington, D.C.: National Geographic Society, 1968), 154.

4. Alf Wannenburgh, *The Bushmen* (New York, NY: Mayflower Books, 1979), 147.

5. I would call attention to this wording, which many of us might reasonably rephrase to read "*although* they were constantly shifting and changing, they had solid survival value." As a rule, anthropologists model consistently the "both/and" thinking I'll be advocating later in this book, and Turnbull is no exception. I would also observe, though, that a newly published biography of Turnbull records his ambivalence with regard to relationships in general, particularly with his birth family. It doesn't seem unfair to guess that the great appreciation he registers for the "social fluidity" he observed among Congo Pygmies may have been colored somewhat by his own wistfulness.

6. Bruce Bower, "Neanderthals Show Ancient Signs of Caring," *Science News,* September 15, 2001, Volume 160, No. 11 p. 167.

7. Wannenburgh, *The Bushmen,* 84ff.

8. Barbara Ehrenreich, *Blood Rites* (New York: Henry Holt and Co., 1998), 22.

9. *Nomads of the World* (Washington, D.C.: National Geographic Society, 1971), 141.

10. Sarah Blaffer Hrdy, *The Woman That Never Evolved* (Cambridge: Harvard Univ. Press, 1981), 190.

11. Hugh Brody, *The Other Side of Eden* (San Francisco: North Point Press, 2001), 244.

CHAPTER 3

1. Maximilien Bruggmann and Peter R. Gerber, *Indians of the Northwest Coast* (New York and Oxford: Facts on File, 1989), 137.

2. Suzanne Abel-Vidor et al, *Remember Your Relations: The Elsie Allen Baskets, Family and Friends* (Ukiah, California: Grace Hudson Museum, 1996), 86.

3. Brian Bibby, *The Fine Art of California Indian Basketry* (Sacramento, CA: Crocker Art Museum, 1996), 5.

4. Huston Smith, *The World's Religions* (San Francisco: HarperSanFrancisco, 1991), 366.

5. Wannenburgh, *The Bushmen,* 51.

6. Bruggman and Gerber, 47.

7. Ibid., 24, rough paraphrase.

8. Bonnemaison, *The Tree and the Canoe: History and Ethnogeography of Tanna* (Honolulu: Univ. of Hawaii Press, 1994), 113.

9. Paul Johnson, *Fire in the Mind: Science, Faith, and the Search for Order* (New York: Vintage, 1995), 15.

CHAPTER 4

1. Brody, *The Other Side of Eden,* 244.

2. Roy Richard Grinker, *In the Arms of Africa* (New York: St. Martin's Press, 2000), 311

3. Gregory Bateson, *Steps to an Ecology of the Mind* (Chicago: Univ. of Chicago Press, 1972), 116ff.

4. Bruggmann and Gerber, *Indians of the Northwest Coast*, 84.

5. *Vanishing Peoples of the Earth*, 202

6. Bateson, *Steps to an Ecology of the Mind*, 114.

7. Brody, *The Other Side of Eden*, 248: "Dreams take the dreamer not to some surreal universe in which the natural order is transcended or reversed, not to a land of fantasy, but to the place and creatures he or she knows best. Moving from the natural into the supernatural, passing through the porous walls that surround reality, the hunter arrives at essential knowledge."

8. Marie Bouchard and Susan Lightstone, "Stories That Used to Be True: Irene Avaalaaqiaq," *Piecework* (Mar./Apr. 1995), 76.

9. Bateson, *Steps to an Ecology of the Mind*, 113.

10. Brody, *The Other Side of Eden*, 57.

11. Malcolm Margolin, *The Ohlone Way: Indian Life in the San Francisco-Monterey Bay Area* (Berkeley: Heyday Books, 1978), 70

CHAPTER 5

1. Roger Lewin, *In the Age of Mankind* (Washington, D.C.: Smithsonian Institution, 1988), 200.

CHAPTER 6

1. Jared Diamond, *Guns, Germs, and Steel* (New York: Norton, 1997), 276.

2. Brody, *The Other Side of Eden*, 82.

3. Peggy Sanday, *Female Power and Male Dominance* (Cambridge, UK: Cambridge Univ. Press, 1981), 163–183.

4. *Mesopotamia: The Mighty Kings* (Alexandria, VA: Time-Life Books, 1973), 26.

CHAPTER 7

1. Cited by Tim Flinders in *Power and Promise* (see www.tworock.org).

2. See in particular Patricia McBroom, *The Third Sex: The New Professional Woman* (New York: Morrow, 1986), 60–61.

3. Gerda Lerner, *The Creation of Patriarchy* (New York: Oxford Univ. Press, 1986), 8.

4. Sanday, *Female Power and Male Dominance*, 5. The inner and outer orientations receive minimal definition here and are explored more fully in the first three chapters of the book.

5. See Sanday, *Female Power and Male Dominance*, 224.

6. Bell Hooks, *Black Looks: Race and Representation* (Boston, MA: Southend Press, 1992) 2ff.

7. German philosopher Karl Jaspers first invoked the term in his 1949 universal history of the world called *The Origin and Goal of History*.

CHAPTER 8

1. Suggested reading: Niles Eldredge, *The Miner's Canary* (New York: Prentice Hall Trade, 1991), and Richard Leakey and Roger Lewin, *The Sixth Extinction* (New York: Anchor Books, 1996).

2. *Nomads of the World*, 181.

3. Diamond, *Guns, Germs, and Steel*, 276.

4. *Mesopotamia: The Mighty Kings*, rev. ed. (Alexandria, VA: Time-Life Books, 1995), 66.

CHAPTER 9

1. Ursula K. LeGuin, *The Telling* (New York: Harcourt, 2000), 119.

2. The term comes from Richard Dawkins, author of *The Selfish Gene*.

3. Elizabeth Wayland Barber, *Women's Work* (New York: Norton, 1994), 102.

4. Bateson, *Steps to an Ecology of the Mind*, 500.

5. Ibid., 15.

6. Kenneth Grahame, *Wind in the Willow* (New York: Henry Holt and Co., 1980), 94.

7. Patricia Jeffrey and Amrita Basu, eds., *Appropriating Gender* (New York: Routledge, 1997), 7.

8. James J. Rawls, *The Indians of California: The Changing Image* (Norman: Univ. of Oklahoma Press, 1984), 25.

9. Cited by Adrienne Rich in "Notes Toward a Politics of Location," *Arts of the Possible* (New York: Norton, 2001), 69.

10. Barrie Thorne, *Gender Play* (New Brunswick, NJ: Rutgers Univ. Press, 1993), 70–74.

11. Rich Heffern, "Thomas Berry: Earth's Crisis Is Fundamentally Spiritual," *National Catholic Reporter* (Aug. 10, 2001), 5–7.

12. *San Francisco Chronicle*, Dec. 6, 1999, reprinted from *Los Angeles Times*.

CHAPTER 10

1. Adrienne Rich, *Arts of the Possible*, 99.

2. Elaine Scarry, *On Beauty and Being Just* (New Haven, CT: Princeton Univ. Press, 2001), 12ff.

3. John Woolman, *The Journal of John Woolman* and *A Plea for the Poor:* (New York: Corinth Books, 1961), 8.

4. John Woolman, 244.

5. John Woolman, 142.

6. John Woolman, 214.

7. Allen F. Davis, *American Heroine: The Life and Legend of Jane Addams* (New York: Oxford Univ. Press, 1973).

8. Allen F. Davis, *American Heroine: The Life and Legend of Jane Addams*

9. John Muir, *My First Summer in the Sierra* (Sellanraa, Dunwood, GA; Norman S. Berg, Publisher, 1972), 157.

10. Muir, *Ibid,* 174.

CHAPTER 11

1. Elizabeth Cady Stanton's "Solitude of Self" speech can be found online at: http://www.pbs.org/stantonanthony/resources/solitude_self.html

2. Elizabeth Cady Stanton, "Solitude of Self" speech.

3. Martin Luther King, Jr. *A Testament of Hope: The Essential Writings and Speeches of Martin Luther King , Jr.* (New York: Harper Collins, 1991), 293.

4. McBroom, 61.

5. McBroom, 53

6. Reported in *Salon Online Magazine,* Jan. 24, 2002.

7. *Salon,* Ibid.

8. Susan Estrich, *Sex and Power* (New York: Riverhead Books, 2000), 34.

9. Sandra Lipsitz Bem, *The Lenses of Gender* (New Haven, CT: Yale Univ. Press, 1993), 125, 153–157.

10. Bem, 153.

11. Judith V. Jordan, personal communication.

12. Ivone Gebara, *Longing for Running Water* (Minneapolis: Fortress Press, 1999), 103.

13. Gebara, 83.

CHAPTER 12

1. Thomas Buckley, "Renewal as Discourse and Discourse as Renewal in Native Northwestern California," in *Native Religions and Cultures of North America: Anthropology of the Sacred,* ed. Lawrence E. Sullivan (New York and London: Continuum, 2000), 33.

2. Buckley, *ibid,* 39.

3 Elise Boulding, *Cultures of Peace: The Hidden Side of History* (Syracuse Univ. Press, 2000), 39.

4. Jean Shinoda Bolen, M.D., *The Millionth Circle* (Berkeley, CA: Conari Press, 1999), 17

5. Peggy Orenstein, *Flux Women on Sex, Work, Love, Kids, and Life in a Half-Changed World* (New York: Knowp, 2001), 285.

6. Ines Talamantez, "In the Space Between Earth and Sky: Contemporary Mescalero Apache Ceremonialism," in *Native Religions and Cultures of North America: Anthropology of the Sacred*, ed. Lawrence E. Sullivan (New York and London: Continuum, 2000), 142–159.

7. Talamantez, 158.

Acknowledgments

Liz Perle, my editor, saw where this book wanted to go long before I did and directed its course with breathtaking assurance. I am profoundly grateful.

Candice Fuhrman, agent and friend, thank you once again for unflagging support.

Harper San Francisco has been my publishing home for twelve years and four books. Anne Connolly, Chris Hafner, Steve Hanselman, Margery Buchanan, Jim Warner, Liz Winer—everybody—Thank you. For twenty-five years, Harper San Francisco books have celebrated the values of Belonging. It's been a privilege to be part of the party.

I am grateful to Craig Bates, Foley Benson, Sarah Dole, Mary Korte and others for sharing their knowledge and love of Native American life ways.

The Charles Schulz Information Center at Sonoma State University opened its doors just in time to be my research facility and home away from home for this book. Its staff is as gracious and accommodating as the building itself.

I wrote this book in large part because I just couldn't buy the argument that gender imbalance—gender strife, if you will—is inevitable. One of the biggest reasons I couldn't is that the men in my own extended family don't buy it either. They don't talk about gender balance or gender empathy, they simply live it, and the effect on sons, nephews, students, co-workers, etc., is palpable and continuing. Thank you, Gib Ramage (my dad). Thank you John Ramage and Steve Ramage, Tom Hawkins and Tighe Smith, Rick Flinders and Peter Flinders.

My mother, Jeanne Ramage, and my "other mother" Carmel Flinders have lived the values of Belonging all their lives, and everyone in their vicinity has reaped the benefits.

And of course my own personal "matrix" for lo, these thirty-plus years has been Ramagiri Ashram and the people who live there, striving as best we can to honor the legacy of our beloved teacher, Sri Eknath Easwaran. To Christine Easwaran, mirror of his teachings, leader and companion at once, gratitude and affection always.

Directly and indirectly—technically, philosophically, spiritually, emotionally—my husband Tim has been indispensable to this whole process.

Ramesh, our son and a writer himself, reminded me at a critical moment, by his own passionate example, how joyous it can be to write—told me straight out, in fact that if the writing weren't joyous, I should take the dog to the beach instead. Good advice. Thank you, sweet boy.

Index

217